Researching and
Writing Dissertations
in Business and
Management

Researching and Writing Dissertations in Business and Management

Michael Riley
University of Surrey

Roy C. Wood
University of Strathclyde

Mona A. Clark
University of Dundee

Eleanor Wilkie
Formerly of the University of St

and

Edith Szivas
University of Surrey

THOMSON

Australia • Canada • Mexico • Singapore • Spain • United Kingdom • United States

THOMSON

Researching and Writing Dissertations in Business and Management

Copyright © 2000 M. Clark, M. Riley, E. Szivas, E. Wilkie and R. Wood

The Thomson logo is a registered trademark used herein under licence.

For more information, contact Thomson Learning, High Holborn House; 50-51 Bedford Row, London WC1R 4LR or visit us on the World Wide Web at:
http://www.thomsonlearning.co.uk

British Library Cataloguing-in-Publication Data
A catalogue record for this book is available from the British Library

ISBN 1-86152-608-3

First edition published by Thomson Learning 2000
Reprinted 2002 and 2003 by Thomson Learning

Typeset by Laserscript Limited, Mitcham, Surrey
Printed in Croatia by Zrinski

Contents

Acknowledgements

The authors gratefully acknowledge the assistance of Elaine Blaxter, Senior Librarian at the University of Strathclyde, for her help in supplying information for this book. We are also enormously indebted to Jean Finlayson who worked patiently and precisely on the original manuscript to produce a coherent manuscript from four diverse sources and styles, and to Leslie Mitchell who worked on this revised version with great efficiency. This book is dedicated to the memory of Ella Wilkie.

Michael J. Riley, Roy C. Wood, Mona A. Clark, and Edit Szivas
Guildford, Glasgow and Dundee, January 2000

Figures

Tables

■ ☐ ■ ■ 1

Introduction: what this book is about (and how to use it)

This book is directed to diploma, degree and postgraduate taught-course students in the business and management fields. It may also be of some interest to research students in these areas. Most students on such courses will, at some point in their studies, have to complete a project, extended report, dissertation or thesis. This book is designed to assist that process by being accessible and easy to use. It proceeds from the assumption that both the process of research and that of writing a dissertation, project or report is best tackled in a systematic manner. At the same time, most academics realize that for many students (and indeed for many academics!) the research process – and particularly the intellectual or 'thinking' part of it – is inherently 'messy'. This is because however well planned a research process is, there will always be an element of creative uncertainty. This need not manifest itself solely in the intellectual dimension but can appear as part of the mechanics of 'doing' research – for example, in what tasks to undertake first, in terms of how data should be interpreted and presented and so on. Many people are intimidated by the prospect of undertaking a piece of independent research work and then writing an extended report on their results. It is not just the research process that scares people but the thought that they must cut themselves off from their normal world for long periods of time in order to write five, ten or twenty thousand words (in some cases more!). The thing to remember about research (and from now on the term is used to embrace the actual writing up of a dissertation, project or report as well as the research process) is that, as far as possible, it should be fun. If this sounds a little perverse, then it is best to think of the research process in highly mechanistic and unsentimental terms. Some parts of the process will be enjoyed more than others but research is, in essence, a process of production in which the manufacture of a commodity or good is directed towards the use to which it is put after it leaves the manufactory. Put another way, think of the DIY expert – the type of person who really thrives on executing home improvements. Often it is the process of work that brings the enthusiast the most joy rather than the end product itself, but without the end product (which might in itself be enjoyed by another) there can be no process.

A colleague of the authors of this book has for many years proffered a piece of excellent advice to students undertaking research projects – 'if you can't get it right, get it wrote'. As this ungrammatical pun suggests, a piece of research or a research report, whatever form it takes is rarely perfect and it is fruitless striving idealistically for perfection. Research is about exploring (and often creating) knowledge; it is an organic process and one where it is rarely possible to check all the angles. By the same token, research – from first idea to completing the report – should not be viewed as an obstacle. If you allow yourself to be intimidated then you probably will be, with all that entails for stress, frustration and unhappiness. To paraphrase the American sociologist W. I. Thomas, if something is defined as real it will be real in its consequences. Within the UK higher education system, dissertations and reports often carry considerable weight within the assessment of the curriculum, and the research and writing process can be blown up out of all proportion, leading to obsessive and unhappy students. Perspective is, therefore, all important. To refer to another anecdotal source, the film director Alfred Hitchcock is reputed to have told actress Ingrid Bergman (who was agonizing over how to play a scene) 'Ingrid, it's only a movie'. Remember, it *is* only a dissertation!

The structure of this book (and how to use it)

There are a large number of research methods texts available, and several aimed at students of business and management. Individual authors have their own way of approaching the research process and thus no single text can hope to 'cover all the angles'. We have tried to cover a wide range of topics in this text, however, and in so doing have adopted a more or less chronological approach to the research process. In Part One we focus on those essential considerations that must be taken on board prior to actually doing anything substantive. Each chapter is self-contained. Accordingly, chapters can be 'dipped into' with ease, and specific topics identified from the contents page or index. In the case of Part One, though, there is some merit in considering a complete read through, for it is here that we have sought to identify and discuss key topics, an awareness of which may forestall many of those problems encountered by students who have not been adequately prepared to engage in a research project.

Part Two of the book contains chapters on individual research methods and approaches, all of which may be legitimately used in business and management research. Many of the major qualitative research techniques are considered here, though again, while we have attempted to give wide coverage to mainstream areas of interest in our approach, we cannot claim to have been exhaustive. Research methods is an academic industry in its own right and in quantitative methods in particular, there is an ever increasing number of rarefied techniques devised for use in highly specialized fields of enquiry. In Part Three of the book, consideration of quantitative techniques is confined to discussion of elementary statistical concepts and techniques. This is not a statistics 'text' in any sense but rather more of a 'ready reference' of certain basic methods that can be employed in the description, presentation and calculation of data. Part Four of the book consists of guidelines on how research work may be presented. This applies not only to written forms of presentation – dissertations, reports, theses and the like – and the associated paraphernalia of referencing, indexing and general written exposition, but to oral presentations of research work. Oral presentation of research work may be a feature of many courses just as an oral examination, a *viva voce*, may be required to defend a thesis at postgraduate level (and, increasingly, at undergraduate level).

In adopting this approach, of birth to berth as it were, from the first stages of the research process to putting it to bed, we hope to clarify a process that often appears both intimidating and overwhelming. This is not a philosophical text in the sense of being concerned with the nature of research methods for themselves, nor is the book littered with lots of references. Where possible, we have tried to illustrate key issues by reference to actual examples of business and management research. References to other works on research methods and dissertation writing *have* been supplied at the end of each part of the book, in order to supply pointers to sources that we have found useful in clarifying aspects of the research process. As a general note, we list below four works in which you will find further discussion of the majority of topics contained in this text. As the book's title suggests, however, our overriding concern has been to produce a user-friendly guide to considerations, techniques, approaches and advice that will, we hope, make the research and dissertation-writing processes as easy and enjoyable an experience as it is possible for either to be.

Further reading

Denzin, N. K. and Lincoln, Y. S. (eds) (1994) *Handbook of Qualitative Research*, London and California: Sage.

Easterby-Smith, M., Thorpe, R. and Lowe, A. (1991) *Management Research: An Introduction*, London: Sage.

Gilbert, N. (ed.) (1993) *Researching Social Life*, London: Sage.

Gill, J. and Johnson, P. (1997) *Research Methods for Managers*, London: Paul Chapman Publishing, 2nd edition.

Part One
Getting Started

 2

What is research for and what does it involve?

'Study and investigation, especially to discover new facts' is the definition of research offered by *The Oxford Minidictionary* (1991 edition). The word 'especially' is important in this context as within academia the meaning of 'research' has been more finely dissected. For example, research may be directed towards the confirmation of existing facts. If a scientist publishes the results of an experiment, results that other scientists view as controversial, these others may seek to repeat the original experimenter's work in order to see if they get the same results. In other words, some research may seek confirmation of existing facts rather than the discovery of new ones. Similarly, in the environment of higher education, research may be defined in terms of a review of existing knowledge in a particular area together with the creation of a new slant on this knowledge. This therefore involves the creation of a new perspective on existing knowledge and need not presuppose the uncovering of new 'facts'. Some people term this 'scholarship' in preference to research but this is only one of the distinctions between these two terms that circulate in the academic community, and new hairs are always being split.

Where does this leave the novice researcher and dissertation writer? This is not an easy question to answer. Many students undertaking research for projects and dissertations do uncover new information in the course of their work. Indeed, many colleges and universities encourage students to undertake investigations which are precisely geared to this goal. One reason for this is that as part of a course's assessment goals, the dissertation or report is not only seen as a useful vehicle for testing students' capacities for independent study and the writing of an extended piece of prose, but as a crucial means of assessing whether students can grasp the essentials of manipulating one or more research technique, methodology or instrument (for example, questionnaires and statistical tests). While under-taking active research to discover 'new facts' is an enjoyable and worthwhile activity, it is no less worthwhile to undertake research which involves a critical review of existing research in an area, that develops a new slant or perspective and one that illuminates the chosen topic (for certain types of higher degree of course, original research making a significant contribution to [new] knowledge is a necessity).

To qualify the foregoing remarks, it should be noted that the majority of students at whatever level want to use the opportunity of a thesis, dissertation or report to undertake research involving active investigation. This is a very laudable desire but it is often the case that people bite off more than they can chew. The process of topic selection (which is addressed in Chapter 3) is therefore very important. The remainder of this chapter investigates some of the main dimensions to the research process.

Some types of research

The preceding discussion steered clear of using many of the distinctions that exist between different kinds of research often encountered in the academic world. Research does have different meanings for different people but there are some general areas of agreement and it is worth examining some of these.

Pure and applied research

Pure research is a term reserved for that kind of research which has no obvious practical implications, that is, no obvious *use* value beyond contributing to a particular area of intellectual enquiry. Such research may produce knowledge that *is* ultimately put to some practical use but the major intention of pure research is to contribute to the canon of knowledge in a particular area *per se*. Applied research is, by way of contrast, problem-oriented, directed towards solving some particular intellectual puzzle that has practical implications. Often, applied research may be sponsored by clients external to the academic world – industrial organizations and the like. Both pure and applied research can, then, lead to the creation of new knowledge and the discovery of new 'facts' about the phenomenon or phenomena under study.

Primary and secondary research

This distinction is quite often found in academic discourse and has already been partly encountered in this chapter. Primary research generally refers to that research which involves the collection of original data using an accepted research methodology. Secondary research normally denotes an activity whereby no new original data is collected but where the research project draws on existing ('secondary') sources alone. Any research activity usually includes secondary research. In research projects where original primary data is collected, secondary research to establish what work has been undertaken in a particular area before is a necessary precursor to research design.

A corollary of the distinction between primary and secondary research is, as implied in the preceding remarks, that between primary and secondary data. Primary data is generally that which is collected specifically in pursuit of particular research objectives: it is 'new' and original data. Secondary data is 'the rest' – books, statistical reports from government and other agencies, documents and so on (see Chapter 7 for details of key secondary sources of relevance to business and management).

Theoretical and empirical research

Following from the distinction between primary and secondary research, that between theoretical and empirical is a little more complex if only because these terms are used with varying degrees of emphasis by members of the academic community. In essence, theoretical research is where research activity contributes to the study of a particular area of intellectual enquiry. It can involve the collection of original data but outside of the natural sciences, theoretical research has more abstract and contemplative connotations and entails acts of interpretation and reinterpretation of exisiting data to extend both the concrete and abstract understanding of phenomena. 'Empirical research' is a term employed to describe that activity which involves the collection of original data for analysis. In this sense, empirical research is synonymous with primary research. The literal meaning of the term 'empirical' is 'based on observation or experiment, not on theory' (*The Oxford Minidictionary*, 1991 edition) though of course, observations, experiments and data can make a contribution to theory just as data, arguably, must be interpreted using a theoretical framework. The main emphasis in this book is on conducting empirical or primary research, collecting original data for analysis.

Descriptive and explanatory research

Another distinction often encountered in the literature on research methodology is that between descriptive and explanatory research (McNeill 1990; Procter 1993). Rudyard Kipling wrote:

> I keep six honest serving-men,
> (They taught me all I knew);
> Their names are What and Why and When,
> And How and Where and Who.

These are good interrogatives to bear in mind during any enquiry process. Descriptive research is largely concerned with what, when, where and who questions, whereas explanatory research goes beyond this and is concerned with why and how questions. Descriptive research is thus essentially informational in character. Descriptive research can involve the collection of original data for analysis but its main purpose is to establish a factual 'picture' of the object of study. Explanatory research is directed towards exploring the relationships between concepts and phenomena and explaining the causality and/or interdependency between these.

Positivism and interpretive research

One of the most frequent distinctions between types of research encountered in texts on research methods (especially in management and the social sciences) is that between positivism and interpretive research (e.g. Easterby-Smith, Thorpe and Lowe 1991; McNeill 1990). This is an important distinction and one to be understood but not agonized over. In their *Dictionary of Sociology*, Jary and Jary (1991: 484–5) identify four principal definitions of positivism, three of which have common, general usage. Paraphrasing Jary and Jary, these definitions are:

- positivism as a doctrine or belief that the only true knowledge is scientific in character, describing the interrelationships between real, observable phenomena (whether social or physical);
- positivism as an approach which assumes that the (research) methods of the natural sciences (for example, measurement and the search for general laws of causation) can be applied unproblematically to the study of social phenomena; and
- the pejorative corollary of the second definition above, where social scientists are seen as erroneously seeking to apply scientific methods to social scientific phenomena.

Positivism has many facets but as viewed by its critics (again, notably, in the social sciences and especially sociology) it is regarded as seeking to apply scientific research methods to the study of social phenomena (of which management is an instance) in order to uncover general explanatory laws in an objective and unbiased, 'value-free' manner. Positivism, then, embraces a number of assumptions which may be crudely summarized as follows:

- there exists a 'real world' of social and physical phenomena;
- this real world is objective and tangible (that is, most people would agree on what constitutes the 'real world' of phenomena);
- this world can be analysed (researched) in an objective fashion in order to increase understanding of the phenomena of which it is comprised;
- the methods employed in such research are (should be) objective and impartial as well as immune from the influence of human values and believes (value-free); and
- if research is undertaken objectively, then the gradual accumulation of knowledge should enable accurate description of the nature and behaviour of such phenomena, including the interrelationships between phenomena in terms of cause and effect, dependency and interdependency and so on: in short, the findings of research should be capable of explanatory generalization.

Hypothetico-deductive method

The main expression of the positivist approach to research is the hypothetico-deductive (research) method which is generally believed to govern the procedures of natural-scientific investigation. Natural scientists (chemists, biologists, physicists) are said to view the world as being external, 'out there', and enjoying a real existence (ultimately) beyond being misconstrued by humans. That is, the rational investigation of the real world of phenomena will ultimately yield universal truths about the character and behaviour of such phenomena.

The scientist, then, begins with a phenomenon to study and generates ideas about its character and behaviour. These ideas are crystallized into a hypothesis. In a general sense, a hypothesis is any statement about the qualities or behaviour of a phenomenon that is advanced for testing. By testing the hypothesis, the researcher seeks to establish whether the statement contained therein is sustainable. The hypothesis is then put to the test, most commonly in the natural sciences by experimentation, but other forms of data collection clearly do play an important role in some fields of scientific enquiry.

Verification and falsification

At this stage, it is useful to make a distinction between the verification and falsification of the hypothesis. Arguably, in classical hypothetico-deductive research, the investigator ought to *verify* the hypothesis, that is, to show that the hypothesis is true. However, an alternative view closely associated with the philosopher Karl Popper is that hypotheses should be subjected to the process of falsification, that is, a process designed, crudely speaking, to show that a hypothesis is wrong/false. The example usually marshalled to illustrate this point concerns black swans. Consider the assertion that 'all swans are white'. How can this assertion be shown to be true or false? One answer would be to verify the assertion by counting all swans. But, even if this were possible, how would the researcher know that they had counted all swans? More significantly, even if all the swans observed were white, it would not necessarily hold true that all future swans would be white (the potential objections of geneticists to this point are acknowledged!). In many, if not all, cases, it is impossible to completely verify a hypothesis. It is, however, much easier to falsify one since it requires only one contrary piece of evidence to refute the assertions of a hypothesis. Thus the observation of one black swan (of course, in reality, there are many more) would refute the assertion that 'all swans are white'. The tension that exists between the verification and falsification principles is an interesting one and serves to remind us of the fragility of the processes by which we claim to 'know' something.

From data to theory

Returning now to the main thrust of the discussion about the hypothetico-deductive method, the purpose of data collection can be seen to be directed towards the testing of a hypothesis with the result that the hypothesis is accepted or rejected. The hypothesis is treated by analysis of the data collected to see if such analysis supports or refutes the hypothesis. If the hypothesis is accepted then this is, technically, a contribution to theory. If it is rejected, a new hypothesis or hypotheses may be formed and the process to test these begins all over again. If (and when) a theory or theories are sufficiently sophisticated, then laws pertaining to the phenomenon which the theory or theories purport to circumscribe may be derived from the body of theoretical knowledge and used to predict the future behaviour of the phenomenon.

A useful development of this view is offered by Gilbert (1993: 25–26) who notes that theories comprise one or more hypotheses, each of which in turn is made up of concepts linked by relationships. Gilbert employs the classic example of Emile Durkheim's 'theory' of suicide to illustrate this point.

The French sociologist Durkheim postulated a causal relationship between economic conditions and suicide, suggesting that economic crises have an effect on suicide rates. Here, Gilbert argues, 'economic conditions' and 'the suicide rate' are concepts linked by a relationship. The relationship is, in this instance, a causal one: changes in 'a' have an effect on 'b'. But relationships between concepts in theories need not always be causal: at a basic level, concepts in a theory may be related in a variety of ways. However, given that a theory is intended to constitute a body of knowledge capable of describing (explaining) the nature of a phenomenon and its behaviour, it will almost certainly be the case that at the heart of a theory will be a series of propositions (concepts) linked by relationships of a causal nature. Returning to the suicide example above, the two concepts – economic conditions and suicide rates – are linked by a causal relationship. All theories must be capable of being tested and a number of hypotheses could be derived from the example to test Durkheim's theory. One candidate would be: 'Changes in economic conditions cause (have an effect on) rates of suicide'. There are limitations to such a hypothesis because of the vagaries of the terms 'changes', 'economic conditions' and 'rates of suicide'. The hypothesis is very imprecise. Also, this is a very different type of hypothesis from that considered earlier: 'all swans are white'. Here, there are certainly evocative concepts ('swans', 'white') but the relationships between the concepts is not of the same order as in the suicide example, to which we shall return for further elaboration later in the chapter.

Hypotheses thus function at different levels. At the simplest level, all that has to be remembered is that a hypothesis is a statement not yet accepted as true: in hypothetico-deductive method it takes a particular form (usually of the kind suggested in the suicide example) but a hypothesis can often be a statement that simply attributes characteristics to a phenomenon – for example, 'swans are white' (though the truth value of such assertions is another matter altogether) (Lacey 1986: 122).

Deduction and induction

A theory, then, is a systematic body or statement of knowledge that explains and predicts the character or behaviour of a phenomenon or phenomena. The term 'deductive' has already been encountered in the context of the hypothetico-deductive method. The terms deduction and induction are, in their own right, important to an understanding of theory construction. Both can also be the source of some confusion but again, Gilbert (1993: 22–24) offers a useful clarification of the terms in a social research context. Broadly speaking, deduction is the process which begins with theory

WHAT IS RESEARCH FOR AND WHAT DOES IT INVOLVE?   **13**

and proceeds through hypothesis, data collection, and testing of the hypothesis to deduce explanations of the behaviour of particular phenomena. Induction is the process whereby the exploration and analysis of related observations leads to the construction of a theory that systematically links such observations in a meaningful way. In Gilbert's terms, 'induction is the technique for generating theories and deduction is the technique for applying them' (1993: 23). Note that in the hypothetico-deductive method, the testing and confirmation of hypotheses effectively constitutes, as noted earlier, a contribution to theory and possibly to the evolution of that theory. Theory must, however, come from 'somewhere' and induction as it were, is the prime suspect.

There are some difficulties with this view that should be noted. For example, if theory is made, confirmed, sustained and developed by processes of deduction (the hypothetico-deductive method) then how can it be made, confirmed and sustained by induction and inductive processes of reasoning? It appears that the role of deduction is confined to *developing* theory but, even here, this is a claim also made for induction. This and related problems are controversial among scholars and anti-inductivists have claimed that inductive arguments in reality proceed using the hypothetico-deductive method (Lacey 1986: 107). Whatever the intellectual intricacies of the situation, the distinction between the two terms is yet another reminder of the need for sensitivity towards terminological nuances associated with the research process.

Major criticisms of positivism

The preceding discussion has gone some way beyond the essential elements of positivism and it is now appropriate to consider positivism's supposed limitations as a philosophical doctrine. It was earlier noted that social scientists and, in particular, sociologists, were among positivism's fiercest critics. This is not to say that such critics are opposed to the creation of general explanatory theories (though some might think this to be an impossible goal) or to objectivity in research. Rather, the critics of positivism have a number of concerns motivated by the underlying view that positivist approaches (including the hypothetico-deductive method) to research are inappropriate to the study of social phenomena. This is because social phenomena are the products of human action and the study of people and their actions is not amenable to the research techniques most closely associated with positivism. At the most obvious level, it is, for ethical reasons, not possible to experiment on people to any great extent or with any breadth of purpose. As a result of this, the methods of positivism are effectively limited in what they can explain and describe about human behaviour. A more potent and less simplistically expressed criticism is that in the world of social phenomena (in contrast to that of natural phenomena) the focus of study is people and human behaviour. People are directed, capable of making choices: they are not inanimate and their behaviour is not readily understood in terms of simple causal factors. Rather, human behaviour is to a large degree constructed through shared meanings and to effectively study such behaviour it is necessary to identify, understand and interpret such meanings.

A further major objection to positivism in general and the hypothetico-deductive method in particular concerns the *actual* status of both as methods of investigation as opposed to the characteristics that are *attributed* to each. The main issue here is the extent to which positivism and the hypothetico-deductive method *are* objective and value-free. Some critics argue that true value-freedom is impossible to attain since any (human) decision about what to study and how something should be studied is necessarily ideological, reflecting the interests and values of the person or people making these kinds of choices. In this view, no decisions of this kind are ever entirely neutral. A related and powerful objection to so-called scientific method is that, like value-freedom, 'scientific method' is a sanitized and idealized model of what actually goes on in reality. In other words scientific research is *not* conducted solely according to the standards of scientific method. The main impetus for this view comes from the work of sociologists of science who have shown that in controversial scientific research where the outcome of experiments designed to test specific hypotheses is contentious, scientists frequently resort to extra-scientific means to attempt to resolve their disputes. Such means often take the form of what many lay people would understand as examples of *unscientific* behaviour, including activities like questioning the integrity or competence of rival researchers. A key point to emerge from many studies that have been undertaken of controversial scientific research is that what comes to count as scientific knowledge is the simultaneous product of both scientific method (as construed in the discussion so far) and rhetorical consensus – that is, agreement as to what will be accepted and acceptable as scientific knowledge.

Interpretive research

The positivist approach to the study of the social world has, and continues to be, influential in the social sciences and management research, where the limitations of experimentation as an expression of positivism's commitment to objectivity have been recognized and experimentation replaced to a large degree by the survey method as the principal means of data collection. If experimentation is the expression of positivist objectivity in the natural sciences, then in the social sciences (especially sociology) this role has been fulfilled by the social survey, often entailing the collection of data (for example, through questionnaires) and the analysis of such data according to the rigours of the hypothetico-deductive method as expressed through statistical testing. As already suggested, however, there has been a retreat from positivism in sociology and many other social sciences. Further, while the influence of positivist approaches on social research should not be underestimated or denied, alternative approaches have always been present, especially in disciplines like sociology and social anthropology. The late flowering of management as an academic discipline beyond merely a body of prescriptive knowledge on 'how to manage' has meant that these alternatives have to some extent defined approaches to management research.

These 'alternative' approaches to research generally constitute different *methods* of collecting and analysing data but sometimes differ more fundamentally in that they involve collecting different kinds of data from those normally associated with the positivist tradition. This is why they tend to be grouped under the heading of 'interpretive' or 'phenomenological' research approaches. Part Two of this book deals with many of the individual research methods normally grouped under the interpretive heading and it is appropriate here to consider some of their shared general characteristics.

It will be recalled that key objections to 'applying' the positivist approach to the study of social behaviour and phenomena, include the following observations:

- social behaviour and phenomena are the product of human action which is of a variable rather than fixed nature (though capable of considerable patterning);
- human action and behaviour is predicated on the articulation of shared meanings;
- to achieve an effective understanding of human action, the social researcher (including the management researcher) must seek to identify, understand and interpret such meanings; and
- human actions are directed and rarely value-neutral in content or motivation.

The elements of this list can be usefully elaborated as follows (see Easterby-Smith, Thorpe and Lowe 1991: 21–22 for a more developed account). First, the interpretive research tradition has, as one of its central tenets, a deep-seated scepticism of the positivist view of the 'real world of phenomena' as external and objective. In particular, the social world is seen as socially constructed on the basis of shared meanings which are subjective. The social world is also prone to greater variations than the natural world: while humans do exhibit regular, systematic patterns of behaviour (like certain molecules), these patterns cannot be assumed to be fixed forever. This leads to a second element of the interpretive approach, namely the unavoidable involvement of the researcher in the observation process. The social researcher being a part of the wider social structures which he or she studies can strive for (and often achieve) objectivity in the broadest positivist sense, but can never divorce themselves entirely from the subjectively constructed social contexts of which they are a part. A corollary of this and the first point is, of course, the previously mentioned view that 'scientific' research in the positivist tradition is itself far from objective in the sense that any human observer of natural, as well as social, phenomena, brings to their observations certain values and beliefs that must, by definition, impinge upon their interpretation of those phenomena. The third characteristic of interpretive research then is the focus on meanings rather than facts alone. The central practical problem for interpretive research is how to access the meanings of those under scrutiny. At a general level, all other things being equal, in any given society a degree of meaning will, as noted earlier, always be shared. For the most part however, interpretive researchers do not study 'society in general' and the researcher's membership of society is so much 'noise' that has to be controlled to allow effective focus on the topics concerned. At the same time, when a group or collectivity of subjects is being studied, the researcher has to absorb a degree of the collectivity's culture and sense of social reality. Researchers may also have to acquire some forms of technical knowledge special to the collectivity being studied in order to maximize the chances of coming to understand the shared meanings of the subjects. Two examples will serve to illustrate these points.

The Sociology of Science

One of the authors of this text (Wood), when a postgraduate research student, was studying the sociology of science and in particular a collectivity of scientists working in a controversial area of nutrition and physiology. These scientists, around 70 in all and most of them based in the UK, were at the cutting edge of their subject. Some of the scientists had claimed to have discovered that obesity could be caused – and in many cases was caused – not, as scientific orthodoxy maintained, by excessive food intake relative to energy output, but by the absence or failure of a special kind of body tissue to burn off excess calories. Thus, fat people were fat because they lacked this special tissue – brown adipose tissue – or because it did not function properly.

The objective of Wood's research was, as part of a wider programme of studies of controversies being conducted by his supervisor and others, to examine the ways in which these controversial claims were treated by the collectivity of scientists working in the chosen area. As noted earlier, sociologists of science had shown that in areas of scientific controversy, scientists tend to resort to extra-scientific means to try and persuade their colleagues and others of the veracity of their own position, or the lack of veracity of opponents' claims. Such was the case in this study, where in addition to challenges to the experimental standards of those scientists making the 'new' claims about the causes of obesity, critics questioned the integrity, competence and motives of the original experimenters.

The point of all this is as follows. In order to function effectively in research terms, Wood had to acquire several types of knowledge. First, he had to undertake a crash training in nutrition and physiology (this involved some degree of independent study plus attendance at a number of undergraduate course in nutrition and physiology being run in his institution's school of biosciences). In this way, Wood could comprehend the scientific basis to 'what was going on' and talk reasonably intelligently to scientists about their work. Moreover, scientific meanings specific to the field under scrutiny could be accessed. More generally, Wood had to acquire some understanding of the general principles that supposedly guide scientists' behaviour – loyalty to the truth, truthful reporting of experimental results and so on – all those things that guide scientific standards. In being able to talk intelligently to scientists about their specific work as well as general principles of the conduct of such work, Wood was able to win the confidence of many of his respondents, including protagonists on both sides of the controversy. Many of these scientists, realizing that Wood was not 'just another sociologist', took him into their confidence, involving him in their experiments, allowing him access to sensitive data from 'work in progress', and even trying to win him over to their point of view on scientific grounds as well as on the basis of other factors.

The Sociology of Work

In their study of hotel employment, Mars and Nicod (1984) wanted to examine the culture of waiting staff as an occupational group. To this end, one of the authors, Nicod, became a waiter, working in various restaurants in order to observe at first hand the activities of other waiting staff. The results of this study showed that, in essence, waiters have a public and a private face, the former largely for the benefit of customers whom they frequently dislike and resent. Furthermore, waiting staff are prone to acts of petty theft usually in the form of items taken from their place of work (especially food items) but also occasionally in the form of money. They have their own social and professional codes of conduct and often employ specialist terms, an occupational argot, to describe certain aspects of their behaviour. In order to study waiters, Nicod chose to work as a waiter, acquiring the technical skills of waiting staff and absorbing their culture. On occasions, in order to maintain his cover (for Nicod was working covertly, without his co-workers being aware that they were being studied) Nicod had to engage in the kinds of acts described above in order to be accepted as part of the occupational group and sub-culture, raising interesting ethical questions (see Chapter 4).

In both these examples, we see the lengths researchers with an interpretive approach felt they had to go to in order to ensure they stood a reasonable chance of accessing and understanding the meanings circulating in a particular culture. A clear issue facing the interpretive researcher is knowledge of when such meanings have been accessed. Put crudely, how does a researcher know they have tapped into the culture of values and meanings of the people they are studying? There is no straightforward answer to this question. Much depends on the group of people being researched. In both the cases described above, the balance of probabilities favours the view that each succeeded in penetrating fairly deeply into the cultures under scrutiny but there can be no absolute certainty on this point, or indeed on the point that they gained complete access to the full realm of meanings employed in each case.

Positivist v. interpretivist approaches

The distinction between positivist and interpretivist research is in some senses real and in others wholly artificial. Both philosophies of research are based on a common desire to understand behaviour but each approach makes different assumptions about the world of phenomena. The main criticisms of positivism have already been discussed. The main criticism of interpretive research was hinted at in the final sentence of the preceding discussion. It is that interpretive researchers can never be absolutely sure that they have acquired the 'world view' of the people they study, nor that they give the meanings they encounter the correct or only valid interpretation. Indeed, a major popular objection to much sociological commentary of the last two decades is that in seeking to interpret people's behaviour, social scientists read into that behaviour too much meaning, or even meanings that are 'not there'. There is probably some justice in this view. The dividing line between interpreting meaning and imputing it indiscriminately to people's behaviour, speech or whatever is a very fine one and reflects the inherent and unavoidable tensions and dangers that arise because of the commitment of interpretive research strategies to the inseparability of the researcher from the researched because of the former's own position as a member of society. The difficulty here is that it is possible to be too subjective. For example, while the issue is often skirted around in discussions of research methods, there is no *de facto* reason why interpretive methods need to be more or less accurate than positivist approaches. The differences between positivist and interpretive research are not just a matter of scale in terms of the numbers of subjects that can be studied, but also a matter of the equal propensity of each for error. All research activity involves acts of faith and requires a critical acceptance of the potential for fallibility. With this in mind, the discussion now turns to questions of the quality of research practice.

The methodological characteristics of successful research projects

Few texts on research methods resist the temptation to advise students on the characteristics of successful and unsuccessful research projects. These general pronouncements often succeed in appearing simultaneously to be useful and vague. In this book, such general considerations are briefly considered towards the end of Chapter 3 while the discussion here focuses on those aspects of sound methodology that underpin them.

There are, it is broadly agreed, three axioms of sound methodology, being (McNeill 1990: 14–16):

- reliability;
- validity; and
- representativeness and generalizability.

To talk of methodological principles is to talk primarily of the means of data collection and the use of data. In this sense, it is possible for illustrative purposes to frame a number of questions pertaining to the items listed above, questions which illuminate the significance of each for sound methodology. These are as follows.

- Is the method of data collection reliable and are the conclusions drawn from it equally reliable, that is, consistent with the data?
- Was the data collected (a) valid data to collect; (b) collected in a valid way using an appropriate technique or techniques; and (c) on the basis of (a) and (b) congruent with the conclusions drawn from it?
- Was the data collected representative in the sense of being typical, thus allowing for (a) the generalization/extrapolation of research conclusions beyond the boundaries of the subjects studied; and (b) replication of results by other researchers?

It is worth noting that these questions, and the very concepts of reliability, validity and representativeness/generalizability, are a reflection of the imperatives of the positivist tradition. Nevertheless, only the most extreme anti-positivist would claim that these criteria do not have meaning and significance beyond research conducted in the positivist tradition. In the broadest sense, there are general and generalized criteria for the appraisal of research technique though this does not mean they can be regarded as unproblematic as the following discussion will show.

Reliability and validity

One of the most useful recent discussions of reliability and validity in research methodology is offered by Gilbert (1993: 26–28). It will be recalled from the earlier discussion 'From data to theory' that Gilbert views theories as comprising one or more hypotheses, each of which comprises concepts linked by relationships. To test a theory, it is necessary to compare the predictions made by the theory with measurements of those parts of the real world to which the theory appertains. In practice, this means measuring the concept or concepts that go to make up the theory. The problem is that concepts, being essentially abstract in nature, cannot be measured directly. Concepts must be operationalized, that is, for each concept there must be some indicator, normally a method of measurement, which stands for the concept and is accepted as allowing for the inference of accurate measurement of the concept. These indicators must be *valid*, in that they accurately measure the concept, and *reliable*, in the sense that they are consistent from one measurement to the next.

What Gilbert appears to be saying is this. As researchers we begin with a theory – like the earlier noted theory of suicide proposed by Durkheim. Here, there are concepts – 'economic conditions' and 'suicide' – linked by a relationship, a causal relationship in that changes in the suicide rates are held to be affected by changes in economic conditions. From these observations, hypotheses can be derived for the purposes of testing the general theory. For example, the previously noted and imprecise hypothesis that 'Changes in economic conditions have an effect on suicide rates' requires the concepts to be operationalized. We would therefore search for some adequate and meaningful indicator of 'economic conditions' and 'suicide rates'. In making our selection (assuming that some element of choice is possible), we would have to be confident that the indicators chosen were both valid (measuring accurately the concept(s) concerned) and reliable (consistent from one measurement to the next). How would we do this?

There are, in fact, no easy or exact answers to these questions (which is why Durkheim's theory of suicide, while ambitious, has been found wanting). One area of agreement might be that the indicators we use will invariably be secondary measurements – for example, government data. But what then? The number of potential measures of economic conditions (however defined – and definition is a problem here) are considerable and include: unemployment levels; economic growth; gross domestic product; the rate of inflation and so on. All of these measurements themselves are the product of data collection and measurement, thus compounding the problem of reliability and validity. As far as suicide rates are concerned, we may

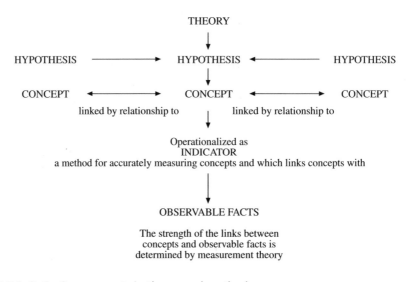

FIGURE 2.1 Core concepts in theory and method

again be reliant upon official statistics which may not reflect a 'true' picture of the suicide rate because of cases of unexplained death, cases where motives for suicide are unclear and which have led officials to classify a death as something other than suicide and so on.

Gilbert (1993: 28) makes the very important point that an indicator links a concept with observable facts (a general conceptualization of the research process after Gilbert is shown in Figure 2.1). The adequacy of this link relies on the indicator's measurement theory which is, broadly speaking, the reliability of the indicator in terms of how it is constructed in the context of the aforementioned reliance on the measurement and collection of other data. The problem for the researcher is thus to know where to draw the line so as to avoid an infinite regression in checking the validity of indicators and, in the long run, there will necessarily be an arbitrary element in any such decision.

So much for the reliability and validity of data collection. The issue of whether conclusions drawn from data are representative and generalizable takes us into slightly different territory.

Representativeness and generalizability

Facts, research methods and research data do not speak for themselves, they are interpreted by researchers and others. To a very large extent, the discussion so far of the reliability and validity of data and research methods has concentrated on questions of the internal consistency of each. A harder test – at least in some respects – of the reliability and validity of data and research methods relates to the wider applications of these data and methods. In essence, the explanatory power of a piece of research is increased the more likely it is believed to be (a) applicable to subjects beyond the sample studied; and (b) replicable – i.e. reproducable – by other researchers.

Applicability in this context is simply another way of asking if the data is both representative and generalizable. If the data from a piece of research is representative, chances are that there is a high probability that it is generalizable (together with the findings drawn from data analysis). Representative in this context therefore refers to an appraisal of the reliability and validity of data relative to its generalizability. In some ways, concerns about reliability and validity in research methodology, especially as they pertain to data selection and collection, are driven by the desire to get the research right without necessarily giving much consideration to the wider applications or relevance of the research. To ask about the representativeness of data is to impose a kind of external test of its validity and reliability by asking if the data and the methods used to collect it, together with any conclusions drawn from data analysis, are wider in their application than the sample of subjects studied.

If this point seems somewhat laboured, it is only because questions of representativeness and generalizability are essentially holistic questions about the integrity of research procedure, but questions which can be equally applied to the separate components of the research process – 'data collected', 'methods by which data collected and analysed', and 'conclusions drawn from data analysis'. Thus while questions of representativeness and generalizability are holistic in the sense of being directed towards the whole research process, they can yield different conclusions for each possible element of that process such that it is perfectly possible for the appropriate data to be collected using appropriate means, and for data analysis to be consistent, but for the conclusions drawn from the analysis to be at odds with these other elements.

More important yet, as Raimond (1993: 88–94) notes, while representativeness and generalizability are inherently bound up with an assessment of whether the conclusions of a piece of research are based on a wide enough range of cases, or are subject specific (or are conclusions that reflect effective choice, collection and analysis of data), in management research, investigations are often small scale, qualitative and interpretive in nature. Representativeness and generalizability are thus very much (arguably very much more than reliability and validity) positivist in their assumptions about the nature of research and the 'real world' of phenomena, and their application as standards to ascertain types of research might be inappropriate.

In short, there are certain types of activity which we describe as 'research' which may not meet the criteria of representativeness and generalizability. For many positivists (crudely speaking), such work should not be regarded as meaningful research in a scientific sense at all. One possible way out of this dilemma is to appeal to the 'test' of replicability, to claim that other researchers using similar methods in the same or similar context will produce the same or similar results.

Falling back on replicability as a validator of research method and technique may not always be possible or reliable however. More importantly, there are many who think that such levels of justification are unnecessary and flawed (because positivist approaches to research are flawed) and do not see the need to adopt an apologetic stance in respect of representativeness and generalizability. A fair point perhaps but one that also suggests a need to recast an understanding of the purposes of research which must surely, at some level, be purposeful only if it seeks to contribute to the generalization of our understanding of phenomena. There is a belief in some quarters of the academic community that many objections to positivist approaches have more to do with (in the words of author Sir Kingsley Amis) promoting academic work that throws 'pseudo-light ... on non-problems'. There is certainly a good deal of justification for this view, which is indicative of the general tensions that exist between those broadly supportive of each of the positivist and interpretive approaches to research. In conclusion, little can be said to reconcile these differences save perhaps the piece of advice offered by Raimond (1993: 89–90) who reminds us that whatever 'research' activity we are engaged in, methodology is what we use to avoid deceiving ourselves. This essentially pragmatic approach is one way of dealing with, but not reconciling, the various generic approaches to research and research methods described in this chapter and with which all researchers must live.

 3

Thinking about doing: choosing a topic

There are many general guidelines that can be offered for consideration in choosing a topic for a dissertation or project. *This is just as well because there is unlikely to be an any more important task that an individual undertakes in the whole research process.* In this chapter, several key areas are advanced as worthy of serious contemplation and action. These are not intended to be exhaustive. The main point to bear in mind is that in choosing the right topic an awful lot of pain can be taken out of the research process.

Can I live with the topic?

Depending on what kind of course is being pursued, the research and writing of a dissertation can cover a lengthy period. For most undergraduate students, the project or dissertation is usually written in the final year and has to be accommodated among a person's commitments to lectures, tutorials, seminars, coursework and examinations (as well as social life!). The writing of a dissertation is an ongoing process in this case, often stretching over several months from September/October through to submission dates after January. For students on postgraduate taught courses, which are usually of one-year full-time duration, the dissertation often takes up the three or four summer months of June to September. Whether diluted or concentrated, a person must be able to live with their topic. For some, the need to constantly return to an ongoing piece of work of some length is a pleasure, a form of relief from other, more short-term, assessment requirements. For many however, the ongoing project is a source of distraction and frustration in which it is difficult to find the necessary motivation and concentration to do justice to the whole process.

One important guideline here is 'choose in haste, repent at leisure' (see 'Take your time in choosing' below). Also important, however, is considered wariness of personal enthusiasms. Often, students who experience the greatest difficulties in researching and writing a dissertation are those who have selected a topic in which they have (a) long-standing interest and enthusiasm but little detailed knowledge; or (b) interest, enthusiasm *and* knowledge. The problem for those in the latter category is that their knowledge is often so great that it leads to frustration and boredom or dilemmas as to what the particular the focus of their study should be. There is some merit in considering whether or not for a dissertation, a new (or at least relatively unfamiliar) topic is not more appropriate than one over which a person already has some command. In respect of those people who fall into category (a) above, enthusiasm is no substitution for hard-and-fast understanding of information relating to the object of the enthusiasm. A good train spotter is not necessarily going to write a good dissertation on the management of change in the rail industry.

The main issue then is that a dissertation topic should sustain interest over the necessary period of time. People can come to hate the whole dissertation process and as a consequence lose motivation, but, if a topic is chosen that retains the interest of the writer, there is a good chance of successful completion. The question here is a deeply personal one and requires a good deal of self-knowledge and honesty. Choosing a good dissertation topic is at least partly dependent on individuals undertaking an audit of their personal skills and interests.

Take your time in choosing

One way of increasing the probability of problems with researching and writing dissertations is to choose a topic too hastily and with little thought. The chief enemy here is the academic environment in which an individual finds themself. It is important to discover what procedures a department operates in respect of topic selection. Sufficient time before these procedures have to be gone through should be allowed for the purposes of contemplation and deciding on a topic. This neatly leads to the next consideration, namely choosing *your* topic.

Adopt a framework for choice

In the light of what has been said so far, it is not wholly illogical to ensure that in selecting a topic, you begin with a number of alternatives. To start with, it is useful to have some preliminary labels for classifying the overall structure of topic ideas. Jankowicz (1991: 32) helpfully suggests that the area-field-aspect approach is useful in this context. An area is a broad field of study that might coincide with a discipline – economics, marketing, human resource management and so on. A field is a component element of the area of study. It may be a recognized sub-discipline (macroeconomics; social marketing; industrial relations) or a major intellectual focus within the area (for example, international marketing; bargaining and reward systems). An aspect is just one facet of a field.

This framework is useful for classifying topic ideas. The natural emphasis falls logically in the last category mentioned above – the aspect or facet, because this is where most research activity takes place. Figure 3.1 shows some examples of the area-field-aspect system of classification. Two observations can be made. The first is that many students initially generate topics in the 'area' or 'field' zones. Some are even

Area	Field	Aspect and topic
Marketing	Brand management	New brand creation – brewer's strategies for creating new family brands of public houses
Human Resource Management	Organizational culture	Empowerment strategies – the role of empowerment in enhancing employee motivation
Finance	Cost accounting	Labour costs – the effect of managerial calculation of the cost of labour turnover on recruitment spend decisions
Public Relations	Promotion	Corporate identity – the effects of television advertising on perceptions of corporate identity
Operational Research	Sales management	Yield management – a comparative study of the effect of yield management on sales of fast moving consumer goods.

FIGURE 3.1 Example of the Area-Field-Aspect model applied to business and management for clarifying project and dissertation topic selection (after Jankowicz 1991)

allowed to proceed on the basis of such a choice (see the section 'Know your academics' below). Occasionally this is appropriate but often it is not in anyone's interest – least of all the student's. Often a first response to the request to select a research and dissertation topic is a deluge (from the lecturer's point of view) of enthusiastic generalities – for example, 'I want to do something on human resource management – or marketing, or business economics, or …' fill in the label of your choice. Too wide a topic causes problems of focus, something rapidly picked up by external examiners. Unless you are doing a Master's degree by research or a PhD, nobody will be expecting you to split the atom or discover a cure for the common cold (see the section 'What is a dissertation for?' below) – so make life relatively easy for yourself and do not try to reinvent the wheel.

The second point to bear in mind is that the curricula of business and management degrees and diplomas usually comprise several disciplines or disciplinary perspectives. Examples include marketing, organizational behaviour and human resource management, finance and accounting, economics and behavioural studies and in the context of Figure 3.1 equate to 'areas'. While this breadth allows a considerable degree of choice it is important to recognize that studying a particular subject in this context does not make an expert of you. A student who studies marketing as part of a broad management degree is perhaps unlikely to cover as much in depth as a student studying for a specialized marketing degree. If you are following a combined subjects course which involves studying a second area then it is worthwhile considering whether that area can bring something useful to bear on the research process. It is always sensible, therefore, to set limits to personal ambition.

If the area-field-aspect system of classifying research ideas is employed to analyse potential topics, some system of arbitrating between these is necessary in order to arrive at a final decision. The next section considers more closely some useful partial strategies for topic selection.

Strategies for topic selection

The four major areas to be considered when arbitrating between potential research and dissertation topics are:

- Complexity and difficulty.
- Access.
- Facilities and resources.
- Expertise.

Complexity and difficulty

Literature searching is an important aspect of the research process (and one examined further in Chapter 7) and it is often undertaken only when a topic has been chosen. Inconvenient and time-consuming though it may be, if you are intending to select a topic from among several potential subjects that interest you, it is wise to undertake some form of limited literature search at this stage. This helps in establishing the degree of complexity that is likely to be encountered in researching a topic.

Complexity and difficulty are terms often used synonymously and while this in many instances may be legitimate, there is sometimes an important distinction between them. In this context, complexity refers to how complicated the research process is likely to be as the result of choosing a particular topic, in terms of the relationship of the parts to a whole. The best way of elaborating this point is to imagine two opposite, ideal-type models of complexity that might be encountered in the research process as a result of choosing a particular topic. The first model is where the choice of a topic initiates a research process that reveals (a) the existence of a substantial literature on the topic; (b) a number of developed academic viewpoints on the topic; and (c) an ongoing debate about the subject. This kind of topic is likely to give rise to complexity because:

- there is a considerable literature to read and understand;
- much of the literature is self-referential (that is, refers less to the study of the topic itself or is less involved in advancing research into the topic than to arguments about how the topic should be studied – or put another way, arguments about the arguments about the topic!); and
- the arguments described in the preceding point are themselves often highly complex and esoteric and may be of a level of abstraction that is difficult and time-consuming to comprehend.

The main problem with this kind of topic is that it is difficult within the confines of a short dissertation for a student to make a significant or original contribution to the issue in question. The second model involves the kind of topic which leads to a research process that in turn reveals a small and limited literature which may be relatively new and under-researched or simply uninteresting (if you generate a topic where you can find few background research commentaries you may have to recognize that you have selected a turkey!). The complexity encountered with this kind of topic is of a different order to that associated with the first model. Here, complexity arises from having to research and write a topic about which little is known. To be convincing, such a piece of research may have to cover many more angles and approaches than one where a framework for research already exists, and some avenues of enquiry may prove to be fruitless.

Of course, most research topics fall somewhere between these extremes. The point is, that in selecting a topic from among a range of potential subjects, a good deal of later heartache can be avoided if a small preliminary literature search is undertaken to assist in assessing the degree of likely complexity of a research process engendered by the selection of that topic. Both kinds (and all) can be difficult in the sense of requiring considerable application, but the degree of difficulty faced in researching a given topic is likely to be influenced by the remaining three key elements involved in the topic selection strategy: access; facilities and resources; and expertise.

Access

Access refers to the ease by which data may be obtained as part of the research process, thereby making the process effective in terms of its principal outcome (the successful writing-up of a dissertation or report). The question to be asked at the topic selection stage is a simple one: is it possible to obtain the data necessary to make the project feasible? The question should be applied to all kinds of potential data that it is believed will be necessary for adequate completion of the project. This includes secondary data (previous published research, statistics) and primary research data. Gaining access for the purposes of collecting original data is considered in the relevant chapters on research methods contained in Part Two of this text. A number of key points are worth bearing in mind at this stage.

In respect of secondary data, do not assume that the vast quantity of statistical data produced by government agencies and others will be necessarily helpful to you – check *before* your finalize a choice of topic. Furthermore, do not be cursory in this check. A whole range of statistical sources on a topic may exist but this does not mean that the agencies and organizations that have produced them have used the same definitions, methods of counting or analysis. You may end up with a rich variety of statistical sources all of which are in disagreement and tell you something different about the phenomenon under scrutiny. Similarly, when it comes to previously published research reports, do not assume that any or all of these reports have a direct bearing on your potential topic. Many industries, particularly in the service sectors, remain relatively under-researched. For a significant number of topics, available literature of direct relevance to your field of interest may be limited, necessitating consideration of the analysis of literature with more general applications to the proposed research area. The importance of a preliminary literature search at the topic selection stage should not be confined to simply *identifying* lists of material using your library's data retrieval system. Some of the literature should also be *viewed* to make sure it is germane to your interests, as the classification schemes employed by libraries when combined with the intrinsic fluidity of content of many academic books and articles need not lead to a natural correspondence between what you see and what you get!

For primary research – original data collection – it is not always sufficient to ask, rhetorically, how easy data will be to obtain. Rather, the acid test is the extent to which it is possible to *guarantee* that it will be possible to obtain the data. If there is the prospect of choosing a topic where ease of data collection will be improved by the use of willing contacts who can guarantee access to sources of such data, this is a plus point that should be kept in mind in reaching a final choice of topic. It is important that offers of help are not taken entirely on trust however. Many students have been left with egg on their faces having been offered help in gaining access to organizations and then being left high and dry when their contacts have not delivered. If you are involved in active research that involves access to organizations, it is as well to remember that the people working in those organizations are often very busy and your research project is low in their list of priorities.

Facilities and resources

It should go without saying that in choosing a topic to research, available facilities and resources must be assessed relative to the goals of the research. It is, however, unfortunately usual for students to embark on research projects without due consideration of resource and facilities issues. More worryingly, in an academic environment where staff are under ever-increasing pressure, is the occasional failure of tutors and supervisors to anticipate facilities and resources problems on behalf of their students.

An elementary audit of facility and resource availability is a useful means of clarifying what is possible in research terms, and in asking yourself the following questions you will have the basis of this audit.

- What will be the financial cost of data collection?
- Who will bear the cost of collecting data?
- Does the department/school of which I am a member provide finance for the development of research instruments (questionnaires, interview schedules)?
- Does the department/school of which I am a member provide equipment and facilities at little or no cost for supporting the research process (e.g. photocopying facilities; the loan of tape-recording equipment for interviews; the loan of tape transcribing machines)?
- Will I need a personal computer and if so, is this available for student use within my institution?
- Will I need special software packages for word processing and data analysis and if so, are these available for loan within my institution or must I purchase them?
- Will my department/school allow me to use the institution's telephone, fax and electronic mail/world wide web facilities in pursuit of my research?

- Will my department/school allow me to use the institution's mail service free of charge for sending letters, questionnaires and other documentation in connection with my research project?
- Will my department/school allow me to use the departmental/school address for the receipt of mail in connection with my research?
- Does the library in my university/college carry sufficient reference and other material to support my research project and, if not, are there any nearby libraries that can be of assistance?

Expertise

Reference has already been made to the role of your own expertise in choosing a topic to research for projects and dissertations. A clinical assessment should also be made of the expertise of academic staff in your school, department or institution, particularly as it relates to the group of academics from which your dissertation supervisor/tutor is most likely to be drawn. This subject is considered in greater depth in the next section. For the moment, it is sufficient to say that, together with complexity and difficulty, access, and facilities and resources, expertise is an important but not overriding element in any choice of topic for a dissertation research project. All four elements represent useful standards against which various topics can be assessed prior to final selection. They are not the only considerations, however, only perhaps the most practical from the point of view of doing the research. Put crudely, they are a convenient shorthand for rapid assessment of competing topics but there are other considerations as this chapter shows, and some balance should be sought in weighing up alternative (potential) topics as, for many people, the question of support and relationships with academic staff can be equally significant factors in topic choice.

Know your academics – an address to students!

In discussing the issue of expertise in the previous section, reference was made to the value of having a knowledgeable specialist in the field for your dissertation tutor/supervisor. This is not always possible in small departments/schools and can be a problem in larger ones. In small departments, a full range of expertise might not be represented. It might, however, exist outside your department. This is particularly true of departments where there is a large element of service teaching (subjects taught by members of staff from other departments). Another problem arises in the overloading of individual staff members with dissertations to supervise. Often, certain areas or topics enjoy a cyclical popularity. Some topics are always popular. Marketing and human resource management seem to fall into the latter category. Whatever the case, this can lead some staff to taking on more dissertations than they can adequately supervise. If this sounds a little strange then consider that even in departments where sound procedures exist for the allocation of dissertation and project supervisors, many members of academic staff do not wish to let students down by denying them supervision. Similar problems arise when certain members of staff, for whatever reasons, enjoy a personal popularity and attract a following.

In a well-managed school or department, none of these problems should arise if the dissertation process is handled effectively and efficiently. It is as well to remember that in addition to having obligations, students have certain rights. Students should always ensure, therefore, that their department has proper procedures for allocating supervisors and that the criteria for allocation are open, readily understandable and realizable. Together with others, they may wish to lobby for the creation of such procedures if they do not exist. It is a regrettable fact of life that many educational institutions are unenlightened when it comes to operating formalized procedures in areas such as dissertation supervision. The academic preference for informality in such procedures is still strong. Having said all this it is important to note that most academic staff in universities and colleges want the best for their students and are well intentioned. Of course, as the saying has it, the road to hell is paved with good intentions but a basic source of conflict between students and their tutors is the failure on the part of the former to recognize that lecturing staff are not rendering individual service but have many other commitments. When it comes to the allocation of supervisors for dissertations, therefore, an effort is required by both parties to accept the decision and strike up a rapport. Some institutions get around the problems discussed so far by allocating two or more supervisors to a student. This system has its advantages (sharing academics' expertise around being the most obvious) but can lead to confusion if supervisors have different expectations of an individual's work.

Two other points should be made here. When it comes to expertise, it is useful to keep in mind the point that, particularly at undergraduate level, the researching and writing of a dissertation is not simply about knowledge and expertise but about the actual process of writing a dissertation. Many academics have, at some time, supervised a dissertation topic of which their knowledge might be limited but most are expert in the art of the researching and writing processes. In short, subject expertise is important but it is only one element of the whole research process. This statement can be qualified further by noting that even where the supervisor/tutor is expert in the subject concerned, he or she might not have an in-depth familiarity with the specific topic, especially if the topic is highly specialized. It is often the case that students who are on top of their research will, at some point, know more about that topic than the supervisor.

The second issue concerns relationships with supervisors (see also Chapter 7 below). Sometimes these can become strained and they may become so at the outset if students feel they have been allocated a supervisor who is unsympathetic, or not equipped to help them. It is foolish to pretend that there are *no* occasions on which some staff do not get on with some students at a personal level and problems of this nature should be tackled at the outset by reference to the course tutor or head of department. Many departments/schools have a procedure for changing tutors and supervisors where personal relationships become strained.

Finally in this discussion, it is sensible for both academics and students to be wary of the academic ego. Many academics do appear to have an unquestioned belief in their own infallibility and this can present problems for students who do not share their lecturers' high opinions of themselves. At the same time, students have been known to be obstinate, obtuse and even bloody-minded. The warning is clear.

Support

You will expect and (usually) get adequate support from your tutors during the research and dissertation/project writing process. It is also important that you establish other sources of support – particularly emotional support – for your work while striving to minimize the potential for emotional disruption. Obviously, this piece of advice has implications beyond the research and dissertation writing processes but these can be particularly lonely and stressful periods in your academic career. By way of offering some useful guidelines, you should:

- engage the interest and support of your parents and friends for your work;
- ensure that you can talk to somebody other than your supervisors and tutors about your work;
- carefully manage any close personal relationships (e.g. boyfriends/girlfriends) so that these are a source of strength rather than disruption;
- tailor your social activities to the demands of your workload (and not the other way round);
- ensure that you do have a social life: too little is as bad as too much;
- develop strategies for coping with work-derived stress;
- *always* ensure that you tell somebody if you cannot cope for *any* reason with your work: if you cannot talk to family and friends, try a member of academic staff with whom you have empathy (this may or may not be your research project supervisor) or your university/college counselling and advisory service;
- *never* let a problem or problems simmer until they reach the stage where they are more difficult to resolve; and
- be kind to yourself and others!

What! No topic?

Some people find it very difficult to generate a research/dissertation topic and there are others who sometimes seize upon this as a sign of weakness or lack of imagination and motivation. However, being unable to generate or decide upon a topic should not be a source of shame. It happens more frequently than many people realize and can be a source of considerable distress. Sometimes the problem lies not in the inability to generate topics but in choosing from among potential topics. To a large extent, the discussion so far in this chapter has leant towards this issue. Not having a topic is a major difficulty; however, a difficulty which might be overcome by turning to four major sources for inspiration and information. These are (see also Raimond 1993: 27–28): previous projects; main themes in the research literature; possible clients and sponsors; and tutors.

Previous projects

You are probably not the first person to have written a project or dissertation in your department/school though on occasions it may seem like it! Many departments keep copies of their students' dissertations and reports and these may be stored in your department or institution's library. If copies of the dissertations themselves are not kept, it is likely that in efficient departments, a database of previous titles is kept. Find out if, for your case, this information (and hard copies of dissertations) exist and trawl the information for ideas. Key advantages of this approach can include:

- the possibility of advancing and/or developing a previous piece of research; and
- locating a piece of research where external contacts and respondents who participated in the research may be willing to help again.

The main disadvantages of this approach are:

- a risk of relying too heavily on previous research and doing little original research to advance it; and
- settling on a dissertation or report that was originally weak in terms of topic choice, execution or some other criterion (to assist with this aspect it may be possible to find out how 'good' such pieces of work were by reference to tutors).

Main themes in the research literature

A second way of generating topic ideas is to search current literature (books, journals – see Chapter 5) to discover (a) what topics are currently popular, controversial or otherwise preoccupying industry or academic researchers; or (b) what topics are not covered or covered only partially. In making this kind of assessment, it will then be possible to gain some idea of what you can link your work to or, alternatively, where you might be able to make a small original contribution to filling out some gap in the literature (but remember not to be too ambitious). Issues of which to be wary include:

- fashionability or trendiness – academics no less than other people enjoy jumping on a good bandwagon and the seeming popularity of a topic does not necessarily mean that it is important and innovative; and
- the existence of substantial literature on a topic may mean that to all intents and purposes, that topic has been exhausted.

Possible clients and sponsors

Without resorting to harassment, it is always worthwhile seeking to discover whether local organizations require an applied research project to be undertaken for reasons of their own. Lecturers are often a good first source of information in this area as many have both local and national contacts.

Tutors

If all else fails, tutors may be a good source of dissertation topics. This is especially true of academic staff who are themselves actively engaged in research. The difficulty with relying on tutors for ideas is that they may suggest something connected to their own work, something in which you have little interest. The strength of their own enthusiasms may also mean that if you link yourself to their work in some way, tutors' expectations will be higher than usual, causing the potential for strain (on the other hand, such opportunities can, for the right people, be a useful discipline).

What is a dissertation for? Purposefulness, success and pragmatism

It may seem odd to have left discussion of the purposes of dissertations and projects until the end of this chapter on topic selection. The reason for doing so is simple: while an understanding of the purpose of a dissertation or project within your course of study is important to *selecting* a topic, it is also one of the means by which the feasibility or viability of a topic is validated. Moreover, to talk of the 'purpose' of the dissertation begs a number of questions about the practical (specific) and metaphysical purposes of the work. Thus, if you have to complete a research project or dissertation as part of your course there will be, as likely as not, a specific set of objectives laid down by your institution which are intended to be realized by undertaking the task of completing a discrete piece of research and presenting your findings. Overarching this, however, is a purpose that is metaphysical in quality, namely the intrinsic satisfaction that is to be derived from undertaking original research for presentation as a dissertation or report. In the experience of most academics, students are keen to complete such a work as part of their studies. This more abstract purpose can be termed the experiential or 'personal learning experience' dimension to the research and dissertation processes. In Chapter 2 we considered methodological 'success' factors in research. Other general success factors associated with the research process include (see also Jankowicz 1991: 9–19):

- the acquisition of concepts and techniques;
- the effective practice and manipulation of these concepts and techniques in a manner directed towards the attainment of specific goals;
- the production of a sustained and extended piece of writing designed to address a specific theme or issue, the production of such a manuscript itself being an exercise in acquiring the skills associated with academic research; and
- an appreciation of the nature of scholarship.

The concept of scholarship is not an easy one to define as it has various usages. Jankowicz (1991: 51) offers a fourfold typology of the characteristics normally associated with the term. These are:

- careful and accurate use of evidence;
- care in the identification and attribution of sources;
- thoroughness in the coverage of subject matter; and
- respect for truth and validity of data and assertions made on the basis of data.

Many authors of research methods texts (e.g. Jankowicz 1991: 42–48; Raimond 1993: 10–15) also indicate certain general characteristics of successful projects and dissertations (note how these parallel the main methodological features of research discussed in Chapter 2):

- a clearly defined topic;
- clearly defined objectives;
- some evidence of originality;
- a sound methodology and good quality evidence/data;
- balance in the reporting of data and evidence;
- relevance and applicability; and
- evidence of the ability to generalize findings.

Note that a recurring theme in discussions of both the research and dissertation process is the need for clarity. Much academic research and writing *is* unnecessarily obtuse and difficult but the ultimate achievement is to be able to write about difficult and complex subjects with clarity – to communicate ideas unambiguously and with interest. Raimond (1993: 16–26) in addition to identifying 'success' factors in the research and dissertation process identifies some of the reasons why projects fail. These include:

- poor time management – especially leaving things to the last minute; failing to frontload data collection in the research process; and not allowing sufficient time to draft the final written documentation for supervisor approval (see also Chapter 7);
- lack of objectivity – notably a failure to achieve sufficient detachment from the subject matter as detailed earlier in this chapter;
- failure to satisfy multiple clients – where a piece of research is heavily linked to a particular organization (especially to the extent of being commissioned by that organization) there is a danger that a mismatch could arise between the organizational client's needs and the needs and requirements of the educational institution by whom the work is being assessed – attempts to resolve these tensions can be clumsy and result in both parties being dissatisfied: it is therefore incumbent on both researcher and tutors to agree the acceptable scope of the final work; and
- letting the audience miss the point – the central problem here is the inexperienced researcher who presents conclusions to their work that are not supported by the evidence they have collected – this is an extremely common phenomenon and requires a careful, programmatic approach to ensure that key issues, with supporting data, are followed through the text to specific conclusions.

Finally in this discussion, having talked about what might be termed the 'theory' of the rationale underlying purposeful and successful dissertations, it is necessary to

TABLE 3.1 Model marking scheme for the assessment of a dissertation in business and management

Allocation of marks (×/100)	Item(s) being assessed
5%	*Choice and definition of topic.* Topic is clearly related to the field of study and with relevance firmly anchored in the articulation of precise objectives and specific hypotheses.
15%	*Literature review.* Literature review is concise and to the point, supplying an adequate context for the study as evidenced in relevance to the earlier stated objectives. The literature review is not simply passive but leads to firm conclusions about the current state of research in the chosen field and an outline of implications of current research for the present study.
10%	*Data collection.* In respect of both the literature review and the claims underlying the study's methodology, competence has been demonstrated in data collection as evidenced in coverage of major sources.
20%	*Methodology.* The methods chosen for the original research are appropriate and clearly explained. Information supplied on the choice and operationalization of methods is comprehensive. Basic parameters of data collected are reported, explained and, where appropriate, commented upon.
20%	*Analysis.* Data is analysed systematically; relevant data is identified and economy is evident in the selection of key findings. Findings from data are related to aspects of the methodology where appropriate, and effects arising from the choice of methods are recognized and commented upon. Where the project or dissertation is an extended literature review or a theoretical critique of existing research, competing and complementary positions in the debate(s) concerned are clearly explained, compared and contrasted, and an assessment of the relative merits of these positions is given together with a clear statement of their implications for the topic under scrutiny.
20%	*Conclusions.* Conclusions relate methodology and analysis of original data to key issues arising from literature review. The dissertation's key hypothesis/hypotheses are revisited in this context and an overall synthesis is achieved, characterized by (a) rejection, acceptance or qualification of the original hypothesis or hypotheses; (b) the relevance of (a) to issues suggested by the literature review; (c) the relevance of original research findings to the implications of the issues raised in the literature review; and (d) a statement of the implications of (a)–(c) together for future research in the form of a short rhetorical commentary or the explicit articulation of conclusions. For dissertations offering an extended literature review/theoretical critique, conclusions should embrace an original perspective on the topic that may be speculative but should be constrained by a clear commitment to remaining within the boundaries of reasonable conjecture.
10%	*Presentation.* The final written product is to the standards specified by the department/institution or, where these do not exist, to the basic requirements of academic writing (see Part Four). The project or dissertation is well written with no grammatical, syntactic, spelling or typographical errors that reflects careful proofreading. The style of writing and presentation is consistent throughout. The text communicates clearly and unambiguously the subject matter of the work.

consider the brutally pragmatic aspects to researching and writing dissertations. Simply put, dissertations and projects usually count for *marks* and this point should not be lost in a haze of academic idealism. Projects and dissertations often attract a sizeable proportion of the assessment for any course and it is thus important to ensure that your work is geared towards maximizing the rewards to be gained from this kind of arrangement. To this end, apart from keeping your eyes on the ball and ensuring that your actions are directed towards creating a product with good mark-earning potential, it is advisable (should it not be volunteered) to obtain from your institution, school or department some tangible statement of the assessment criteria applied in evaluating dissertations and projects. Table 3.1 lists an idealized marking scheme for a dissertation assessment in business and management.

■ □ ▨ ■ 4

Choosing a research method

The preceding chapter considered some of the issues to be taken into account when choosing a dissertation or research project topic. Research is an organic process, and attempts to inject some structure into this process, to make it more mechanical or rational, is by no means an easy task. Choosing a topic is inextricably bound up with the process of choosing a research method or methods, to bring the topic to life through the collection of data. This short chapter examines some of the main issues that bear on the selection and use of research methods. These issues not only have implications for the choice of particular methods but may feed back into the process of topic selection. This chapter and the two that follow it therefore form the first part or span of a bridge between settling on a topic and researching it. The second part of the bridge is the successful management of the research process which is discussed in Chapter 7.

Topic and methods together

In some cases, the choice of topic can simultaneously decide the choice of research method(s). For example, if you are interested in some performative aspect of employment in an industry (i.e. how employees 'do' their job) then the methods available for executing such a study and gaining the quality of data necessary are, realistically, fairly limited. On the assumption that you do not wish to rely only on employees' accounts of how they do their job, then some form of observational technique will need to be followed. If the study in question was of the 'real' feelings of bank tellers towards their customers, then covert participant observation may be the only serious method available, with the researcher joining (should the host organization permit) the staff of the company under the guise of being a genuine employee and observing and recording the feelings of co-workers in a naturalistic manner. If, by way of contrast, you are interested in factors affecting the speed of transactions between bank tellers and clients, then direct observation may be an appropriate technique.

The range of methods

In some cases then, the choice of topic will simultaneously decide the methods employed to gather data, in other cases there will be a degree of choice. For the most part, the degree of choice will to some extent be constrained by the focus of a topic and the quantity of data required to effectively study that topic. The range of key research methods discussed in Parts Two and Three of this book can be seen as occupying points on a continuum running between the quantitative and qualitative and reflecting the number of respondents studied and the level of personal involvement of the researcher (see Figure 4.1) (Worsley 1977: 89). This is a useful means of conceptualizing the degree of choice available in the selection of appropriate research methods where the choice is not immediately implied by the nature of the topic. Clearly indicated by this scale is a 'level of inappropriateness' of techniques relative to the number of respondents that are to be consulted in a research project. Thus, working up the scale, participant observation is rarely if ever appropriate to studying large numbers of people. Working down the scale, appropriateness is more difficult to define relative to number studied. Social surveys and the questionnaire method *could* be appropriate in some circumstances to small numbers of respondents in a study. As McNeill (1990: 121–122) notes, different claims can be made for each method shown on the scale in terms of reliability, representativeness and validity (see Chapter 2):

> Where the survey researcher may claim reliability and representativeness, the ethnographer will claim validity. The survey enthusiast will point out the dangers of bias and unreliability in ethnography, and stress how the representativeness of a sample can be calculated precisely. The ethnographer may concede all this, but would point out that it is not much use being able to produce the same results over and over again, and to say how representative they are, if they are invalid in the first place.

Of course, it could be argued with equal force in certain circumstances that the reliability and representativeness of the questionnaire social survey method diminishes the smaller the number of people covered by its application, but reliability and representativeness are unlikely to be improved by increasing the number of people included in an ethnographic study employing observation and participant observation.

In choosing a research method then, there are always trade-offs and compromises. An observational study of a small group of people cannot usually be representative, yet ethnographic and observational methods are not normally intended to be used for representative studies in the sense of representative of the population as a whole. Within the boundaries of an observational study, however, findings may be perfectly valid and reliable. Another consideration worth noting here in respect of representativeness, validity and reliability of findings, is the accumulation of data and evidence. This is a variation on the well-known duck aphorism – i.e. if it walks like a duck and quacks like a duck, it *is* a duck! The accumulation of consistent research evidence and findings (research undertaken over

PRIMARY DATA COLLECTION	Social surveys (questionnaires)	Structured interviews	Unstructured interviews	Focus groups	Observation	Participant observation
SECONDARY DATA ANALYSIS	Biographical analysis	Public records	Content analysis	Conversation analysis	Interaction analysis	Video analysis

RESEARCH METHODS Continuum						
PRIMARY DATA COLLECTION	LOWER		*Level of personal involvement of the researcher*			HIGHER
	LARGER		*Respondent group size on research project*			SMALLER
SECONDARY DATA ANALYSIS	MORE		*Level of subjectivity/interpretative flexibility*			LESS

FIGURE 4.1 Methods of data collection showing a continuum of research methods and techniques relative to respondent group size and researcher's level of involvement (after Worsley 1977).

time and by different parties in different locations) about a particular phenomenon or topic makes it difficult to argue that these findings are not to some extent representative of that phenomenon/topic.

Multi-method approaches and triangulation

Triangulation is a term used to describe the use of a number of different research methods in a single research study in the belief that variety will increase the validity of findings. This is an interesting notion and one for which the logic or rationale remains unclear. The term 'triangulation' is borrowed from surveying where it is used to denote the use of three reference points to check the position of an object. The use of more than one research method to examine a particular phenomenon may improve understanding of that phenomenon and each technique may reveal facets of the phenomenon that would not be yielded by the use of alternative methods. These are the main advantages of a multi-method approach. However, the generation of a greater range of data can lead to confusion and a loss of focus in research and there is no *de facto* logical reason for supposing that a multi-method/triangulation approach increases the validity of findings, especially if one or more of the research focus, research design or implementation of research methods are in some way incomplete or faulty in the first place.

Quantitative and qualitative methods

The distinction between quantitative and qualitative methods is one encountered frequently in discussions concerning the choice of research methods. Jary and Jary (1991: 513–514) distinguish between the two in an interesting manner. For them, qualitative techniques rely on the *skills of the researcher* as an interviewer or observer in gathering data whereas quantitative methods place reliance upon the *research instruments* employed to gather data and analyse/measure it (for example, questionnaires, experiments). This is a useful and clear distinction which goes some way to overcoming the perception by many of the experimental and questionnaire methods as fundamentally qualitative in conception (because in social as well as business management research they involve researcher skills in both the construction and administration of the questionnaire/experiment except when, in the case of the former, self-completion is expected of respondents) but quantitative in ultimate execution (because results are expressed in largely quantitative – usually statistical – terms, especially in the case of questionnaires). In reality, when research is written up, the nature of sampling (see below, Chapter 8) demands that a text contains at least some simple descriptive quantitative data even if the major means of analysis is qualitative in nature.

Gaining entry

Any choice of research method will to some extent depend on how easy it is to implement that method, that is, how easy it will be to gain access to the quantity and quality of respondents. As a rule of thumb (though by no means a certain one), access to respondents is more difficult to achieve when fewer are required in preference to many (see Figure 4.1). Access to respondents has already been touched upon in Chapter 3. Here, the concern is with the strategies that might be employed for 'opening doors'.

Having identified the kinds of respondents you need for your study, it is necessary to make the appropriate approaches to secure their co-operation. With some types of respondent there are few problems – for example, for some interview and questionnaire survey type studies it is often possible to approach people 'cold', either by letter, domestic calling or by approaching them in the street (as many market researchers do). For many kinds of managerial and organizational research, however, gaining access to people can be less easy.

This is particularly true where an organization's employees are concerned and the permission of organizational leaders or their managerial representatives is necessary to gain access to employee respondents. If research is explained properly, then employers and managers in many organizations are often willing to help students, provided the form of the research is relatively uncontroversial. Data that might be considered controversial by managers and employers can often still be gained from respondents in small-scale behavioural studies by 'casual' means. For example, if studying employee empowerment in organizations, much information on pay rates and workers' attitudes to their employment, including common grievances might be garnered. As a research strategy, this 'Trojan Horse' method has to be used with some care if used deliberately as it is one thing *not* to enlist the support and sanction of organizational office holders in positions of authority and quite another to mislead them by claiming to research one topic and then studying another. Of course, this does not mean that topics that are seemingly uncontroversial to those allowing access to their organizations need be interpreted uncontroversially by the researcher. Similarly, a hard-edged topic can be softened in appearance when seeking to sell it to an organization that can offer access for research.

General rules for obtaining help for your research from organizations and the people within them include the following.

- Identify (probably with the aid of tutors) suitable organizations and personnel within them who are likely to be sympathetic to your needs.
- Make contact with the key staff member(s) who can help you and/or whose authority you need in order to gain access to the organization.
- Specify clearly (but not necessarily comprehensively) your needs, including the level of access you require and what respondents you need to consult (and in what manner, i.e. using what research instrument): prepare to negotiate and compromise over levels of access – be practical in your ambitions.
- Gild the lily – offer some returns to the organization and/or respondents, however abstract. For example, if possible, take on board some concerns of the organization in your research, offer them a full copy of your report or dissertation and so on.
- Adopt a suitably courteous manner in your dealings with others. Adopt the role of willing apprentice, showing modesty and an eagerness to learn. Even exaggerating your ignorance can help you get the best out of others. This type of behaviour is all a matter of impression management, a term borrowed from the dramaturgical sociology of Erving Goffman (1959). Exploit your position as a learner and whatever you do, do not start *demanding* things of organizational officials or respondents as this will almost certainly alienate them. It still occasionally happens that a student is sent packing with a flea in their ear from organizations which had initially been helpful because the student fails to recognize that organizational officials or individuals providing assistance with research have priorities of their own and are usually busy with these to the extent that dealing with demanding and ungrateful researchers becomes a luxury they can live without.

Three other, more specific, issues need to be considered in gaining entry to an organization or group of respondents for the purpose of collecting data. They are: confidentiality; the utilization of research findings and the ethical collection and use of data.

Confidentiality

If your research involves collecting data from people (by whatever means) then consideration must be given to the issue of confidentiality. Confidentiality is something on which individuals and organizations tend to require assurances in return for their co-operation. It is also possible (though by no means certain) that guarantees of confidentiality can increase the reliability and truthfulness of respondents' inputs to your research. In any case, there are certain rules you should always follow as a matter of course. These include:

- offer anonymity to all respondents who participate in your research whether these be individuals or organizations;
- always honour this undertaking: never be tempted to breach it; and
- take steps to ensure that data analysis is, wherever possible, undertaken on the basis of removing 'give-away' indicators of the source of the data, so that you yourself are working with 'anonymous' data.

This last point is particularly important since, if you as researcher analyse data in aggregate form you may in many cases forget its origin. This has the advantage of allowing you greater sensitivity to regularities in the data. The origins of data can always be checked back if this is germane to the research.

Utilization of research findings

Confidentiality and anonymity where offered and accepted should be carried over into the writing-up and utilization of your research. Individuals who are quoted or referred to in your report(s) should have their identities disguised if the research is in any way controversial or if information and data have been given on the grounds that it is reported anonymously. You will read many studies where respondents are given pseudonyms or simply referred to as (for example) 'Manager A', 'Manager B' and so on, in order to protect the identity of the interviewees. Promises of this kind of anonymity also often allows respondents to speak more fully of their real feelings. What applies to individuals in such contexts also applies to organizations. In many published research studies based on empirical investigation in organizations you will find that the name of the organization(s) have been changed. This is usually (and often) at the request of the organization's management who, while having no objection to the dissemination of research findings, require some protection of their 'business secrets' or practices from rivals.

If, once written up, your research is to have a wider audience than your tutors and other students or academic users, it is necessary to agree appropriate strategies with respondents. Normally, the procedures already described will be sufficient but if your research has been sponsored by a particular organization or organizations, they may wish to have a copy of your report. Before agreeing to such sponsorship, you should come to some arrangement over how the research findings may be used, if at all, outside this organizational context (this is particularly true for MSc, MPhil and PhD theses where publication of some or all of the findings in journal or book form may be a possibility).

Ethics

Many professional associations issue their own codes of ethics on the conduct of research (e.g. the Market Research Society, the British Sociological Association). The themes discussed above are essentially ethical issues and ethics is a subject that has come to occupy researchers and others in respect of how they conduct their research work (in the natural sciences this is most obvious in the campaigns of those who claim to represent animal rights and seek to halt scientific experimentation on animals). Ethics is a complex area and one where debates among concerned parties are characterized by more than just a degree of sanctimoniousness. Many social researchers agree that in dealing with respondents in a research context it is sometimes necessary to be less than fully truthful in outlining one's intentions (see Hornsby-Smith 1993 for a useful review). This is the key: it is always best to avoid telling lies about your research or intentions. Indeed, it is not unreasonable to say that one should never tell an untruth or deliberately mislead others (especially respondents) about the research work being undertaken. Within the limits of common decency it is permissible, however, (in the words of that civil service mandarin of the Thatcher years of government, Sir Robert Armstrong) to be 'economical with the truth'. A position of partial truth-telling is reasonable provided it does not lead to casualties in terms of confidentiality of sources or the abuse of respondents' trust and goodwill. At undergraduate level, the kinds of research undertaken will not usually raise too many ethical issues of the kind where only partial truth-telling is necessary to maintain the integrity of the research programme.

A note on samples and piloting

The nature of sampling – the selection of appropriate subjects for study in a research programme – is examined in depth in Chapter 8. However, it is important to consider when selecting a research method or methods the extent to which difficulties may arise with sampling, so an understanding of this topic is in many ways integral to the topic-research method selection process. This is particularly so if the method(s) chosen for use in research require *piloting*. A pilot study is a simple way of testing whether the articulation of the method(s) selected for use in a research programme is adequate to meet research objectives. Piloting is notably useful in (a) clarifying the effectiveness and relevance of questions in a questionnaire (see Chapter 9); and (b) performing a similar function for proposed interview-based research. In the case of the latter, piloting allows the researched to evolve a series of questions (the interview schedule) that maximizes the opportunities for securing the views of respondents.

Where the likely main sample is in some way restricted in numbers, piloting can be achieved by using a group of individuals who possess similar characteristics to the intended sample. It is always worth piloting a research project if time allows, but consideration must be given to the effort–reward relationship involved. If the effort that has to be expended in conducting a pilot eats into the amount of time set aside for the main project, or the projected rewards to be gained from piloting are assessed as small, then piloting may be an unnecessary burden. Nevertheless, some consideration of the desirability or otherwise of piloting research instruments should always be made as a matter of routine if only to focus the mind on issues concerning the quality of such instruments.

Writing a research proposal

Whether or not your department or school expects it, and irrespective of the level of study to which you are committed (undergraduate/postgraduate) it is always useful to clarify your objectives by the formulation of a research proposal. At its best, a research proposal is a short but informative statement of intent *and* a guarantee to yourself and others that certain basic tasks have been undertaken prior to commencing research for a project or dissertation. These are the tasks that have been outlined so far in this book and they subsume the issues of sampling and piloting a research project. A research proposal is also useful as a personal reminder of what has been done and what needs to be done. If executed properly, the research proposal can be valuable as an *aide-mémoire*, as something to refer back to in times of depression, to remind you how structured your topic and research programme is and how straightforward it will be to execute! In short, the research proposal is one means of keeping 'your eye on the ball'. In some contexts it may assume greater importance, as a tool for persuading others of the feasibility of your work: this is particularly true in circumstances where a research proposal is a prerequisite to having your project accepted and a supervisor allocated. In these circumstances, the proposal should also aim to convince second and third parties that you have done your homework and are thus capable of achieving your aims. Research proposals may usefully comprise the following elements.

- Your name.
- The working title of your dissertation/research project.
- Statement of objectives. In no more than 100 words, concisely state the objective(s) of your dissertation/research incorporating explicitly the key hypothesis/hypotheses to be examined.
- Background. Again in around 100 words, state the antecedents of your study, i.e. the reasons why this topic is being proposed relative to previous key research (read the previous and later discussions in this book on 'Literature Searching' to clarify the importance of this aspect of your work).
- Methodology. In around 200 words outline what methodologies are to be employed in the research, incorporating, at the end, a short list of considerations relative to data collection (where is data coming from?); any special facilities or resources required; and any special expertise you need to acquire or has to be supplied from external sources.
- Methodological support. Briefly identify any progress made in obtaining access to data (established contacts, etc.) and whether any research instruments have been designed and piloted.

- Chapter outline. Identify the proposed number of chapters with working titles, clearly but briefly identifying the content of each.
- Timescale. Outline within the period during which your research/dissertation will be undertaken key stepping stones, specific scheduled times for the completion of key tasks.
- References. Where references have been cited in the 'Background' (and they usually will be) and other sections, identify these in a short list (see Part Four of this text for guidance on referencing).

Finally, it is worth repeating the advice that topic choice and choice of research method(s) are the most important decisions you will probably take throughout the whole research and dissertation writing process. Frustrating though it may be on occasions, it is therefore important to spend some time getting these aspects of your work right.

Describing research objectives through mapping sentences

Once you have selected your research and dissertation topic it becomes imperative for you to express your thinking on it through clear objectives. This is never an easy task because it requires you to do two things simultaneously. On the one hand, you must express the purpose of the research and define the variables that you are working on, whilst on the other hand, it is necessary to set the parameters, the outer limits of the universe you are working in. The success of the task of writing clear objectives will influence every other aspect of the research, including personal peace of mind. The message is get the description as refined and clear as is humanly possible at the beginning of the research as it will save a lot of heartache later!

Beyond objectives and hypotheses

The normal tools of research description are the objectives and the hypothesis. Whilst the latter is not always necessary they are both fundamental to description and performance. However, a further descriptive tool exists which might be termed 'the really useful working description'. Known as the mapping sentence it is a tool which has evolved out of the psychological theory known as Facet Theory (see Donald 1995 for a detailed discussion) and in many respects it mirrors Set Theory in mathematics. Put simply, the idea of the mapping sentence is for the initial description of the research to be expressed and wholly encompassed in one sentence. At first glance it might seem absurd to describe a research project in one sentence but the challenge it contains is the very process that forces the mind of the researcher into thinking it all through. It is easier, for example, than having to describe to someone the plot of a film you saw last week in 25 words or less! Instead of having just objectives and hypotheses you have an additional tool, an 'operational description'. It is very useful.

Initial description of the content of the research

The most important task of research design is to undertake an initial description of the domain or area which concerns the researcher. For such a description to be useful it must describe the boundaries of the area, identify the main components within the area, and the probable relationship between those components. To be more specific, a description must:

- describe all the variables in the area of interest and by so doing define the parameters of the study;
- describe the range of variation that is possible for each variable; and
- describe the nature of the relationship between the variables, e.g., causal, antecedents of, consequence of, similar to, different from, etc.

In other words a description should:

- display the logical sequence of the methodology;
- cover all variables (of all types); and
- cover all the variation within each variable.

The mapping sentence

The technique for achieving this level of description is the mapping sentence. The mapping sentence lays out your research in an operational way; a 'rough guide' would be an appropriate label. There are three stages in writing a mapping sentence. These are, first, *to describe the variables*. Normally there will be at least three types of variable: the independent variable and the dependent variable to which must be added the subject variable (i.e. characteristics of the sample you are controlling). So at a very minimum there are three variables to describe. The second stage in writing a mapping sentence is *to lay out the range of variation for each of the three variable types*. The final stage is *to express the logic of the methodology* of the study in terms of the variables. This means writing the sentence itself.

Some examples of mapping sentences

Our first example is *based on an experiment*. The experiment is concerned to identify the factors which influence the recall of TV advertisements. In this example there are four types of variable. The first stage is to identify the possible variables.

Subject variables:

- gender
- age
- economic class.

Intervening variables covered by subject sampling (an intervening variable is the variable that research suspects may influence the causal relationship under scrutiny):

- experience of the product
- no experience of the product
- interest in the product
- no interest in the product.

Nominated independent variables:

- time from image recall
- gender of principal figure
- single or group feature
- price quoted/not quoted
- colour of background
- humour–no humour
- length of advert.

Dependent variable:

- Number of advertisements recalled by subjects.

Having identified the variables and expressed the range of variation, the mapping sentence can be written. The style of the sentence is based on imagining one person undergoing the experiment.

| A subject | male | having | experience of the product | |
| | female | | no experience of the product | |

| and having | an interest in | the product will recall more |
| | no interest in | |

advertisements depending upon	time for image recall
	gender of principal figures
	single or group feature
	price quoted–not quoted
	colour of background
	humour–no humour
	length of advert

Laying it out in this way allows the researcher to see all the variables and to select the ones of interest. It is not written in stone and does allow for additions and subtractions to be made. For example, you may wish to use only women in the sample so 'male' goes from the subject variable list. You may also wish to add another independent variable, say, style of music. The structure of the sentence does not change but the content can.

Our second example is *based on an attitude survey*. In this example a researcher is looking into attitudes to healthy living. The first stage is to identify the variables.

Subject variables:

- age
- gender
- economic class
- social origin.

Intervening variables handled by the sample:

- employed and/not employed
- nature of work.

Independent variables
A positive attitude towards:

- personal fitness
- healthy eating
- sleep
- no smoking
- regular sport.

Dependent variable:

- intention to join a health club.

The sentence can be written as follows:

A subject	age gender economic class social origin	who is and who has	employed not employed sedentary work manual work

will display a positive intention to join a health club, if they have positive attitudes towards	personal fitness healthy eating sleep no smoking regular sport

Our third example is *based on analysis of data*. In this example the researcher is interested in whether the price of air fares influences the choice of a particular country (X) as a tourist and business destination. The first stage is to identify the variables.

Subject variables:

- trends in visitors from USA
- trends in visitors from Europe.

Intervening variables (controlled):

- stable currency conditions.

Independent variables:

- price of air fares.

Dependent variable:

* change in the rate of tourist visits
* change in the rate of business visits.

The sentence can then be written as follows

A change in the price of air fares from	Europe	
	USA	
determines whether a subject visits X for	business	
	tourism	

when currency conditions are stable

There are a number of ways to express the same thing and the one chosen should be the most useful.

Why try to describe your topic before you start?

* A precise definition of the universe you are looking at gives the researcher a sense of confidence not least because such definitions make the project easier to communicate to others.
* A description helps to identity what information you will need to collect or what observations you will need to make.
* It will help to identify relationships between the variables you are examining.
* A good initial description will enable the researcher to edit the topic as information and knowledge is accumulated in a way that allows for additions and subtractions but *not* wholesale restructuring.
* A good description makes it easier to align the topic with previous work in the same area and with established theory.

The whole purpose of mapping sentences is to help to refine the original research idea or question into a practical proposition. Once this is done then the researcher can usefully consider further important elements of the proposition – especially the use of classification systems and typologies.

 6

The uses of classification systems and typologies

Nothing stands alone. Every variable, including the ones you are investigating, belongs to a group. Indeed, part of the process of defining the variables we are interested in lies in locating the group of which they are part. This group itself will be a subgroup of some larger group. To draw an analogy from the world of crime, when the police pick up a suspect they immediately check out 'known criminal associates'. These other criminals are part of a subset of a general category of people – criminals! Being able to place the variables in your research in their appropriate sub-group orientates your research into a wider setting enabling it to be properly appreciated.

Classification systems

Being able to place the variables we are interested in within a group or within groups whilst simultaneously understanding how these groups relate to other groups and exist within larger formations, is the bedrock of research. In other words, good classification approaches allow the researcher to specifically locate their variables and to define the 'universal set', i.e. the broadest category, in which their work exists. By this means the researcher can focus on variables yet never lose sight of the bigger picture.

All knowledge is classified, that is, it is systematically grouped by established criteria. If, for example, we think of science, metallurgy has ferrous–nonferrous categories, zoology has mammals–reptiles. Physical science has developed through differentiating compounds which are then arranged in groups according to the differences and similarities in their actual physical nature, for example organic compounds, inorganic compounds. All branches of science have developed classification systems bases on the discovered differences and similarities of their subject material. By contrast social research does not possess natural categories based on secure definitions. Therefore categorization in social research is itself a social process which requires consensus and yet which is biased by subjectivity.

This assertion of subjective bias in social classification needs to be qualified. In the first place, some of the material used by the social scientist is factual, for example, sex and age. Furthermore, much observed behaviour is the same so that even when allowing for individual differences there are great areas of similarity. Progress in social science has produced a consensus on certain categories. The standard system of social class A, B, C1, C2, D, E would be an example of this.

In a very real sense the social scientist has to be careful about the classification of their variables because proof will depend upon association with a defined population. The physical scientist can generalize from experiments on, say, a particular type of molecule or an atom to all such molecules and atoms and therefore does not need concepts such as population, sample and the normal distribution. If a hypothesis is proven for one molecule it is proven for them all! The social scientist needs these concepts precisely because the variations in the behaviour of the variables under examination are not anchored in safe definitions nor securely confined within group boundaries which means that generalizations to the world beyond the study have to be substantiated. That variation is, or is not, confined to a specifically defined population is the very essence of statistical proof. Statistical measurement is the nearest the social researcher can get to the certainty of, say, the chemical formula of cell structure.

What is subjective about social classification is the labels we might give to an agreed piece of behaviour and consequently people may place the same observed phenomenon in different categories. This is the point when social classification systems meet personal psychological classifications systems. How people classify objects, ideas and other people is central to our understanding of social research. We all make sense of the world by placing everything we see into a known category. We are not constantly aware of this process nor of what categories we carry around in our heads; but they are there nevertheless. This process is of particular importance in qualitative research.

We can think of classification systems in four broad types as follows:

- *Scientific classes* (the result of cumulative scientific enquiry).
- *Classes laid down by social research* (the result of social science good practice).
- *Classes set by social norms* (classes accepted by society).
- *Psychological classes* (the mental processes of categorization and evaluation).

Typologies and classes

In everyday conversation we hear the expressions '... the type of' or 'the kind of ...'. The speaker is implying a typology, that is, the existence of a set of subdivisions of a particular category. A typology is the subdivision of a specific category into degree. These subcategories must all share the nature and definition of their principal but be sufficiently different to allow for clear boundaries to be placed between the subcategories. An example is helpful here. Consider a conventional typology of power frequently found in the discourse of organizational behaviour:

- physical
- resource
- position
- expert
- personal.

It is important to understand that power itself will be contained in a typology of social forces which exists at a higher level. The nature of a typology is that it is a special case of classification. Classification systems can use both similarity and differences as their basis. For example, hockey, judo, snooker, rugby are all 'sports' or 'pastimes' but they are not actually related to each other in any generic sense in the way that, say, judo, boxing, wrestling might all be subcategories of a typology of fighting sports. If we now look within any typology or classification system we can see that each part or category has three functions. These are:

- *the differentiation function* (what it is and what it is not);
- *the evaluative function* (like-dislike-indifferent); and
- *the instrumental function* (what is its purpose – influenced by the context).

Looking even closer into a classification system the heart of it lies in what actually differentiates one category from another. The differentiating factor can be something about the nature of the category or something which lies between each category or both! Indeed they may be the same thing. The evaluative and instrumental functions can become differentiating factors. It is perfectly acceptable to have categories formed by evaluations and by defined purposes. The more normal case is for these functions to follow directly from the differentiation process.

To begin with the nature of the variable itself, the key concept here is similarity, difference and distance. How, on what basis, is one category similar to or different from another? Furthermore, how far are they apart? What is the distance between them? Another way to look at categories is to find their boundaries. Locating where the boundary lies between membership of one category and membership of another is itself a research process. This process has its own typology.

Boundary properties

There are three modes of boundary formation which correspond to three forms of groups or category differentiation. In one the boundary emanates from the dissimilarity of contents in the categories. In another, the boundary is formed by some repulsion force that keeps the categories apart and in yet another there exists some actual barrier which is not part of either category, between the categories so that they cannot be joined.

In the first mode of boundary formation, the separation is founded on attribute differences. This is the 'oil and water – can't mix' mode where the categories have nothing in common. The differentiation is by attribute difference or by the absence of an attribute of one category in the other. In the second mode, which might be called the 'chalk and cheese – won't mix' mode, the separation is based on ethnocentric properties. Here the difference is created by forces within each category. In other words, the categories repel each other. This phenomenon is often found in social groups where strong identity creates self-favouritism and consequently own-group bias. In the final mode, which might be called the 'over my dead body – can't mix, even if you wanted to' mode the separation is due to a barrier or barriers to the effect that the categories are kept apart by intervening forces which are not part of the categories themselves (for example, competition between groups; dominance-subordination relationships between groups in hierarchies; and socially decreed separation such as caste systems). It is important to note that these categorization modes are not mutually exclusive. As they co-exist it is imperative that the researcher considers them all in deciding on a classification scheme.

Purpose in classification

Unlike scientific classes, objects, ideas and people can fall into a variety of classes at the same time. Indeed one of the inherent problems of qualitative research is to know what style of classifying a subject a person is using when they are talking about something. Objects, social activity, data, people and ideas can be classified in many ways, for example by:

- what they are
- what they do
- the situation they occur in
- when they are present or absent
- their particular attributes

- consequences
- duration
- time
- value
- antecedents.

Principles of classification

The following could be considered the general principles of classifying objects, social objects and ideas.

- Define the universe in which the classification system lives. Here you are setting out the parameters of the whole classification system by saying what is included and what is excluded.
- Each class is defined on the basis of internal similarity and external differences.
- The principle of internal similarity and external difference is applied to all classes within a typology.
- The process of class differentiation is always a case of pair comparison, e.g. $A = B$, $B = C$, $A = C$.
- Common source does not ensure class similarity (e.g. because my brother and I have the same mother tells you nothing about me and my brother).
- A definition of a class simultaneously defines what is excluded from the class.
- The search for class differentiation is the search for class boundaries. Boundaries indicate the presence of a class.
- The evaluative component of a class can change with its purpose.

The importance of classification in research

Classification is the basis of all research. We can measure nothing if our variables are not in some form of order. As a process, classification is important for three reasons. First, because research demands clear definitions of the variables being investigated. A large part of that defining process is putting variables into classes. Second, the very process of finding a class for a variable is itself research – part of methodology. Third, placing the variables within a classification gives the research a sense of security. It sets parameters to the research task. These arguments reinforce each other precisely because they represent a circuitous process; research matter needs classifying before it can be measured and when it has been measured it is reclassified knowledge! Thus research is a classification process (see Bailey 1994, for an elaboration of the discussion in this chapter).

To conclude with the big picture, work can expand beyond feasible boundaries. Research is particularly prone to this effect. This is why defining the 'universal set' at as early a stage as is possible places the research task within practical boundaries. This task of setting limits on the research task is part of the research process and must be seen as such.

■ □ ▨ ■ 7

Managing the research process: a basic framework

The research process in which you engage for the purpose of writing a project or dissertation will not manage itself and only rarely will others – especially academic staff – manage it for you (although among some students there is a popular conception to the contrary on both counts!). For the purposes of the discussion in this chapter, management of the research process is discussed under six headings. The aim is to provide a basic framework to consider in managing the research process: other aspects of such management will arise later in the text, most notably in Part Four where the writing up of research is discussed. The six headings are:

- Administration and time management;
- Managing relationships with other people;
- Managing places and spaces;
- Using libraries (including sources of information);
- Literature searching; and
- Research equipment.

Administration and time management

To begin with, a (perhaps subtle) distinction will be made here between management and administration. Although these terms are often used interchangeably, it is possible and reasonable to make a case for differentiating them. Management will be taken here to imply a proactive approach to a mixture of task elements that make up the research process, involving the co-ordination of all these elements in an effective and successful manner. Administration will be used differently to denote those procedures that are devised and followed to establish and maintain records, documents, equipment, relationships, places and all other aspects of the research process necessary to underpinning successful co-ordination – i.e. management – of that process.

Though it might be a somewhat fanciful notion, it is often believed that there are three principal kinds of administrative worker: (a) the totally organized person who clears their desk every day and knows where everything they possess can be found: this person is often excessively tidy and fastidious; (b) the person who lives their work life in a state of organized chaos: their office or home may look recklessly untidy but they too know where to find things; and (c) the totally disorganized person who, irrespective of whether their environment is messy or tidy, can find nothing. Whatever your individual method of working, it is important that in addition to proactively managing the research process, some effort is made to institute procedures for the maintenance of those facilities and resources essential to making progress.

The administrative function therefore permeates the whole research process and cannot be ignored. Furthermore, it can broadly be divided into two dimensions: the strategic and the operational. Strategically, it is important to ensure that, a topic having been chosen, some sort of schedule is drawn up indicating a timescale for the completion of key tasks. The purpose of the schedule is not primarily to remind (or haunt!) you about targets to be met and those that have not been met by the time planned for. This is one role of the schedule but its main purpose is to help you plan the order in which tasks should be performed, i.e. to prioritize tasks.

The driving force of the research schedule will almost always be the process of data collection. If primary data is to be collected as part of the research, whether through interviews, questionnaires or some other method, all this will have to be arranged and will take time. Data collection is rarely something that can be left until the last minute, particularly if it involves gaining access to other people. Any schedule of activities should, therefore, 'frontload' data collection though other activities should not be ignored. Table 7.1 is adapted from Jankowicz (1991: 66) and shows the main activities that have to be managed in any research process and thus constitute the core of any schedule.

The operational counterpart of the research schedule is the research or project diary or log (Jankowicz 1991: 73; Barrat and Cole 1991: 28–29). This can take the form of a small exercise book or ledger or, depending on your attitude to paperwork, may be kept as part of a larger loose-leaf file in which documentation associated with the research project is stored. The purpose of the research diary is to act as a day-to-day record of your activities, record data and the development of ideas, help in the planning of activities including appointments and as a general almanac of your progress. The research diary is most useful if it is small and portable since it can be taken almost anywhere. While it may sound a little bizarre, ideas can come to a person in many different places, often in a very fleeting manner. It is, therefore, always useful to have, in addition to the project diary, access to paper and a pen so these ideas can be jotted down before they are forgotten. It is not uncommon for some academics to keep jotting pads or scrap paper by their beds and in other parts of their home precisely to record these moments of inspiration: any ideas can subsequently be transferred to the research diary.

The themes discussed so far in this section, like the research process as a whole, require effective time management. Table 7.2 records some of the main elements of time management. Good time management requires self-discipline but like other aspects of the learning process, the key factor to bear in mind is the need for realism. It is just as easy to attempt to do too much as too little and when developing the self-

TABLE 7.1 Schedule of activities typically involved in the research process for an empirical study (after Jankowicz 1991: 66)

Beginnings
- Check institutional/departmental regulations
- Choose topic and likely methods; establish preliminary hypotheses
- Undertake preliminary reading and literature review
- Write dissertation proposal and have it approved

Early development
- Make necessary contacts and seek permission for access, where appropriate, to subjects
- Make initial contacts and agree research ground rules in respondent-based research, including confidentiality rules
- Acquire specialist information, e.g. company written documents, etc.
- Confirm topic and methods
- Establish scope of literature review, confirming key sources and their availability
- Begin note taking from secondary literature sources
- Commence design of research protocol

First core activity stage
- Work literature review up quickly, drawing out implications of review for key hypotheses and research methods
- Make any necessary revisions to hypotheses and to choice and/or application of research methods – this is the second last sensible point to determine the final form of these – the last if you do not pilot your study
- Continue note taking and developing contacts, including determining availability of respondents in respondent-based research

Second core activity stage
- Piloting of research if necessary
- Final adjustment (revision only if essential) of hypotheses and research methods based on pilot
- Main data collection commences
- Data subjected to preliminary review upon completion leading to further data collection if required
- Data subjected to systematic analysis and preliminary conclusions drawn
- Assess preliminary conclusions against data to see if they hold up
- Consider whether further data collection is necessary
- Assess relationship between methods used, preliminary conclusions drawn and issues arising from literature review in order to establish whether all are congruent

Writing up
- Systematically prepare manuscript
- Check drafts with tutors (and sponsors and or respondents if relevant)

Production
- Typing or wordprocessing (ensure necessary arrangements are made in advance if you are relying on somebody else to do this for you)
- Edit and revise typed manuscripts carefully
- Check final manuscript and if required, have it bound

Delivery
- Ensure correct number of copies are delivered to appropriate persons
- Oral presentations where appropriate

TABLE 7.2 Main elements of effective time management

Responsibility	Accept responsibility for the management of your time to avoid blaming yourself and others for those diversions that put you 'off course'.
Holism	Effective time management is not simply about the management of academic work and output but brings complete benefits. Accordingly, personal time management should accommodate the totality of activities in which you engage – eating, sleeping, drinking, going to the cinema/theatre and so on.
Kindness	One objective of time management is to ensure kindness to the self. Time management is not principally about schedules, about timetabling, but about maintaining a consistent though flexible routine. Accepting responsibility for your own time management should mean that guilt is eliminated from the process: that extra night off or the spontaneous afternoon social occasion should be enjoyed to the full in the knowledge that your system of time management and your self-discipline can cope with such exceptions to normal routine.
Mutuality	There is a tendency to think of time management as a solitary exercise, one designed in the area of work especially to isolate you from others. However, while some academic tutors might be reluctant to admit it, perhaps the most important learning that goes on is when formal educational encounters are followed by informal discussions in a social context. In short, such learning is a shared social experience, particularly among members of the same peer group, and even the most tentative academic two-hour discussion over a coffee or beer can reinforce and develop learning.
Mechanics	At the end of each lecture, day or week, or whatever short time-period you choose, it is useful to spend some time – either alone or with others – to briefly review what you have learnt during that time and identify areas you do not fully understand. Many students leave this process to their assessed work believing that reading books and articles will compensate for any lack of understanding: sometimes they will but this is no substitute for putting your lecturers (nicely) on the spot by getting them to clarify your understanding.
Evangelism	Whenever possible, set your own standards and deadlines and tell other people about them – but not in such a manner as to encourage them to think of you as smug! It is always a good idea to have a piece of assessed work ready a week before the tutor's deadline then, just before submission, you can look at it 'cold' and make any *minor* adjustments necessary. In short, wherever possible, get slightly ahead of schedule.
Obsessiveness	Obsessiveness is to be avoided. Formal academic work can be completed too quickly; adherence to personal time management standards and schedules can be stressful and damaging.
Rhythm	To paraphrase the song, if you have rhythm, you have music! Know yourself and exploit this knowledge to your benefit. If you have subjects and topics you especially enjoy, ask yourself if you would rather leave assessed work for such subjects to later in your schedule and do other less enjoyable work first.
Dissertations	If you have read this far, you will have noticed that much of the preceding discussion is couched in terms of general academic work: the same principles apply to the management of the dissertation and you should not go back over the points above and make your own notes as to their relevance to the management of the research/dissertation writing process. Bear two points in mind, namely (i) do not waste a lot of time thinking about doing work; and (ii) do not waste time avoiding getting to the point!

discipline necessary to successful time management, as with anything else, it is important to conduct a self-assessment of those things that motivate you and to institute, if necessary, a schedule of 'treats' to be realized upon completion of particular tasks.

As the headings employed in this chapter suggest, the management and administration of the research process has several dimensions. Good administration is, in essence, however, the effective administration of information. This is not simply a matter of maintaining files. Some people feel comfortable with many detailed files covering all aspects of their research work. Others rarely work from more than one large file for any single project, whatever form this might take (a large arch-lever file suitably divided is useful as it is loose-leaf and permits a lot of storage: while it might not be possible to keep everything in such a file – for example, photocopies of academic articles – there will be little residual material to store).

The most common types of information required and encountered in any research project include:

- academic books, articles and other published information;
- documentation, sometimes but not always in the public domain;
- correspondence with contacts, interviewees and others; and
- research materials – for example, interview schedules, completed questionnaires and interview transcripts and so on.

In the section on literature searching, the range of information that might have to be dealt with as part of the research process is elaborated further. For the moment, it is enough to note that the amount of paperwork a research project can generate is often underestimated, even, on occasion, by experienced researchers. The methods of holding information should thus be as refined and as simple as possible. Organizing the research process is a complex business and simplicity is to be encouraged for reasons other than maintaining as few items of documentation as possible. In particular, while files are important, while information storage is important, more important yet is the ease and rapidity with which recorded information can be retrieved and consulted. In this sense, simplicity is associated with reduction: the filtering and condensing of information. Filtering refers to the process of identifying essential information and documentation that must be kept and stored for use in the research process. The process of condensing information alludes to the need to ensure that you actively view all information as capable of reduction to its elements. This can be a lengthy and at times dull activity but is essential to concentrating your information into readily usable forms.

Furthermore, the condensing of information does not refer merely to the notes that you might take from published sources of information but to other forms of documentation as well. For example, interview transcripts will be distilled for the elements they contain that are salient to the research; only single copies of 'round robin' letters requesting information will be retained; fieldwork notes will be filleted for essential information which will be represented in condensed form, and on it goes.

The two general pieces of advice here are simply expressed. First, it is easier to work with a small amount of essential documentation germane to the research process than it is with large amounts of paperwork. Second, the skills of filtering and condensing information for storage and rapid retrieval are essential to administration and overall management of the research process: the temptation for novice researchers is always to acquire and retain too much information, usually because the processes of filtering and condensing information seem tedious and unnecessary. Having said all this, some words of qualification are necessary and again might be expressed in two 'rules of thumb': (a) do not dispose of any essential materials you may wish to repeatedly consult throughout the course of the research process – if in doubt, retain! and (b) while recommending as reduced a system of information storage as possible, it is always dangerous to put all one's eggs in a single basket. Your master file(s) containing all essential documentation should therefore be copied, each copy or copies being stored in different locations.

Managing relationships with other people

Managing the research process is not simply a matter of managing yourself and all the paperwork that is generated. It involves getting the best out of all those people who can help you with your work, whether these are respondents to your study, or supervisors and others in positions of authority. Social skills relevant to particular research methods will be examined at the appropriate points in Part Two of this book. At this stage it is necessary to indicate the need to establish *systematic* relationships of trust with all those who might be able to offer you assistance with your work. Many students undertaking research projects for the first time seem to think that other people will drop everything to assist them with their research. This is rarely the case. Whoever you deal with, you should seek to follow a number of general guidelines in dealing with others.

First of course, it is necessary to identify key players: your supervisor or tutor, the subject librarian at your college or university responsible for management or whatever subject you are researching, key respondents – both real and potential – to your study, and so on. Second, having identified key players, it is necessary to establish a working relationship with each. The emphasis here is on the word 'relationship'. A student's relationship to their supervisor or subject librarian is to some extent a formal, almost contractual one. Academics and librarians are expected to help students as part of their normal duties. Establishing a positive relationship means trying, within reasonable limits, to transcend this ordinariness and normality without becoming a nuisance or appearing to be over-familiar. Race (1991: 39–41) makes a number of valuable points in respect of student–lecturer/supervisor relationships including the advice to students to (a) remember that academics are human; (b) show interest in academics' subject specialisms and views; and (c) reward 'good' behaviour (i.e. thank tutors and supervisors for their help and advice). In establishing any kind of relationship it is, of course, necessary to introduce yourself to those who may be able to help you. Your dissertation supervisor/tutor will probably be already known to you. However, it is quite possible to spend a number of years pursuing a course without either meeting or being taught by all members of staff in your department. If you find yourself allocated a supervisor who you do not know well, make an appointment to see him or her as soon as possible and take with you a clear, brief note of your aspirations for the research project you are going to undertake (perhaps in the form of your research schedule). Remember the point made in Chapter 3 about the many commitments of academic staff: your supervisor may be your supervisor, but he or she is also a number of other things to many other people. Remember this too when it comes to establishing relationships with library staff and others who can help you. For example, if your institution has a word-processing laboratory within its computer centre and this facility is open to all students in order to allow them to process their work, it is clearly important to make contact with the centre's management and/or technical staff. This contact may again be formal or informal but the point is, as with all others who may be able to help you in your work, to get yourself known and make a positive impression. The same applies to key respondents in organizations that you might want to tap for information or access in order to undertake your research. Write letters of introduction to respondents: if you do not know who 'they' are, then some attempt at formal introduction, outlining the nature of what you are doing and asking for co-operation, is a good way of establishing relevant contacts. Your correspondence should not be of the oily or fawning kind but polite and to the point (i.e. courteous and short), so that the person to whom it is directed can readily understand your needs and is able to respond: do not give potential respondents the excuse to consign your letters to their 'pending' tray because of lack of clarity.

Thirdly here, mention has already been made of the importance of courtesy. Sometimes, people you deal with when undertaking a research project can be intimidating, unforthcoming and obtuse. So, of course, can the researcher! It is important to maintain composure and good manners at all times. More significantly, in making contacts with key individuals who can help your cause, it is critical to ensure that relationships are *maintained* even if the assistance of some individuals is not required all the time. This is one way of impressing upon others your sincerity so that they do not look upon you simply as someone who *has* to rely upon their support because of the absence of alternatives. Maintaining such relationships is easier with people in your immediate environment – supervisors, library staff and the like – than it is for external contacts. In respect of the former, you can put in a number of appearances or requests for information or help to impress upon supervisors and librarians the level of your commitment. Do not overdo it, however, as this courts the danger of being branded a nuisance. There is a tightrope to be walked in relationships with others that requires you to develop judgement. Do not force your demands and requests on others, but do outline your requests clearly and firmly. Most research involves the researcher interacting with others and the successful management of these relationships is important to the success of the overall research process.

Managing places and spaces

The 'places' dimension to management of the research process is as much psychological as physical in nature. There are two key issues here: comfort and familiarity. In respect of comfort, it is important to try and establish places where you can work on your research with maximum peace of mind and the minimum number of distractions. If this sounds rather obvious, then the key word here is 'places' in plural. Many academics do their research work at home, away from the demands placed upon them by their work environment. At the same time however, a good deal of research time is spent in libraries (and most university and college libraries, despite efforts to the contrary, rarely provide the tranquil environment necessary to maximum productivity) and on fieldwork visits, collecting data. Fieldwork visits usually involve working in unfamiliar environments. For example, the interviewing of respondents usually takes place in the latter's place of employment, on territory with which the respondents are familiar and comfortable.

Whether writing up material, reading, visiting contacts for the purpose of collecting data or any other aspect of the research process then, it is useful to establish as much as you can about the environments you will encounter and thereby maximize your feelings of comfort and well-being.

On the 'home' front, this means things as basic as familiarizing yourself with the locations of relevant material in libraries, how to use library catalogues and so on. When it comes to research fieldwork, it is not always possible to achieve the levels of familiarization with other environments that would be most desirable. It is surprising, however, just how far it is possible to go in anticipating the circumstances in which you might find yourself. If you are interviewing respondents or administering a questionnaire on someone else's premises, then having obtained the permission of the relevant authority figures, some reconnaissance may be possible. For example, if you are interviewing factory workers then it might be possible to visit the unit in question to observe the layout and experience the ambience of the environment. Remember, however, that access to organizations for the purposes of research can be difficult, especially if for the purpose of making contact with front-line employees. To summarize therefore, it is useful to make the environments – the places and spaces – in which you have to operate as a researcher, work for you as much as possible, and this requires awareness, planning and reconnaissance wherever possible.

Using libraries

Libraries can be intimidating places. Most students attend a library induction course early in their academic careers and many universities and colleges offer supplementary courses on library use for students beginning their projects and dissertations. Sadly, many students (and some academic staff!) rarely familiarize themselves to any large extent with the facilities of their library and are thus deprived of knowledge relating to the full range of available information. All libraries differ to some extent in the kind of literature searching sources (indices, abstracts and so on) they hold but a library is nevertheless a first stop in any hunt for information.

Because of the variability in library holdings, the information presented here is largely generic. Table 7.3 lists principle generic information sources some of which are not always found in libraries (e.g. company reports). Table 7.4 lists key catalogue abstract and indexing services. Table 7.5 lists some key journals in the business and management field.

TABLE 7.3 Generic information sources for research (adapted from Jankowicz 1991: 127)

Data available from organizations
- Government departments (e.g. Department of Education and Employment; Department of Trade and Industry) and government bodies
- Private companies
- Public sector organizations; local government offices
- Trade associations and employer representative groups
- Local employer networks
- Trade unions
- Research organizations (e.g. market research companies) and professional bodies (e.g. Chartered Institute of Personnel and Development)
- Consumer organizations (e.g. Consumers' Association)
- Pressure groups and voluntary organizations (e.g. Low Pay Unit)

Data available from primary literary sources
- Research monographs (books on a single theme or topic)
- Academic journal articles
- Conference papers
- Unpublished research reports (often available from authors) and university dissertations (available on inter-library loan)
- Newspapers and magazines
- Annual reports of companies, public sector organizations, local government and pressure groups and voluntary organizations
- Organizational 'house' magazines

Data available in secondary sources
- Textbooks
- Books of readings (collations of articles on specialist themes)
- Encyclopaedias, bibliographies and dictionaries (especially of specialist subjects)
- Academic journal review articles
- Academic journal annual indices
- Annual review books (of topics in academic disciplines)
- Abstracts (see Table 7.4)

Data available from library and related reference sources
- Subject guides
- Citation Index for discipline(s)
- On-line databases
- Specialist in-house or national information services

Many of the above are now likely to be contained on CD-ROM products or can be accessed via the Internet.

TABLE 7.4 Types of catalogue abstract and indexing services which may be available in your library and elsewhere

A   LIBRARY SUBJECT INDEX

Lists the subjects covered by your own library. Each subject will be given a classification code using an established scheme e.g. Dewey or Library of Congress. Use this if you know the subject but not the author or title. As library books are arranged in a numbered sequence, the classification code will allow location of the book on the shelves.

CLASS CATALOGUE

Lists all the books held by your library within each subject classification.

AUTHOR CATALOGUE

An alphabetical list by author of books held in the library.

TITLE CATALOGUE

An alphabetical list by title of books held in the library.

JOURNAL CATALOGUE

A list of journals held in the library arranged by title or classification number.

OPAC: ONLINE PUBLIC ACCESS CATALOGUE

A computerized database which offers all or some of the above functions on one system.

What if it's not in your own library?

B   NATIONAL LIBRARY CATALOGUES: THE BRITISH LIBRARY AND THE LIBRARY OF CONGRESS (USA)

As copyright deposit libraries they aim to receive a copy of every book published in their respective countries. Useful information to note if requesting items, via the Inter-Library Loan service, includes author, title, publisher, date of publication and ISBN (a unique identifying code). National libraries often have good collections of older material.

BRITISH NATIONAL BIBLIOGRAPHY, BRITISH BOOKS IN PRINT, CUMULATIVE BOOK INDEX, BOOKS IN PRINT

List books published and in print in the UK and USA respectively, from 1950 onwards. They have subject, author and title sequences.

Finding out about theses

C   ASLIB INDEX TO THESES

A quarterly publication listing theses prepared for higher degrees in British universities and former polytechnics, includes an author and subject index.

A subscription version via the web may be found at: *http://www.theses.com*

DISSERTATION ABSTRACTS

A monthly publication listing doctoral dissertation submitted to University Microfilms International. Participating institutions are predominantly North American, although some European and British institutions also contribute.

A guest version is available on the web at:
http://wwwlib.umi.com/dissertations/gateway/main

CURRENT RESEARCH IN BRITAIN (CRIB)

Lists research currently being carried out in UK universities. Includes the subject, institution and contact details of the researcher.

Finding journals and journal articles

D ULRICH'S GUIDE TO INTERNATIONAL PERIODICALS

An annual three-volume catalogue of journals, published throughout the world, listed by title and by subject.

BUSINESS PERIODICALS INDEX, RESEARCH INDEX, ANBAR, LEISURE RECREATION AND TOURISM ABSTRACTS, BRITISH HUMANITIES INDEX, EMPLOYEE RELATIONS INTERNATIONAL: A BIBLIOGRAPHY AND ABSTRACTS JOURNAL, JOURNAL OF ECONOMIC LITERATURE, ACCOUNTING AND TAX INDEX, MARKET RESEARCH ABSTRACTS

Indexing services which sometimes include summaries of the article. They provide a subject, author or company approach to journal articles.

Finding information using computer systems

E ELECTRONIC DATABASES: CD-ROMS AND COMMERCIAL ONLINE SERVICES

Many education institutions are linked to the academic computer network called JANET. This offers the facility of searching the library catalogues of all member institutions, as well as access to many other computerized files of information. The INTERNET serves a similar function but on a larger scale.

Electronic databases useful for the Business student to which your library may have a subscription:

ABI-INFORM: a general management and business database covering many of the core journals.

BUSINESS AND INDUSTRY: includes many trade journals in full text, and is particularly helpful when looking for market or product share data.

GEOBASE: geography, planning and environmental issues.

TABLE 7.5 Key journals in the business and management fields

Academy of Management Review	*Journal of Accounting Research*
Accounting and Business Research	*Journal of Finance*
Administrative Science Quarterly	*Journal of Industrial Relations*
Applied Economics	*Journal of Management Studies*
British Journal of Industrial Relations	*Journal of Marketing*
Econometrica	*Journal of Marketing Communications*
Economic Journal	*Journal of Marketing Research*
European Journal of Marketing	*Management Decision*
European Journal of Operational Research	*Management Science*
Harvard Business Review	*Marketing Intelligence and Practice*
Human Relations	*Organizational Studies*
Human Resource Management Journal	*Oxford Bulletin of Economics and Statistics*
International Journal of Accounting	*Oxford Economic Papers*
International Journal of Advertising	*Oxford Review of Economic Policy*
International Journal of Human Resource Management	*Personnel Review*
International Journal of Retail and Distribution Management	*Service Industries Journal*
International Labour Review	*Strategic Management Journal*
Journal of Accountancy	

Literature searching

Any search for information must be directed. Familiarity with the range and totality of sources of information is useful but once introduced to the potential number of sources, many students new to the research process behave like young children given a free hand in a sweet shop: they gather as many items as possible without regard to quality or whether or not they can consume them. It is possible for researchers to become 'information junkies' and this can delay the research and writing process because having gathered a large amount of information, there arises a desire to try and 'fit it all in'.

Accordingly, it is necessary to approach information sources with specific questions or requirements in mind. This focuses the 'information need'. Prepare for disappointment with some types of information – particularly statistical data published by government and other agencies. Sometimes, the information is not available in the form desired (if at all) and has to be inferred from that information which is supplied. Similar frustrations are often encountered in the extent to which information is of contemporary relevance: in short, up-to-date, 'of the minute' data is often difficult to obtain. For example, with official government statistics there is often a time lag between collection of data, and its analysis and publication, which means that the most recent analysed and published data is one or two years old (sometimes more).

A related point here is that information of any kind should be scanned for its contemporary value. This is a fairly obvious thing to do with such things as statistical data but students often fail to apply the same tests of modern relevance to books, articles and the like. Of course, some books and articles never date: those which report original research studies are the main problem. Some pieces of research pass into the mainstream of a discipline's theory development and remain classics. Others remain valuable in their own right but become dated in terms of the validity of their conclusions, usually because the phenomenon or phenomena they study has changed or been influenced by the course of history. Authors of best-selling textbooks get round this problem because their publishers invite them to issue new editions of their work from time to time, when they can update information and the conceptual development in the field about which they are writing. With reports of original research it is, however, necessary to develop some discrimination as to what remains important. An additional qualification to these observations is that for the purposes of reviewing the literature in a subject or field, then an original research report whether in book or article form stands as an important element in the historical development of that field in its own right. The required skill to establish how important, or dated, or relevant these works might be is not easy to define but may be encapsulated in the term 'discrimination'.

Returning now to the concept of 'information junkies' introduced earlier, it is appropriate to note that many of those new to the information process encounter a genuine problem with literature searching in terms of the extent to which the process itself generates uncertainty and doubt. Approaching information sources with particular questions in mind can lead to familiarity with the range and totality of information pertaining to a particular topic (especially if the topic is a very narrow one) and this familiarity itself can generate questions and issues not originally contemplated when the topic was chosen. This in turn can give rise to the temptation to refine the initial question(s) posed and ultimately the topic itself. Some ongoing refinement of the research process at this level is desirable and probably unavoidable. It is certainly useful to refine a topic in the early stages of the research process if this leads to a genuine enhancement in understanding of the topic or the issues it raises. It is also often the case however that people become submerged in the information gathering/literature searching process and become confused and disoriented. A common symptom of this confusion and disorientation is constant tinkering with the fundamentals of the topic. Unless, therefore, literature searching as part of the process of topic selection has not revealed serious barriers to the adequate realization of your topic (see Chapter 3 above), you should adhere to your original topic and research plan as far as possible, yet still take any early opportunities to refine your topic where this seems sensible. If literature and information searching raises any doubts in your mind about the feasibility or limitations of your original topic and research plan, then you should seek the advice of tutors on how to proceed.

Searching the web

The world wide web is frequently portrayed as the solution to all information problems, but before you dive on to the nearest computer it is worth thinking about the type of information you are looking for, and planning your research strategy. It should be remembered that searching can be slow, particularly if logged on in the afternoon. It is also worth bearing in mind that nobody is centrally regulating the system, thus it includes much information that is not only of poor quality but also inaccurate and out of date. Added to this is the problem that it is not a static database. Favourite web sites will move without any notice, or disappear completely. A whole new system of referencing must be learned to enable readers of your work to find your information sources. Having said all that, the web is a marvellous tool if used sensibly and with realistic expectations and will help you to find information from a variety of sources. Informational web pages such as those written by libraries will give summary information to help you work effectively within the unit. News web pages will provide snapshots of current affairs events and company web pages will provide annual reports and accounts, product data and graduate recruitment information. The following, stage, approach is recommended.

(1) Begin by checking if your own library or academic department has created its own web pages and look for lists with titles such as 'useful sites' or 'links'. These will save you time by allowing you to focus on high quality sites immediately relevant to the interests of your institution.

(2) Identify *Gateway* sites which tend to be organized by subject and have the added benefit that a human has usually quality checked the site. Start by looking at:

BUBL   http://bubl.ac.uk

This covers all subjects, provides good brief descriptions of the sites listed and regularly check the links.

Biz/Ed   http://www.bized.ac.uk/

This is an educational service for students and lecturers of business and economics.

(3)   Try using the search engines such as Yahoo, Alta Vista, Infoseek or Excite. These are predominately a computer-based approach to indexing, with limited human intervention for organizing or assessing the sites. It must be remembered that they do not duplicate each other, but are separate databases of sites with some overlap. Make use of the 'Advanced Search' options whenever possible to refine the search. e.g. Excite allows the search to be limited by language, country or type of site (non-profit organization, educational or commercial) and can specify whether a word or phrase must be/must not be/should be present in the site description.

A note on notetaking

Although it may appear rather obvious, effective literature searching is utterly dependent on the development of strategies for both recording the outcome of searches and, more importantly, the recording of key points from literature that is identified as useful. In the earlier discussion on research administration, the question of economy in the storage of research-related data was touched upon. For materials that you record, some similarly economic system of recording *what* you have read is required. Some people use file cards in various combinations, others simply have a file of notes. The method of recording information is important and the following guidelines might be usefully kept in mind as a means of delineating some key elements in such activity.

- Notes taken from whatever source should be ordered in some systematic way. If the notes are simply made and stored on an author-surname alphabetical basis, it is useful to maintain a brief index of key-word themes against which relevant authors' names are listed. For example if you have read five books by A. Adams, B. Bullfrog, C. Crouch, D. Dimwit and E. Edwardes and you keep your notes in an arch-lever or similar file ordered by surname, you might, if your topic was, say, labour turnover in retail bookstores, have the following key-word index:

Key-word theme	Information in:
Extent of turnover	Bullfrog; Dimwit
Effects on unit	Dimwit; Edwardes
Reasons for leaving	Crouch; Edwardes
Managers' attitudes	Adams; Crouch; Edwardes
Cost of replacement	Adams; Bullfrog

- Take notes systematically, preferably breaking them up into numbered points. Periodically, and certainly at the end of each point, you should make a note of page(s) of the book or article from which the point is summarized.
- Always keep a full record of each item you read and use as well as a reference for items you do not use but to which, as a result of change of mind, you might wish to return. A full reference should be taken in each case (file card indexes or computer word-processing facilities are useful means of recording but take a hard copy of the latter each time you update it, just in case of computer failure!). Part Four of this book contains guidance on referencing: referencing is the undoing of many a researcher who in failing to record items adequately during the research process has to engage in a last minute scramble to track down discarded material.
- Never throw away a document, even after taking notes, unless you are absolutely sure you will not need it again. If there is an article or book where only a *small* part is relevant, consider photocopying that part of use for retention – but check that you understand copyright law first!
- Do not over-write notes. The tendency for inexperienced researchers and writers is to note down too much from their documentary sources and to over-quote, a fault frequently transferred over to the final dissertation. As people gain experience of literature on a topic it becomes easier to prune notes, but unless you are writing a theory-based dissertation where the final text will be heavily dependent on quotations for making sense of the subject (an event that occurs only infrequently even with theory-based dissertations) then note only a few outstanding quotations. Main notes should capture the essence of an article or book/book chapter.

Research equipment

It is important in topic and research method selection to ensure that you have access to the necessary equipment for executing your research programme. Beyond the mundane everyday stationery items, the most common pieces of equipment used in research are the personal computer, programmable calculator, micro- or mini-cassette recorder or similar, and a tape transcribing machine. If you have your own personal computer (or even if you do not but intend to use another machine) ensure that you have access to appropriate packages. Software is now sufficiently advanced to allow a range of products for the analysis of data from questionnaires and for drawing charts, figures and diagrams – as well as more routine tasks such as word processing. A programmable calculator is valuable for obvious reasons but most usefully for its statistical functions which allows rapid calculation of basic statistical parameters (Part Three of this book covers statistics).

For interview-based research a portable tape recorder is vital and the best suited is a micro- or mini-cassette 'dictaphone' style machine which can literally fit in a pocket. Interviews may be recorded (but see the section on conducting the interview in Part Two, Chapter 12). These machines do not tape for long so a supply of tapes and an ability to change a tape quickly without disrupting the interview process is important. Voice-activated tape machines are to be avoided as they are invariably temperamental. The transcribing process is considerably eased with the aid of a special transcriber machine which allows the adjustment of tape speed to keep pace with handwriting/typewriting speed. It is likely that your departmental secretariat may be willing to make available their machine (assuming they have one) or that a local office equipment firm has a hire scheme. The cost of such machines is usually prohibitive for individual purchases.

Finally then, after seven chapters, it is time to proceed and explore in some detail key research and data analysis methods. It is worth repeating once again that what follows is not exhaustive and will be less useful if the issues raised in this part of the book have not been thought through. In comparison to getting started, doing the research is relatively easy, a view we hope will be supported by the treatment of those topics that comprise Parts Two and Three of this text.

References for Part One

Bailey, K. D. (1994) *Typologies and Taxonomies: An Introduction to Classification Techniques*, London: Sage.

Barrat, D. and Cole, T. (1991) *Sociology Projects: A Students' Guide*, London: Routledge.

Donald, I (1995) 'Facet theory: defining research domains', in Breakwell, G., Hammond, S. and Fife-Schaw, C. (eds), *Research Methods in Psychology*, London: Sage, 116–137.

Easterby-Smith, M., Thorpe, R. and Lowe, A. (1991) *Management Research: An Introduction*, London: Sage.

Gilbert, N. (1993) 'Research, theory and method', in Gilbert, N. (ed.), *Researching Social Life*, London: Sage, 18–31.

Goffman, E. (1959) *The Presentation of Self in Everyday Life*, New York: Doubleday and Archer.

Hornsby-Smith, M. (1993) 'Gaining access', in Gilbert, N. (ed.), *Researching Social Life*, London: Sage, 52–67.

Jankowicz, A. D. (1991) *Business Research Projects for Students*, London: Chapman and Hall.

Jary, D. and Jary, J. (1991) *Dictionary of Sociology*, Glasgow: Collins.

Lacey, A. R. (1986) *A Dictionary of Philosophy*, London: Routledge.

Mars, G. and Nicod, M. (1984) *The World of Waiters*, London: George Allen and Unwin.

McNeill, P. (1990) *Research Methods*, London: Routledge.

Procter, M. (1993) 'Measuring attitudes', in Gilbert, N. (ed.), *Researching Social Life*, London: Sage, 116–134.

Race, P. (1992) *500 Tips for Students*, Oxford: Blackwell.

Raimond, P. (1993) *Management Projects: Design, Research and Presentation*, London: Chapman and Hall.

Worsley, P. (1977) *Introducing Sociology*, Harmondsworth: Penguin.

Part Two

Key Qualitative Research Methods

8

Sampling – choosing your subjects

Most research projects involve the study of something that is real and tangible, whether animate or inanimate. In the majority of research cases it is not possible to study all the elements in a particular set (i.e. to undertake a census) for reasons of practicality. For example, if one wished to study the attitudes of small business owners in a certain part of the country towards the introduction of a minimum wage for their employees, it would not be practical to study all small-business owners in the area, even if one could identify each and every business owner who constituted this population. In the case of this particular problem, the set, or more properly the population of known small-business owners in the region, can form the basis from which a sample is drawn. Note these terms. A sample is a sub-set of a larger grouping, a population. Samples are frequently studied in order to learn something of the characteristics of the larger groups (population) of which they are part. Such samples, if selected in certain ways can be used as a legitimate basis for drawing inferences about the populations from which they are drawn – in essence, within certain boundaries, we can make claims from samples that are generalizable to the populations of which the samples are part. This is not true of all methods of sampling and to understand this point more fully, it is necessary to distinguish between probability (or probabilistic) sampling techniques and non-probability (or non-probabilistic) sampling techniques, also sometimes known as purposive sampling.

Two general types of sampling technique

Probability sampling is where each element in a population is randomly selected when constituting a sample and has a known, non-zero chance of being selected (Arber 1993; Chisnall 1991). For example, if we were to return to our earlier problem of studying the attitude of small-business owners in a particular region towards the introduction of a minimum wage for their employees, then we might find there are 50,000 small-business owners in that region. If we require a sample of 500 and this sample is to be selected randomly, then each member of the 50,000 population has one chance in 100 of being selected as a result of the sampling process.

Probability sampling is the basis of inferential extrapolation. Put simply, it is the most effective means by which detailed study of a sample can lead to legitimate and justifiable generalizations about the population from which that sample is drawn. A key element of sampling, as with research in general, is to ensure that a sample is representative of the population from which it is drawn. Note that this does not mean representative of social characteristics in general. If we were studying the career paths of managers in the UK manufacturing industry then our population would comprise a very large number of men and any random sample would reflect this. The fact that women managers as a proportion of managers on the entire industrial workforce or as a proportion of all levels of manager in the manufacturing industry was very small in the sample is neither here nor there (except in so far as it is a very interesting finding in its own right!). A sample need only reflect (indeed ideally should reflect) the characteristics of the population of which it is part when that sample is generated randomly – i.e. when the sample is generated probabilistically.

We have so far made several references to the 'population' the set from which a sample is drawn. We need to consider how a population is defined. The qualitative aspect of this process is to determine carefully the limits of inclusion and exclusion given the focus of study. Let us consider a study that had as its objective the analysis of the feelings of young employees in the UK retail sector towards their pay with a view to establishing whether such workers felt their pay was 'fair'. What is our population? Ideally it is all young workers (however defined) in all retail outlets and company headquarters. Let us assume that there existed a list of all retail outlets and headquarters in the UK, and a list of all young (say 16–24 years of age) employees. Each of these would constitute in their own right a sampling frame. Sampling frames constitute, as it were, the quantitative aspect of the process of defining a population. Casual reflection reveals, however, many of the problems attendant on defining the population from which a sample is to be drawn. In our case, even if the sampling frames referred to actually existed (they do not) then would we treat all 16–24-year-olds the same? Consider the possibility that this age segment of the working population in retail comprises distinct groups, each evincing different feelings towards whether they are paid favourably (these groups may emerge on the basis of gender, ethnicity, motivations for working or any number of variables). None of this is problematic provided such differences are hypothesized at the outset of the study and reflected in the research objectives of the inquiry. Difficulties in establishing the population and hence the sampling frame from which a sample is to be drawn reflect the importance of clarifying research objectives and highlight the significance of techniques like mapping sentences (see Chapter 5).

Non-probability sampling

Non-probability or purposive sampling is technically defined as where the chance of selection for each element in a population is unknown, and for some elements, is zero (Arber 1993; Chisnall 1991). In general, non-probability sampling may be crudely understood as everything that probability sampling is not. Key issues are that items in non-probability sampling are not selected randomly and this has clear consequences for the extent to which the characteristics of sample data can be generalized to the population from which they are drawn. Specifically, to make claims for the wider population on the basis of study of elements selected using purposive sampling is dangerous, as it cannot be assumed that the characteristics of the elements are randomly distributed throughout the population. The application of statistical tests to such data is also problematic, but not impossible, as non-parametric statistical tests can be employed (see Chapter 17). Thus, the way in which a sample has been selected including its representativeness to the wider population, as well as aspects concerning sample size, must be carefully borne in mind when interpreting any statistic or, indeed, the results of any statistical test.

The two types of sampling technique elaborated

The various versions of sampling techniques that fall under each general type are shown in Table 8.1 in the wider context of the process of sample selection. Each method of sampling is, in this section, considered in turn.

Probability sampling methods

In this part of the discussion we deal with the varieties of random sampling so it is important that the preceding discussion has been properly understood. Now is the time to revisit the themes outlined earlier if there are any doubts over the distinction between probability and non-probability forms of sampling.

Simple random sampling

The most basic form of probability sampling, a simple random sample (SRS) is the selection of elements from a population where each element in that population has an equal, non-zero chance of actually being selected (Arber 1993; Oakshott 1994). The first clear requirement of this approach is a sampling frame in which every member of the population is clearly and separately identified. The second requirement is a method by which to achieve a random sample! Two approaches are as follows. First, there is the lottery method whereby the names, numbers or other identifying means

TABLE 8.1 Sub-types of the principal categories of sampling

Probability sampling	Non-probability sampling
Simple random	Quota
Quasi random[1]	Convenience
Stratified	Snow-balling
Multi-stage	
Cluster[1]	

(1) But note points in text on technical concerns over randomness and bias that arise with these two methods.

of each individual member of the population are mixed thoroughly in some receptacle and the number that is required for the sample is drawn forth. Parallels with the National Lottery or with the game of bingo are clear. Second, there are random numbers. Here, a unique number is allocated to each item in the population and then random number tables or computer-generated random numbers are used to select the sample. Random number tables are found in most statistics texts and in specialist collection of statistical tables (e.g. Murdoch and Barnes 1986) and are simple to use as they involve selecting a random column in the table as a starting point and scrutinizing the numbers in that and subsequent columns, bringing into the sample those correspondingly numbered items in the population.

Quasi-random sampling

Also known as systematic sampling, quasi-random sampling occupies a somewhat ambiguous position in our dual model of probabilistic and non-probabilistic methods of sampling. First of all, as the term 'quasi-random' suggests, this method is not wholly random. In effect, only the first item selected from the population for the sample is chosen at random. Thereafter, subsequent selections are related systematically to the first. The key word here is 'systematic', and the core concept is the sampling interval (Arber 1993: 79). The sampling interval is the systematic element in quasi-random sampling and can be determined arithmetically relative to the size of the population being studied and the required sample size. Thus, assume we have a population of 1000 regular customers visiting one of a city's shops. The shop in question is keen to ascertain the views of these customers as to the quality of their experience while shopping in the store and have been advised by their researchers to take a 5 per cent sample. Thus a 5 per cent sample of 1000 equals 50 – this is our target sample size. The sampling interval is calculated by dividing 1000 by 50 – yielding 20. Thus to proceed with the sampling procedure, a random number between 1 and 20 is selected, then the twentieth value after this is selected and the twentieth value after that. For our example, assuming a random start of 12, this yields the following values:

12	212	412	612	812
32	232	432	632	832
52	252	452	652	852
72	272	472	672	872
92	292	492	692	892
112	312	512	712	912
132	332	532	732	932
152	352	552	752	952
172	372	572	772	972
192	392	592	792	992

We have already noted that in respect of our probabilistic and non-probabilistic model of sampling methods, quasi-random sampling by its very definition causes us a classification problem. A second difficulty is the insistence of some writers that quasi-random sampling utilizes a sampling frame, and by others that it is usually employed when such a frame is not available. In our example above, we assumed a sampling frame of 1000 regular customers. But what if we take the example of a hotel and we wish to interview guests as they arrive at the hotel? The problem is at least implicitly recognized by Cunningham (1991: 64–65):

> ... suppose that a hotel wishes to interview guests as they arrive as to their first impressions of the hotel. Suppose it is decided to interview 10% of guests daily. If we identify these using simple random methods, we may end up choosing to interview the second, third and fourth arrivals. However, since these may well arrive together, we would have to ask some of them to wait while others are interviewed. This is unlikely to improve first impressions of the hotel. The systematic alternative is to take every tenth guest.

Examining Cunningham's example closely we can ask whether or not he is assuming a sampling frame (the total number of guests staying in the hotel each day) or whether his 10 per cent selection approximates to establishing a 10 per cent quota of all guests registering in the hotel on a given day (see the later discussion on quota sampling). The two are somewhat different. In the case of the first there are difficulties that might arise from 'no-shows' or from casual callers who (assuming spare capacity in the hotel) are accepted as guests. Clearly such factors affect the size of an assumed sampling frame. In respect of the second, a 10 per cent sample (more or less) will be achieved selecting every tenth guest who registers at the hotel but here, clearly, the sampling frame is relatively open. We need not worry too much about this provided we are aware of the effect that our strategy has on the selection of our sample. Systematic selection generally results in an unbiased sample provided that the selection of every nth item does not yield a grouping of items with like characteristics – the probability of this happening is fairly low but is nevertheless more common than might be supposed.

Stratified sampling

The objective of stratified sampling is to ensure that in a population under study, the sample drawn from that population is as representative as possible in terms of characteristics of that population which are germane to the variables under study or in terms of a recognized 'distortion' in the population that might not be reflected so precisely were a simple random sample selected. A recurring example in manufacturing industry is worker selection for labour relations' research. Overall, in the total population of workers in manufacturing industry, male employees outnumber females. However, significant differences exist amongst the sub-sectors of manufacturing industry and differences also arise from occupational segregation and from geographical location.

Let us imagine you were studying job satisfaction of employees in five independently owned firms and you were fortunate enough to know not only the size of the population, but certain essential characteristics. Some of these characteristics might be:

- a population of 100 employee operatives, 20 in each firm;
- a gender breakdown of 70 per cent female and 30 per cent male employees;
- an age breakdown of 70 per cent of workers less than 30 years;
- an employment status division of 60 per cent part-time workers and 40 per cent full-time employees; and
- a division between employees in the sales and administrative departments of the order of 70 per cent and 30 per cent respectively, of which 50 of the former and 20 of the latter are female.

While a straightforward random sample of any population will, on average, be representative of that population, it need not be as closely representative of all the population's essential characteristics as you would wish. The actual numbers or proportions that arise are slightly more open to choice than when a stratified sampling approach is used. In the example above, a random sample which may, perhaps, not be very large would be almost certainly in danger of failing to adequately represent certain crucial features of the population. For example, labour researchers know from prior research studies that female workers tend to have views on certain aspects of their employment experiences that differ from those of male workers. The same might be true of administrative workers and sales people. Thus, to ensure that the sample is representative, and such potential sources of difference are reflected in the overall results, it would be preferable that the sample selection procedures proceed on the basis of stratifying the population.

Immediately, however, we hit a problem for it is clear that the population should not, ideally, be stratified by every characteristic that can give rise to a possible source of variation as this would overly complicate procedures and, in the scheme of things, could not be guaranteed to improve either the accuracy or overall value of the results to a cost-effective advantage. Furthermore, in the list of population characteristics itemized above, none of these characteristics are mutually exclusive (i.e. an employee of either gender may be working part time, less than 30 years of age and working for the sales department) and this has to be kept in mind in any stratification strategy. Considering what we (think we) know from prior research, we might conclude that age is not an especially important factor in our study since it is thought this is unlikely to be a major source of variation in our investigation regarding workers' attitudes. Furthermore, since *our* population contains a significant proportion of employees aged under 30, we can assume to some degree that a randomly chosen sample would reflect this proportion more or less accurately providing the sample chosen is sufficiently large. Similar reasoning can be extended to the division between part-time and full-time workers.

Note here how we have used our contextual knowledge deriving from prior research to inform some of our sampling decisions. After the process of reasoning outlined above we are left with the knowledge that in many previous studies of employee attitudes to work, gender and occupational group have been important sources of variation in perspective. Thus, we must take this into account in the next stage of our sampling procedures. First, let us assume that the ratio of female to male workers in our population approximates directly to the national breakdown for that industry, and wish to ensure that in our sample this ratio is maintained as we regard it as potentially significant in the quality of data produced (we do not consider this to be the case for age or employment status). Similarly, in the case of occupational divisions, we want to ensure that a proper balance is maintained between those working in the administrative and sales departments. Now we are ready to stratify our sample. We know there are 100 workers in total (the population) and 70 per cent of these are female and 30 per cent male while 30 per cent are administrative workers and 70 per cent work for the sales department, with 10 of the former and 20 of the latter being men. Here, our population equates to our sampling frame (for the sake of argument we assume that all members of the population of interest have agreed to be available and be interviewed if selected), so we stratify the sampling frame according to gender and occupational group.

At this point it is worth recalling that our population is spread over five firms. This in itself may well be an important source of variation in data (for example, we are interested in employee attitudes to their work and this may vary according to the practices of management). We *could* stratify according to firm but to do this would be to invite all sorts of dangers. Even if (as has been fortuitously suggested for the sake of argument!) each firm has an equal number of employees in each department, it does not mean that any or all of the other ratios pertains to each and every firm. Thus, to set up a stratified sampling frame incorporating a 'firm' factor is not possible, demonstrating one of the limitations in adding a potentially useful stratification criteria due to lack of data on the population. Nevertheless, we would have to be sensitive to the possibility of this source of variance when analysing our data. Table 8.2, then, shows the final form of our stratified sampling frame.

Once the sampling frame has been stratified, the sample in this case is selected systematically. An alternative would be to take a simple random sample from each stratum proportional to the size of the stratum, or, in some cases, a disproportionate sample for reasons which are discussed later. First, let us deal with the situation represented by our example and say we require a 25 per cent sample – in this case, as our population is 100, equal to 25. The sampling interval is calculated by dividing 100 by 25 – yielding 4. Thus, we proceed with the sampling procedure. To expedite this procedure, it should be noted that first all the members in the population are numbered according to the stratified list, i.e. the 50 female employees in the sales

TABLE 8.2 Stratification by gender and occupation

Stratification by: Gender	Occupation	Population: Number in gender/occupational set	Sample: Number by gender and occupation
Male	Administrative	10	3
	Sales	20	5
Female	Administrative	20	5
	Sales	50	12
Total		100	25

department are numbered 1–50, the 20 female employees in the administrative department take the numbers 51–70 and so on with the male employees in the sales and administrative department being numbered 71–90 and 91–100 respectively. We then select a random number between 1 and 4 and the fourth value after this is selected and the fourth after that – and so on. For our example, assuming a random start of 3, this yields a selection which conforms to respondents numbered as follows:

3	23	43	63	83
7	27	47	67	87
11	31	51	71	91
15	35	55	75	95
19	39	59	79	99

The number in each set of the stratified sampling frame is shown in the final column of Table 8.2.

We have spent some time discussing stratified random sampling because it is frequently presented as an accurate and simple technique for ensuring greater representativeness in 'awkward' populations. Indeed, a further development of the process described above is to impose a disproportionate sampling fraction where you wish to achieve more cases in respect of certain groups (or strata) than would be obtained by applying a uniform sampling fraction. For example, in the above situation a fraction (or interval) of 1 in 4 was applied, but had you wished to obtain more than 3 cases in your sample in respect of male administration workers then a smaller sampling interval, or even a census, could have been applied in respect of that strata.

There are several reasons for applying disproportionate sampling fractions. As has been shown a principal benefit of stratification is to ensure greater representativeness of the sample in respect of the population from which it is drawn. Thus, the basic technique of stratification might be employed to ensure all significant groups, including minority groups, are included in the overall sample selection. If these groups constitute in themselves an interesting area for study, then a disproportionate sampling fraction may be applied in order to ensure a greater number from this group are selected for analysis than would be the case if a uniform sampling fraction were applied. Other reasons for using a disproportionate sampling fraction are when one group displays considerably greater variation within itself than others. For example, if female administrators are known to hold widely divergent views on some topic germane to the purposes of the study, then it might be deemed necessary to sample them more intensively in order to ensure a more precise understanding of their opinions is obtained. This aspect brings into play the concept of variance and the accuracies that can be achieved with different sample sizes. For more guidance on these technical issues the reader is referred to later sections in this chapter which deal with sample size and to Chapter 16 which deals with measures of dispersion.

Finally, one other reason for taking a disproportionate sampling fraction relates to where the costs involved in sampling one stratum are far greater than the costs

SAMPLING – CHOOSING YOUR SUBJECTS

involved in sampling another strata. If, for example, it proves for some reason to be considerably more expensive to interview one category of operatives than another, then the more expensive group may be sampled less frequently, albeit randomly, in order to contain costs. These are judgmental decisions every survey planner must take. The important point to remember is that if disproportionate sampling fractions are used, the statistics computed for each stratum must be re-weighted when statistics relating to the overall sample are calculated. Again, the reader is referred to Chapter 16 where the nature of such computations is explained.

To conclude this section on stratification we can see that in the right hands stratification can be an extremely useful tool. However, it is not always an easy procedure to manipulate or apply as many contingencies can arise in determining the forms of stratification to use. Contingencies may of necessity be based on (a) subjective decisions; and (b) what we think we know about the characteristics of the population. In respect of the latter, the researcher is caught in something of a bind. In short, comprehensive knowledge or understanding about the characteristics of the population under scrutiny is essential if stratified sampling is to be used effectively and successfully, while cursory or superficial knowledge, carelessly operationalized in the stratification of the sampling frame, can lead to a situation whereby criteria for stratification are selected that reflect only the researcher's preconceptions about their topic of study. Appealing though it is, therefore, stratified sampling has to be recommended along with a stern warning about its potential limitations and the technical complexities involved.

Multi-stage sampling

Multi-stage sampling is, as the term implies, where the sampling process involves two or more stages and is often associated with studies where the population of interest is geographically widespread. It is effectively a technique that aids the random sampling process and offers the benefit that a full sampling frame is not required at the outset. To explain, suppose you were wanting to interview members of management teams in recruitment agencies in the UK to establish the nature of their perceptions about graduate applicants. Recruitment agencies are reasonably well distributed throughout the UK and to select a random or systematic sample would lead to much travel and great cost. Also, it is unlikely that you would have, or want to compile, a complete list of all managers in all recruitment agencies throughout the country. To overcome these difficulties the country is broken down into smaller areas – for example counties or local authority regions. Indeed, stratification of areas such as counties on local authorities by principal geographical regions is often introduced in order to minimize geographical bias. A number of these areas is then randomly selected. If the number of areas or counties selected is still too large and too dispersed, then these areas in turn can be further broken down and a random sample selected of the still smaller units. This 'staging' continues to a level where a random or stratified sample of individual units can be selected for study. The effect of this process is to end up sampling a number of units (or individuals) from a very limited number of areas. Thus, it is important to ensure that the final sample selected from the last stage of sampling units is proportionate and as representative as possible of the (remaining) population as a whole in order to avoid area bias. When making the final selection, a systematic sampling approach is often indicated as potentially more useful than simple random sampling. For example, if the last stage units are five city conurbations with a known number of recruitment agencies in each (say 10 in the first, 9 in the second and so on to 6 in the fifth) then we find:

City	Number of recruitment agencies	Cumulative numbering
A	10	1–10
B	9	11–19
C	8	20–27
D	7	28–34
E	6	35–40
Total population:	40	

If we are interested in a 25 per cent sample, that is 10 agencies, our sampling interval will be $40 \div 10 = 4$. Beginning with a random 1, this would yield a selection of agencies numbered as follows:

1	21
5	25
9	29
13	33
17	37

This would translate to our sampling units as follows:

City	Number of agencies	Number in sample
A	10	3 (i.e. the 1st, 5th and 9th on the list)
B	9	2
C	8	2
D	7	2
E	6	1
Total population/sample:	40	10

Cluster sampling

Turning now to cluster sampling or clustering, which is a form of sampling similar to multi-stage sampling, in that it involves two or more stages in the sampling process. Also, as with multi-stage sampling, clustering is a technique often used when a large geographical area is at the heart of the sampling requirement or where the focus of research interest constitutes a dispersed population such as may be represented by a range of institutions or discrete organizations (IT companies, banks, management schools). The essential difference between generalized multi-stage sampling and cluster sampling is that at the final point of selection, clusters are small enough for everybody in that cluster to be interviewed. In the previous example we may have interviewed every member of the management team in all 40 of our agencies but, more likely, and ideally, we would have taken a random sample selecting only certain staff from each cluster.

A disadvantage of cluster sampling is that since all the cases in the final stage units are selected the procedure does not entirely follow the strict rules of random sampling. It therefore presents us with the classification problem (see Table 8.2). There is a danger that individual clusters may display problems of undue homogeneity. For example, all managers in one recruitment agency may be prone to adopting similar attitudes. But these are technical aspects that again require personal judgement when deciding upon the expediency of adopting certain sampling techniques.

It is not uncommon for student researchers to follow more flexible *ad hoc* techniques similar to these methods rather than using the methods themselves. The former course of action is acceptable provided no pretence is being made to probabilistic sampling with all that implies for the validity and reliability of conclusions drawn from data. 'Something' is either selected randomly or it is not: there is only limited scope for compromise between probability and non-probability (purposive) sampling, the last of these to which we now turn.

Non-probability (purposive) sampling

The key feature of non-probability sampling is that items chosen for a sample are not chosen randomly but purposively. The best known form of purposive sampling is quota sampling but under the general 'purposive' heading we can also include convenience and snowball sampling.

Quota sampling

At some time in your life you have probably been shopping in a busy street when approached by a market researcher with a clipboard. Chances are this researcher is engaged in quota sampling, which is a non-probabilistic method of sampling that aims to achieve a sample that is representative of the population under scrutiny by pre-specifying quota controls on certain known characteristics of the population. The sources of these 'known characteristics' are usually official statistics drawn from (primarily) government surveys. However, there are a myriad nongovernmental sources of statistics on many and varied aspects of different populations. The 'known characteristics' of a population under scrutiny are usually interpreted in terms of their proportionality and it is this proportionality that guides the setting of quotas in sample selection.

For example, suppose you are interested in surveying a record shop's customers for some purpose. You may employ three independent quota controls: age, gender and place of residence. Suppose you have three age categories 16–34, 35–49 and 50–65 and know (the figures are hypothetical) that overall (nationally) some 70 per cent of all record shop customers are in the 16–34 range, 20 per cent in 35–49 and 10 per cent in the 50–65 range. Similarly you may know that on a similar scale, 60 per cent of these customers are female and 40 per cent male and that 60 per cent live in urban and 40 per cent rural areas. These guidelines would provide the quotas of people you must survey in order to ensure that the appropriate proportion of people within each category is represented in the sample. In this way the quota for each variable is filled. In a street survey, the researcher generally tries to fill quotas via observation of the passing populace. This can lead to various forms of bias: it may over-represent those who frequent city centres regularly (usually housewives as opposed to business people); interviewers may select their quota on the basis of extra-quota variables (for example, a researcher may be seeking to interview a number of women in the 35–49 age group and they will gauge the ages of passers-by intuitively – this would be seeking to match a quota variable: however, the researcher may only stop those who look friendly or approachable and thus likely to participate in the survey – an example of an extra-quota variable – in this case perceived personality type – determining selection); and the boundaries of quotas may be under-represented in certain cases. Thus in the case of age, in order to avoid possible offence by mistaking the age category of a potential respondent, researchers 'play it safe' and select those they feel have a greater probability of being in the mainstream of the age group.

Street-research is not the only application of quota sampling. In our record shop example, we might first determine the sample size to be selected and then second, a method of filling our quota(s) to reflect proportional balances pertinent to the characteristics described. Of course, the advantage of quota sampling is that it can be adjusted to a variety of scales, which of course will be related to the size of our declared sample and hence the objectives of our research. With our retail example we may be undertaking some kind of national survey (unlikely), a regional survey, or most likely, a survey within a single strictly determined area such as a town or city. Whatever the case, our quota controls will ensure a correct proportionality is maintained relative to the closer population parameters. Ideally, we will also guard against imbalance in the total sample by ensuring that our quota controls are adequately interrelated (sometimes known as the 'interconnectedness' or 'interfacing' of the quotas). The objective is to avoid situations where, for example, one age group might carry a disproportionate number of one gender or one category of place of employment. Unless the exact extent of the interrelated population parameters is known and can be applied (e.g. the proportion of male and female customers in the 16–34 age group and so on) then the process of allocation based on simple independent quotas can give rise to imbalances in cross-tabulations that do not match reality. The simple procedure of applying independent quotas is a less scientific one.

However, if quota sampling has several disadvantages it also has a certain value as a technique. First, it is generally cheaper than probabilistic methods of sampling (because travel and hence interview costs can be more readily contained). Second, it is a quick method of obtaining data that does not require a full sampling frame. Third, quota sampling has a useful immediacy. Thus, if a researcher is investigating something that is extremely topical, the delays attendant on probability sampling might not apply and respondents may be encountered when the issue under scrutiny is fresh in their minds.

Convenience sampling

Convenience sampling means different things to different commentators on research methodology. At its simplest, convenience sampling means quite literally taking as a sample whoever is available to receive the administration of the research instrument (a questionnaire, an interview). In a more focused sense, convenience samples are non-probabilistic samples that might be selected to focus on a particular issue or issues. They are convenient precisely because they are by definition at the core of a study's concerns or because they meet the general parameter of a study's objectives. Nothing can be generally inferred from data gained from convenience samples except in a wholly speculative sense. Mars and Nicod's (1984) study of the occupational culture of waiting staff (see Chapter 2) employed the research method known as participant observation (see Chapter 13 below), which entailed the researcher (Nicod) actually becoming a waiter in several establishments for short periods of time. To some extent, Nicod was constrained in his endeavours by the establishments in which he could obtain employment as a waiter. In a very broad sense, the hotel and subjects (waiting staff) he chose to work in/observe were selected because they were 'convenient' to the researcher in meeting his objectives. The term 'convenience sample' can be interpreted in many different ways and cover a multitude of researchers' sins! It is a generally unsatisfactory term but can be broadly defined as follows:

- a convenience sample is a non-probability sample;
- quite often a convenience sample is not a sample at all in the sense that those selected are chosen on the basis of some distribution of multiple characteristics: rather, the sample is chosen because they share certain very clearly defined core characteristics; and
- convenience sampling is most often used where research objectives are inherently qualitative in nature and focus upon the elaboration of theoretical concepts and issues in micro-social contexts.

Snowball sampling

Snowball sampling is one of the most interesting and useful techniques of sampling where small groups are the focus, the research objectives are essentially qualitative and the population of interest is either likely to be small and/or possess rare or unusual characteristics. In sociological research, 'snowballing' has been used to identify samples as varied as drug-takers, prostitutes and scientists! Snowball sampling involves identifying a member of the population of interest and asking them if they know anybody else with the required characteristics. This person (or those people) are then contacted and, if appropriate, included in the sample while themselves being asked to suggest the names of like respondents who may be known to them. In the case of the scientists mentioned above, several studies of controversy in science have employed snowball sampling in order to identify a network of respondents who view each other as the key players in the area of experimentation or theorizing under scrutiny (Collins 1984). Snowball sampling is an especially useful technique for investigating controversial areas and/or for identifying networks of respondents who might otherwise be reluctant to publicly participate in a research project.

Sample size

Often the novice or student researcher is too ambitious relative to their research objectives and resources, selecting too large a sample for realistic study. More often than not, the time and money available for research will impose heavy limitations on the sample size that can be taken. The method of survey will also play a vital role. Clearly it is more possible to choose a larger sample where the instrument of survey is a postal questionnaire rather than where it involves intensive face-to-face interviews. On the other hand, there is a danger for many students of taking too small a sample for meaningful study. This can arise especially where the aim is to analyse data across a range of interrelated characteristics involving cross-tabulations, or where certain statistical tests such as the Chi-square test (see Chapter 18) are to be applied, or where claims of an inferential nature concerning the wider population are to be made.

For many students and, indeed, experienced researchers, the problem of determining sample size is a complex one. Again, it involves matters of judgement balancing cost and time against desired accuracy and purposes of the survey. The decision also depends very much on the nature of the population to be explored. In short, if the intentions of the research are to explore a variety of issues or characteristics about a group, this must be taken into account in determining sample size. Each characteristic may be subject to a diversity or range of options, which will need to be considered in any breakdown or cross-tabulation process. The researcher will want to ensure enough cases fall into each cell. Also, the accuracy with which estimates are to be obtained or population parameters inferred are crucial. If, in an opinion survey, all the opinions held by a group on the particular topic are the same then a sample size of only one is required to obtain a representative view. This is, of course, an extreme and highly unlikely situation, but it makes clear the point that in general in order to determine sample size it is necessary to know or have some estimate, of the variance among the population in respect of each characteristic to be explored. The statistical term 'variance' is described in Chapter 16, but in principle the more wide ranging a population is in respect of its key characteristics or opinions to be evaluated, then the larger the sample that is required to obtain reasonably accurate estimates. Another factor is the accuracy with which the estimates are required. If the researcher is content with a rough-and-ready guide of, say, the income level of a group then the sample size need not be so large as if a highly accurate evaluation is required.

As has been said there are no hard and fast rules on what sample size should be selected for a particular study. As well as considerations concerning accuracy and variations in the population, time and cost will come into the decision process. More often than not, these are highly important limiting factors. If you only have so much time and money at your disposal, then you can only conduct a certain amount of research and therefore your sample size may have to be confined to what is practical.

Summary

Sampling is an extremely complex topic but the selection of an appropriate sample is central to the success of any research project. Sampling method and sample selection should reflect explicitly the objectives of the research project. In summary, three key problems that sampling presents to the novice researcher and which should be confronted and ultimately avoided are as follows.

- *Inappropriate sampling method.* Here the choice of method, from the basic distinction between probability and non-probability sampling to the selection of a specific method is extremely important. However, there is a tendency among novice researchers to select a sampling method that does not reflect the objectives of the research, for example in selecting a non-probability sampling method when a probability sample would be more appropriate.
- *Sample size.* Often, the novice researcher is tempted to select either too large a sample relative to their resources or, at the other extreme, too small a sample for meaningful study given the aims of the project. Unfortunately, there are no hard and fast rules, but the decision should take into account whether it is a quantitative or qualitative type of study or approach that is being pursued. If the aim is to make inferences about the wider population then a larger sample is likely to be required. Many projects, however, and particularly student projects, involve taking only small samples. This is because of limitations on resources, particularly time and money, especially where in-depth interviews are involved. The disadvantages of only taking small numbers are self-evident, but the procedure does not necessarily preclude a student from conducting a useful piece of research or presenting findings that contribute to the foundation of knowledge on a particular topic.
- *Inappropriate method of sample selection relative to the research instrument.* Here the concern is the all-too-common tendency to select a sample that mismatches the research instrument. Novice researchers are particularly fond of questionnaires as a research instrument but these are not always the most appropriate means of meeting research objectives. Large samples are often inappropriate in cases where personal interviews are the primary research instrument and small samples where the research instrument is a questionnaire designed to obtain quantitative results.

To conclude, then, sample selection should be guided by research objectives and the chosen research instrument. Where doubt exists, it is usually best to err on the side of conservatism such that the potential for disaster is minimized by ensuring that the sample chosen for study meets a minimum number of requirements in respect of the designated research objectives. In this way, it is possible to maximize the possibility of generating a minimum useful quality of information from your sample, even if you are unsuccessful in achieving all your aims.

9

Questionnaire design

One of the problems for questionnaire design is that the questionnaire, for many, is synonymous with research. Often researchers jump for the questionnaire without thinking about other forms of data collection. The first message therefore is to be sure that you actually want to use this technique. Although it is more versatile than most techniques it does not have the qualitative depth of some alternatives. Among its many attributes the questionnaire is especially good at collecting information on facts and opinions from large numbers of people.

Think before you start to design the questionnaire

Once you are commited to a questionnaire you are involved in two processes: a creative process of writing questions and a design process of devising a structure which is rational in terms of the questionnaire's objectives and intended subjects. Like any other research technique if the objectives are not clear then the results will be as unclear as the objectives. Before even starting to design your questionnaire a number of aspects of your topic have to be considered and clarified. Some of these aspects will appear to be obvious but elementary mistakes are even more harmful to research than errors in design detail. Put simply, there are three fundamentals that you have to get straight before you start. These are:

- what do you want to know about your topic?;
- how much do your intended subjects know about your topic?; and
- in what human terms will the answers be expressed, or to put it another way, what are you actually measuring?

What do you want to know about your topic?

In research you are seeking knowledge about a topic but must be clear as to exactly what it is you are looking for. What kind of information do you want? The following items may act as a checklist.

- Evidence that your topic exists?
- The extent of your topic?
- How your topic is defined?
- How significant your topic is?
- How much do subjects know about your topic?
- How do they feel about your topic?
- Do they believe in your topic?
- How do they value your topic?
- Who or what do they compare your topic with?
- How do they differentiate your topic?
- How do they see the purpose of your topic?
- How will your topic change?
- What causes your topic?

The list is not exhaustive – more questions could be asked, yet some of the questions appear too obvious to be important. Yet they are important. You need to check your research objectives and mapping sentences (see Chapter 5) against these questions. It is another check of your 'grip' on the research.

How much do your subjects know about your topic?

It would be ridiculous to ask people questions on subjects they know nothing about. It happens! This is an area where expert assumptions have to be made. In other words, the researcher has to have a rough idea of how much the intended subjects know of the topic. However, these assumptions are not just about knowledge. Some thought has to be given to how the intended subjects learnt their knowledge of the topic. Did they learn it through some form of education, or from experience, or both? There is a connection between how one remembers something and the way it was learnt originally. Is it remembered for what it is or is it remembered by association or comparison with something else? If you ask people to evaluate your topic you have to have grounds for suspecting that they will have feelings towards it.

Assuming your subjects know about your topic some thought needs to be given as to the form in which they hold this knowledge. Three dangers lie in wait for the researcher here: nostalgia, reality and 'ought' models. To put it another way, your topic can be seen 'through rose-tinted glasses' 'through self-constructed reality' and 'by reference to how it ought to be rather than how it is'. These aspects are not matters of interpretation to be applied to data once it has been collected. They are aspects that can be accommodated by a questionnaire and need to be part of the researcher's preliminary thinking.

In what human terms will the answers be expressed? Or, what are you actually measuring?

Questionnaires can take many forms particularly when psychological aspects are being measured. Whilst it is beyond the scope of this chapter to review every type of questionnaire (see Moser and Kalton 1993, for an authorative discussion of quantitative and qualitative surveys; also of value are the works by Slater 1982 and Rosenfeld, Edwards and Thomas 1993) it must be clearly understood that you should be absolutely certain as to what is being measured, and accept that in most circumstances, only one form of response can be measured by one questionnaire. Accordingly, you should ask yourself, 'am I measuring ...':

- Knowledge?
- Some aspect of behaviour?
- Opinions?
- Priorities?
- Attitudes?
- Beliefs?
- Values?
- Perceptions?
- Feelings?
- Evaluations?

Earlier it was stated that researchers must be sure of the type of knowledge and information they are seeking. It is not always easy to measure social phenomena such as attitudes and values. A common problem occurs with the difference between opinions and attitudes (see Chapter 11). Problems of this nature have to be approached through study of theory and of the theoretical assumptions of the alternative measuring instruments that the researcher is contemplating.

Questions to be considered at the planning stage

Every researcher worries about the response rate of their questionnaire. 'The sample size has been calculated (see Chapter 8) but will I make it?' is a common question every novice researcher asks throughout. It is not a matter of luck! Questionnaire design plays a part in success as far as response rates are concerned and it is not just a case of making the questionnaire look pretty! In designing the structure of a questionnaire there are three questions to be considered. First, how to induce people to fill it in. Second, how are the responses to be aggregated? Third and most importantly, will the questionnaire achieve the objectives? These questions are in fact criteria by which you could judge your questionnaire design.

Designing questions

Alas, circumstances dictate that there are no firm rules you can apply to questionnaire design. However, it is possible to identify the kind of design decisions that have to be made. The list below is not exhaustive but covers key issues.

- Whether the questionnaire is to be postal, face-to-face interview or telephone based.
- The length of the questionaire.
- Where to put personal details.
- The degree of disguise.
- Whether to fire blanks.
- Whether to use check questions.
- Running order or sequence.
- The need to aggregate the data.
- The need to compare the data with other data.
- The need to computerize the data.

The best way to answer these questions is to imagine yourself filling in a questionnaire. This is where a degree of awareness of the subject's knowledge can contribute. That said there is no substitute for piloting the questionnaire (see Chapter 4).

Writing questions

There are no easy answers here, only pitfalls to avoid. As in the case of design, question writing is aided by the ability to think out what information you are seeking and the ability to visualize how your intended subjects might perceive your topic. However, four pointers as to what a question is supposed to achieve can be helpful. These are:

- focus;
- raise attention;
- eliminate alternatives; and
- draw an unambiguous respose.

These criteria presuppose that the subject is interested, aware and has knowledge of or about, the topic you are surveying.

Types of question

There are basically two types of question – open and closed. The closed question restricts the answers to a small set of responses and requires the questionnaire designer to have a fair knowledge of the range of options the subjects might have in this area. It does, however, generate precise answers. The open-ended question has the merit of not imposing restrictions as to the possible answer but is harder to aggregate and computerize. It has the merit of offering richer and deeper responses.

Wording pitfalls

There are some common pitfalls to be avoided in constructing questions. The most common are as follows.

- Avoid vague wording, e.g. 'frequently', 'normally', and achieve clarity and precision – you may understand the question but will your respondents?
- Avoid implied questions of belief. Questions should not depend on the subject believing in the question, e.g. 'Healthy eating is good for you'. 'How much do you spend on vegetables in a week?'
- Avoid leading questions, e.g. 'Most people think'; 'Wouldn't you agree that?'; 'Isn't it the case that?'
- Avoid typical examples as a means of guiding your subjects.
- Avoid letting the subject answer 'it depends on'.
- Avoid double-barrelled questions – asking two questions in one, a common failing amongst novice questionnaire writers.
- Avoid hypothetical questions, e.g. 'What would you do if?'
- Avoid asking respondents as to what they think the views of others might be on a topic or topics – this is an inherently unreliable method of obtaining data.
- Avoid periodicity – when asking questions requiring respondents to specify a quantity, offer a range of possible responses couched in numerical rather than verbal terms (e.g. '2–3 times a month', '4–5 times a month'; 'more than five times a month' rather than 'sometimes', 'always', 'never').
- Avoid simplistic approaches to asking questions about behaviour and attitudes that might be construed as obviously socially desirable or undesirable as respondents may give the answer that they consider socially desirable.

Some common problems

In broad terms the commonest problems fall into three categories which are: first, phrasing questions, second, determining the levels of classification of choices, and third, handling the possibility of 'don't know'. There are, alas, many more pitfalls.

Problems of phrasing questions

In what direction do you phrase factual questions? Do you ask 'How long have you lived at your present address?' or, ask 'When did you move to your present address?' The first question is easier to answer but will be less accurate than the second.

Problems of expressing levels of degrees of a choice set

Experience of questionnaire design shows that a number of problems reoccur irrespective of the nature and purpose of the questionnaire. The three problems outlined below are all problems of classification.

Problem 1: the key decisions

Often questionnaires contain choice sets like the one below containing classes of numbers, i.e.:

100–199
200–299
300–399
400+

If this choice set is to work you have to make certain important decisions, which are (a) do you need equal intervals? (b) how wide should the classes be? (c) how many intervals do you need? and (d) where do you set the boundaries. The last category needs special consideration. If it is open ended then calculations become difficult. If it is closed the implication is that a finite limit exists which may not be how your subjects interpret the topic (see Chapter 16).

Problem 2: handling the unspecified

What do you do when the classification you are using cannot contain all possibilities? The answer is you need to ask about 'other' categories. If you need to ask about 'other' categories you also need to ask your respondents to specify what it is, which effectively means employing a supplementary question. The possibility of having to use the 'other' category has to be considered very seriously because it may have implications for some other part of your questionnaire. If a large proportion of answers fall into the 'other' category then the questionnaire itself is less valid.

Problem 3: handling rogue items

In setting out a classification you often come across items that do not fit easily into the mainstrean of your class boundaries. There are a number of options here such as:

- combine the item into another class and tell the reader;
- tell the reader it is not to be considered at all; or
- use the 'other' device.

Handling the possibility of 'Don't know'

It was suggested earlier that part of the initial thinking process was to access how much your intended subjects actually knew about or cared about your topic. If there is any reason to think that their knowledge might not be comprehensive or that their attachment might be variable then the questionnaire must build in the opportunity to express this with a 'Don't know' option. This avoids the possibility of subjects inventing answers to question they find difficult or spoiling their questionaire out of frustration.

Mode of questionnaire

It is easy to fall into the trap of associating questionnaires with the postal mode of survey without first considering two alternatives. These are, face-to-face interviews and telephone interviews both from a structured questionnaire.

The great merit of face-to-face interviews is that the researcher has more control but more importantly can strengthen open-ended questions by allowing longer answers and asking supplementary questions. Researchers who combine quantitative and qualitative data in the same instrument should give the face-to-face interview technique serious consideration.

Telephone interviews are widely practised in market research and are becoming more acceptable in academic research. This technique has the special merit of achieving greater subject focus on each question because of the isolation of each question from the other. It is especially useful to measuring opinions and levels of knowledge and awareness. Indeed, as a technique it is almost universally confined to opinion surveys where knowledge of the subject is either confidently assumed to be known or obtainable at the same time as the opinion. It is a simple direct technique for simple direct research problems. In other words it is largely confined to opinions and should not be considered when anything of a deep psychological nature, such as attitudes, are to be measured. The basic rule here is that only when each question is regarded as a separate item can a telephone method be considered. At a more pragmatic level, the length of the study is a determining factor. Face-to-face and telephone interviews are demanding on the subject and therefore cannot be used in circumstances where a great deal of information is being collected (for further discussion, see Chapter 12).

Simple common sense rules in questionnaire design

Although there are no hard and fast rules experience teaches us to apply common sense to the task of questionnaire design. Key things to ensure are as follows.

- Use simple and concise language.
- Do not make unrealistic demands of those who are to fill in the questionnaire.
- Each question should ask about one 'thing' only.
- Each question should have no escape route, i.e. don't know, no comment, it depends.
- Be polite.

- Be straightforward and guard against double meanings.
- Get the question order right.
- Make the layout easy to follow.
- Give clear instructions.
- Test (pilot) the questionnaire first.

Survey design

The whole task of creating a questionnaire must be seen as part of a larger process which involves its application. This is the survey process. There are many approaches to designing a survey and variation will depend to a large extend on the complexity of the subject. The following list is a suggested process.

- Stage one: identify the topic and set some objectives.
- Stage two: pilot a questionaire to find out what people know and what they see as the important issues.
- Stage three: list the areas of information needed and refine the objectives.
- Stage four: review the responses to the pilot.
- Stage five: finalize the objectives.
- Stage six: write the questionnaire.
- Stage seven: repilot the questionnaire.
- Stage eight: finalize the questionnaire.
- Stage nine: code the questionnaire.

Survey administration

- *Stage one*: Select the sample.
- *Stage two*: Prepare the mailing system. This requires the questionnaires to be numbered, a return date set and mailing facilities to be organized. Consider whether to include a 'return' envelope to avoid respondents having to bear the costs of postage.
- *Stage three*: An optional course of action is to record which questionnaires (identified by their number) are returned when. This might allow for subsequent interpretation of the return rates of any sub-categories of respondents in the sample.
- *Stage four*: Again, optional, you might choose to follow-up postage of questionnaires (after a suitable lapse of time) with a telephone call to check with respondents that they have arrived. It is increasingly common, where resources permit, to telephone potential respondents *before* the questionnaire is issued in order to establish whether the targeted individual/organization is willing to co-operate. Such a strategy is usually prohibited by cost for large samples being employed in dissertation research. After the closing date for the return of the questionnaires has passed, telephone follow-ups to prompt return is permissible provided that this does not affect the research design (i.e. the people who respond may be as important in analytic terms as their responses).

Coding a questionnaire

The purpose of coding a questionnaire is to allow a computer to undertake the hard work of aggregating the answers. The principle behind coding is based on two concepts, the variable and the range of possible answers. Every question or part of a question represents a variable. For example:

- Gender: male/female – is one variable
- Nationality – is one variable

Furthermore, questions may have more than one answer. Answers may be as simple as 'Yes' or 'No' but there may also be a wide range of possibilities. Therefore we need to tell the computer to recognize and place the whole range of possible answers in separate codes. The numbers used in codes usually begin with 0 or 1 then follow a sequence, e.g. 1, 2, 3, ... 10, etc. They are normally written as 000, 001, 002 and so on. When a code is assigned to a variable every possible outcome must be coded. For example the variables gender and nationality would be coded thus

Gender	Male	=	1	Nationality	British	=	1
	Female	=	2		French	=	2
					German	=	3
					Other	=	4

and, when entered on the computer would look as follows:

Question No.	Variable 1 Gender	Variable 2 Nationality	Description
1	1	2	Male, French
2	1	3	Male, German
3	2	2	Female, French

On reflection – some final thoughts

Mistakes in questionnaires can vary from the mere irritatingly inconvenient to the catastrophic where the whole thing is ruined by one error. Piloting is your best safety net, but piloting implies analysis as well as just checking that subjects can understand and complete the questionnaire. The analysis of a pilot study can be a model for the analysis of the complete sample. If the form of analysis cannot be done from your pilot information because of the structuring of the questions it cannot be done on the main sample. The best advice is to analyse the pilot as completely as you envisage the sample; it might seem inappropriate to do statistical analysis on a sample that is too small to warrant statistical inference, but the point is to practise your analysis and to make sure outputs (especially if computerized) are what you actually want.

10

Quality and quantity – some miscellaneous methods

There are many occasions in which we want not to 'count', or quantify some social phenomenon or interaction, but to investigate feelings, attitudes, values, perceptions, motivations – those unobservable, fluid and intangible factors which help explain human behaviour. Only words can do that. Although one can 'measure' an attitude, from the extremely negative to the extremely positive (-5 = extreme dislike; 0 = neutral; $+5$ = extreme liking) (see Chapter 11 on Attitude Measurement) that does not tell us whether my $+5$ is as strong as your $+5$, or if my 'neutral' is for the same reason as your 'neutral.' The more interested and involved we become in studying human affairs, the more we realize that it is often not the actual numbers or observable states of affairs which fascinates us, but why they come about, and the only way in which we are going to find that out is by asking questions, collecting data, in the form of words rather than numbers. We observe and record conversations, actions, events, and then try to interpret them and their meaning through a range of concepts and theories which owe their explanatory power to factors other than statistical techniques or formulae. Instead we use an array of interpretative techniques which seek to 'describe, decode and translate ... the meaning ... of certain more or less naturally occurring phenomena in the social world' (Van Maanen 1983: 9) in situations where the *frequency* of the phenomenon is not the issue.

This is the type of method of research we label qualitative, describing explanations based on non-numerical data. Often, quantitative and qualitative methods are employed in the same research project, qualitative methods being employed to elaborate the quantitative dimensions of the research. For example, Foxall and Hackett (1994) conducted a survey to establish consumer satisfaction with Birmingham's International Convention Centre. This asked 86 visitors to grade 28 features of the Centre on a spectrum of 1–5 (very unsatisfactory to very satisfactory). Under factors such as 'atmosphere' and 'location' were variables which would require further qualitative analysis to establish what were the actual feelings of the staff relative to these variables, what they meant by 'helpfulness of locals', and how the design of the Centre or the lighting levels affected their moods and perceptions of their experience of it. Unstructured discussion with the visitors could reveal all sorts of likes and dislikes about colour schemes, furnishings, what it was that led them to talk about the 'friendliness' of staff. After all, one man's friendly behaviour could be labelled by another woman as 'threatening' behaviour. In other words, whilst the statistical survey gave some indication of the importance of 'atmosphere' in the Centre experience, the meaning of that word encompassed a number of highly subjective and personal factors, some of which were of no relevance at all to some visitors, and others which management had never thought could be an issue.

In other kinds of research project, it is often the case that one starts with a qualitative analysis, does some quantitative work based on ideas which have come out of the initial analysis, and then finally sees how the findings of the quantitative analysis relate to further qualitative studies. Qualitative research can add totally new dimensions to an issue or question under study. Indeed, depending upon the objective of the research, qualitative methods may be the most appropriate technique or even the only possible technique. Qualitative research produces for us evidence as to the world of symbolism and meaning for individuals and groups – a way of understanding what has been called the 'buzzing blooming confusion' of experience. But by its nature it can be far more difficult and more demanding of the researcher than quantitative research. For example, the personal involvement and interpretation increases the possibility of human error and bias. The observer, or listener, may be more tempted, quite unconsciously, to 'see' data fitting what he or she hoped it would fit. The same observable data – someone's behaviour, sentence structure – may never be repeated again, let alone in front of another observer, and its veracity can thus be readily questioned. Also, it is extremely easy to fall into the trap of ending up with a mass of anecdotal data which may not relate to any existing theory of social interaction nor offer any new hypotheses. However, the advent of some extremely good computer software programs for qualitative analysis has certainly contributed to 'making sense' of the complexity of what could amount to literally millions of words!

Unlike the mathematically and logically 'tight' tools of quantitative analysis, there are no formal, fixed rules governing qualitative research and analysis. Each method carries its own advantages and constraints. We have already identified where it is appropriate to use questionnaires as tools of inquiry. Now we can lay down some principles and guidelines with reference to other techniques.

The case study

The case study is a separate research strategy which may or may not involve observation (see Chapter 13 below). However there are many case studies in which the people involved never come face to face with the researcher – indeed, they may even be dead! – and the study is undertaken through the medium of the written word, or other forms of recording information. You may wish to look at official documents – for example, an assessment of the parliamentary debates which took place on the process of the passing of legislation to introduce (in 1999) a national minimum wage. Or it may be the media coverage and associated organizational documentation relevant to some past industrial dispute, or to a controversial advertising campaign as has occurred in the past with the Benetton chain. Thus the approach requires its own particular research design, which, as always, will be dependent upon the questions you want answered. An initial problem may be that it is often difficult to know where to begin and where to end the case being analysed. This is partly because the 'case' in hand may entail examination of a complex behavioural phenomenon – for example, a case study of how the local council authority deals with a spectacular national event like the opening of the Millennium Dome. It may be an 'event' or it may be a 'process' – the decision-making process as it took place with reference to a contentious new marketing policy, or the implementation of a new training programme in a retail chain. However as a general guide, once you have defined the issue, or problem, or area of interest, the parameters of the unit of analysis – the case study – should be quite clear. A good example of the generalizations which can be drawn from a case study is demonstrated in a study of the 1982 World Fair in Knoxville, Tennessee (Richter 1994: 223). This revealed the severe political problems which arose because of the speed at which the tourist infrastructure was developed, and which led the host community to be caught up in an inflationary spiral and housing squeeze which resulted from this development.

Single case and multiple case study design

The decision as to which of these to go for depends upon (a) the reason for the choice of subject and (b) how much 'external validity' is felt to be necessary, meaning how much you might wish to generalize from a particular case study. Obviously evidence and theories drawn from a multi-case study may be far more powerful, but the objective of the exercise may not be to make generalizations, but purely to investigate a 'one-off' situation. The single case study can be one way of testing an already well-formulated theory, investigating an extreme or unique case, or observing a phenomenon which has previously not been accessible for study or has not even existed. On the other hand, the multiple case study, whereby a number of individual situations are investigated, may prove very fruitful because of the ability to compare and contrast findings.

Another form of 'case study' research is that in which the case or 'scenario' is not a situation which exists, but one which might exist, given certain known facts and trends. A good example of this is one which probed how social, managerial and technological changes might affect the shape of leisure and recreation management up to the year 2000, starting from the base line of 1974 (Moeller and Shafer 1994: 477–479). A panel of experts, 900 in all, in the biological, social and environmental sciences, and in recreation management, offered, individually, a list of 'events', related to their own expertise, which they predicted would have a 50:50 chance of occurring by the year 2000. Their responses were summarized and re-submitted through four rounds of questionnaires, with each member of the panel having a chance to re-evaluate their initial predictions (this is otherwise known as the 'Delphi' technique). The final results showed events falling into five categories – for instance, natural resource management and work and leisure patterns – which the experts predicted would have a major impact on recreation management 25 years on.

One cannot generalize from a case study in the same way that one can from statistical analysis. It is obviously not possible to make inferences about all 'cases' on the basis of empirical data collected from a sample of one. However, one can 'test' theories already in existence though a comparison of the results of the study, and the results of that comparison can strengthen the validity of theories, help identify other cases to which the results are generalizable, suggest refinements of theories – or falsify them completely.

Critical incident technique

This technique does share similarities with the case study approach, but by definition it concentrates on observing and analysing human behaviour within very limited parameters. The activity observed must have a clearly defined beginning and end, and be sufficiently complete in itself to allow for the possibility of valid and reliable inferences or predictions to be drawn from it, to allow for useful generalizations to be made about the individual or individuals involved in the act or incident. For the incident to be 'critical', the observer must be able to identify what was intended to happen, and what the effect in fact was. A good example might be if you were to ask a number of marketing managers working for a motor manufacturer with an international presence what their views were of the overall marketing policy of the company. After establishing a context, the managers might be asked how the company responded to a particular marketing problem – for example, how it entered a new market, or marketed a new model of car. This particular 'critical incident' or situation would then encourage responses which give you some basis for hypothesizing about decision-making and problem-solving within the organization at several levels, about the communications system, about whether and how power was used or delegated, and so on. Using this technique does mean that you should have access to other data which helps substantiate the interview. You will be well aware of the problems of recall in both practical and psychological terms. Our memories do fade, and we have a tendency to remember that which reflects to our credit in our behaviour – which is why using autobiographies as a secondary source can be very suspect.

Diary methods

Diary methods have been widely used in research into diet and nutrition, managerial activity and industrial placement. The diary is a record of either an individual or a group's actions over a period of time, which could be over a day, a month, a year, or even longer. It can be purely quantitative material – the amount of time taken each day on a particular task – or it can be a powerful source of qualitative data on feelings, motives, perceptions, identified as significant by the writer(s) at a particular time or times. Thus the diary technique can be very valuable to the researcher or observer if he or she might not or cannot be present at crucial times, or might not necessarily perceive the same significance the writer does. Generally, diaries have a starting date and a completion date, as far as the researcher is concerned, and take the form of the written word, although it could be spoken in that it could be recorded on a tape as opposed to in a notebook.

The diary can be used in association with other methods of data collection, and it can also be a useful adjunct to the research process, or it can purely be a record for you of the meaning, pattern and progress of the process itself, or it may be that you wish to record a sudden idea, or insight, before it goes the way of all flesh. All of this can be extremely useful when it comes to formally writing up your core data. However, there are some snags about using the diary technique and you have to be fully aware of these before you embark upon it. Key points to observe are as follows.

- You have to make sure, in a diplomatic way, that those who you ask to contribute to your research in this way are reasonably literate! Otherwise you may find difficulty processing the data you collect.
- Although the use of the diary as described above suggests that it is a 'stream of consciousness' process rather than a structured record, it is necessary that you give some guidance to the diarist as to what to record. This will come from the objectives of your research, the hypotheses you are testing, and the data you require to support a theory. For example, if you are studying authority relationships in a bank, then it is important that your respondents know whether to record their feelings about these relationships between staff alone, or between staff and customers . Rosemary Stewart's (1988) seminal study of what managers do, which made use of the diary technique, obviously depended upon some initial parameters defining what tasks were considered to be about 'managing'.
- You have to ensure that the diarists complete the task you set them by encouraging them in any way appropriate. If you have asked someone to keep a diary daily over a period of even a week, it is essential you maintain contact. For practical reasons, you need to establish that no snags have developed which might affect the quality of the record, and for purely psychological reasons you want the diarists to feel that what they are is doing is valuable so that they will continue with what could be, after the first flush of co-operation wears off, quite a time-consuming and tedious job. Experience generally suggests, however, that individuals are happy to co-operate, if only because someone has actually shown an interest in their thoughts!

You must emphasize, as in all research which is aimed at recording people's attitudes, opinions, and emotions, the complete confidentiality of the data. This is even more important in circumstances where you have asked individuals to record their immediate reactions and feelings.

Projective techniques

If projective techniques have any use at all, and there are some genuine doubts as to the scientific basis for their validity, they are of most use in trying to predict future behaviour rather than explain past behaviour. They are also very specialized in their interpretation and application, and are thus much less likely to be used in the type of research project or dissertation in which you will be involved. However, an awareness of their existence and what they claim to do can suggest further insights into people's attitudes and feelings. Thus they could be, if not an actual research tool in themselves, another way of extracting data, without necessarily being applied formally. You may be familiar with these techniques through the work of David McClelland (1961) on motivation theories, where he used projective techniques to measure an individual's need for achievement. The technique involves, for instance, getting respondents to write stories, explain what photographs mean to them, project what they would do in certain circumstances. A good example of this is that given by Easterby-Smith *et al.* (1991: 91). In a test to select public house managers for a large brewery chain, a question might be posed such as 'Suppose someone came into your pub whom you know well as a good and valued customer. He says "lend me £20 because I've got a certainty for a horse running in the 3.30." What would you do?' The answer desired by the interviewer is one which shows that the interviewee has the wit to decline, but in a manner that does not offend the customer. Another situation on which you might want to use this technique could be to offer a range of menus to respondents, and ask them to articulate a view as to the sort of occasion on which they would offer such a menu. The responses would, indirectly, help you assess the symbolic meanings attached to certain foods and recipes by individuals. Thus at least thinking about projective techniques can help you frame questions, whatever the general interviewing technique you use.

Content analysis

Content analysis is a technique which is favoured by those researchers who are somewhat unhappy about a completely holistic approach to theorizing and explanation, and thus like to see some 'hard facts' come out of their evidence. However, it is also a very useful technique in its own right, and one with which you will be probably be familiar through its use in identifying the authorship of literary works – or anonymous letters in criminal investigation! It involves identifying and counting certain key words or phrases in a piece of writing or in the recording of an interview, conversation, or surveys which include unstructured responses. It also may involve counting the number of centimetres, or the amount of time devoted to certain news items in the media – readers' letters on a particular topic, 'soaps' or police series on TV. These selected words, phrases or items, by their type or frequency, then allow the researcher to hypothesize some deeper meaning behind them, in addition to providing clear quantitative data. The simplicity of the idea that a certain author uses certain words and phrases linked in a particular grammatical or semantic style unique to him or her and that can be used to identify his or her work, is both useful and not in the least new. Some of you will no doubt remember it as a task you undertook in English Literature at school when you analysed Shakespeare or Wordsworth. However, for social scientific and management research it is a tool which helps us towards a different type of understanding. We might, for instance, extract from a large amount of unstructured interviews and discussions on the qualities people expect of a 'good' car, the fact that the words 'comfortable', 'fast' and 'roomy' keep cropping up. Thus the frequency of certain ideas or views allow us to deduce their importance to the interviewees without our 'putting words in their mouths' through getting information from a structured questionnaire in which we have determined what are to be the key concepts.

It goes without saying that, although concerned with literary focus, content analysis can be extrapolated to the examination of images as well as words so, for example, the particular images used to promote a sense of the quality of a new motor car in a manufacturer's or retailer's brochures can be revealing in the 'messages' they seek to communicate. Content analysis therefore can throw up interesting new hypotheses, because a completely new view, idea or concept may be revealed as important, or because on reflection a much deeper meaning may come through, be possible of being interpreted, than was initially thought by the researcher. The recognition of this possibility is reflected in the highly sophisticated form of content analysis called 'semiotics', which aims to get at the underlying message of a text or some other medium of communication. The application of semiotics might be seen in looking at the visual and verbal language used in various forms of advertising. If, however, you are attracted by this technique and think it might be applicable to your chosen research topic then Weber's (1990) *Basis Content Analysis* is a useful book. The computer programs which deal with qualitative analysis, by virtue of the way they process data, also give insights into how to use this technique.

Of course, content analysis has its disadvantages. For example, it assumes that if an idea, view or action is not mentioned, then it does not exist. It can also be exceedingly time-consuming, perhaps with little reward, as it may only throw up a few consistencies, or even none. And ultimately, if you are interested in interpretation and meaning, this is still basically a quantitative technique, with the inherent technical issues surrounding sampling. It will not tell you why certain views and ideas occur, or whether different words and phrases might still have the same meaning for different individuals or whether the same words and phrases might have different meanings for different individuals. Certainly, some researchers may be much happier with numbers because they seem more tangible and accurate, and may be more politically acceptable, as in content analysis researchers go by numbers and frequencies, rather than by feel and intuition. But content analysis can often be a good starting point for creating hypotheses and a good finishing point for testing them, and it may be that your intuition as to the meaning and interpretation of frequencies offers a breakthrough in explanation.

Grounded theory

Grounded theory is a term used to describe any type of social theory that is built up from naturalistic observation (observation in this context can encompass more 'interventionist' research instruments, for example certain types of interview). This method is the more commonly used, and more likely to be used, in management research, where extended interviews of the sort described above as a method of research are relatively common. Easterby-Smith *et al.* (1991: 108–111) provide a useful breakdown of the seven main stages in such analysis, commenting that the approach benefits from the fact that the data collected generates theories, rather than being the consequence of theories. This method 'works' because these theories come from the language and ideas produced by those being studied and thus could be said to be more 'real' and revealing. These seven stages are, briefly paraphrased, as follows.

(1) Familiarization – read and re-read your data, looking for first thoughts, new thoughts, associations, contradictions, interesting, strange connections, corre-lations – anything which will help you begin to formulate your ideas and further questions which might need answering.

(2) Reflection – establishing relationships, if any, between your data and previous research or academic studies – or even 'common sense' knowledge and understanding. At this stage, you may feel that you have only intuitive feelings or explanations, but don't assume they are not valuable. Great leaps in science have often come from 'intuition', a word which does come from the Latin word 'to contemplate.' Even sheer guesswork can sometimes bring results!

(3) Conceptualization – this is when you need to think about the concepts or variables which seem to be important for understanding what is happening. Concepts or variables help you classify or order your information as well as suggest where explanations might come from (for example, the variables referred to earlier when we referred to the concept of 'atmosphere' – which itself was a variable – as it was understood by those who visited the Birmingham International Convention Centre). Two variables used were 'friendliness of staff' and 'lighting levels'. If these variables come up consistently in data, then it suggests that they are very important factors in explaining what is meant by the 'atmosphere' of a place, and thus theorizing about what might contribute to atmosphere in other locations or in other eyes or minds.

(4) Cataloguing concepts – which means exactly what it says. Whatever form of cataloguing you use, this is a useful piece of self-discipline if you are new to such research techniques, even if it is not, in some researchers' minds, an essential step in the process. Not only does it provide a quick reference, a glossary, it also helps you establish whether the language recorded in your data can be matched with the language you might wish to use as an academic.

(5) Recoding – the process of refining and redefining, during which further interpretation and analysis takes place. As previously mentioned, new categories and sub-categories may be required as you 'contemplate' your data. Some may require to be further sub-divided, others can be combined or abandoned. For example, the concept of the 'image' of a shopping mall may mean quite different things to different respondents.

(6) Linking – at this stage you are seeing the light at the end of the tunnel, Patterns are beginning to emerge, certain concepts are showing an affinity with each other, you can begin to draw out useful generalizations which may be seen to relate to other theories and models and which suggest academic literature you

know, or further literature searches upon which you might embark. By this stage also you should be able to produce a first draft for your supervisor – or even a fellow student or friend – to comment on. Given the essentially subjective nature of this type of research, it does help to have comments as early as possible on your findings, however tentative.

(7) Re-evaluation – which naturally arises out of the last point. As has been pointed out, this should be both an ongoing exercise, as well as one which arises from the observations of others. It could result in a change of emphasis, in a re-allocation or relabelling of concepts, a new idea or approach which arises as a consequence of reflection. This process would apply of course to the writing up of any research project, but at the end of the day, the quality of your findings depends on how you personally and uniquely perceive and interpret data. The meaning, or inferences, you draw from a conversation is quite (qualitatively) different from the meaning, or inferences, you might draw from a set of statistics.

General principles of secondary data analysis

We have thus far concentrated principally on primary qualitative data – that collected directly by the researcher. Secondary data is that which has been collected, collated and analysed by others as opposed to that which you have collected yourself. Hakim (1982: 34) defines secondary data analysis as 'any further analysis of an existing data set which presents interpretations, conclusions, or knowledge additional to, or different from, those presented in the first report on the inquiry as a whole and its main results'. The data can come from academic or non-academic sources, and may be quantitative or qualitative in nature. Many standard textbooks on research (e.g. Gilbert 1993) limit their discussion to quantitative, secondary, statistical data. Secondary data can, however take other forms and could encompass qualitative data: articles in academic journals and the popular press, other branches of the mass media, literature, formal and informal documents government publications, speeches, letters, and so on. It is easy to see why, given all possible sources, there is often a 'grey' area between what is considered to be primary and what is considered to be secondary data or source material, unless one sticks to a narrow definition of 'data' as always statistical in format. However, for the researcher the possible sources for useful material to support a piece of research are only limited by his or her imagination and the ability to get at the material. Generally secondary data has come about as the result of research by others, but it does not always need to be 'research' undertaken for formal academic purposes. A good example of an exception is literature, fact or fiction, which has been written purely as literature, yet which offers hard information on some aspect of, say, the history of certain types of occupation, or the use of certain products and services.

In certain aspects of your research, it may only be secondary data to which you have access, because the data you require, for financial, logistical or time reasons, is impossible for you to collect yourself. Or it may be that data collected for quite a different purpose to that to which you yourself are directed could be very useful if it is looked at with new eyes, analysed and evaluated using different tools and techniques, towards different ends. As far as statistical data is concerned, it may be that a formal or public organization, for instance, the government's Central Statistical Office, or the Economic and Social Research Council, will have data collated over a period of years on very large sample sizes which allows you then to select data on particular sub-groups, or allows you to support your research with data collected over a period of time previous to your study.

The most useful hard statistical data is usually 'official' or 'unofficial', although this does not suggest a hierarchy of credibility. 'Official' statistics are produced by government departments to help with the day-to-day running of the country (for example, *Social Trends*, produced annually, which identifies factors like how the British occupy their leisure time, or the most-visited tourist attractions in the country) and 'unofficial' statistics come from, for example, marketing organizations, public opinion pollsters, pressure groups, university departments and research units.

Therefore, depending upon a number of factors which we will discuss below, the data you are interpreting and applying may be of a far superior quality and detail than any that you are able to gather yourself, whilst that being no reflection on your talents and abilities. It may be that you are just not (yet) a sufficiently sophisticated and experienced researcher to undertake certain studies which you feel could be of value to your own, so there is no opprobrium attached to picking someone else's brains, as you will certainly get the credit for recognizing that the data you have worked on is of relevance and value. Remember the importance attached to your literature search in your dissertation, where you not only articulated the extent of your reading of relevant academic studies, but also the extent of your ability to evaluate the contribution of these studies to your own research.

There are two key questions to be answered if you intend using secondary data. First, how do you establish its quality, and second, how do you make it 'work' for you? Taking the first question, the following is a useful checklist (derived from Procter *et al.* 1988, and Stewart 1985) which can be applied to all types of data, qualitative and quantitative, from whatever source you might consider to be useful.

• To whom is it attributed? Who collected it, wrote it, collaborated in its compilation?
• What are their 'credentials' for being taken seriously? These may not necessarily be credentials of the academic or 'official' type, but some other qualification or quality which would lead you to value what is being said or written, to consider it as appropriate source material. For example, motoring writers for the press reporting on the test drive of a new model might be viewed with suspicion because they often receive benefits from the manufacturers and thus might not be quite so objective in their assessments.
• What was the objective, or objectives of the exercise being undertaken? A study by an employer representative organization such as the CBI or Institute of Directors purporting to show that the National Minimum Wage has 'cost' 250,000 jobs in a

year is, of course, of great industrial relations and public policy import. But a covert objective of such a report could be to undermine trade union or government attempts to increase the minimum wage. In such cases, extra attention must be paid to the credentials and vested interests of the group or organizations producing the report.

- For whom was it produced, if any one or one group in particular, and did that group have any vested interest in either the research being undertaken or the outcome?
- Can what you are interested in justifiably be classed as suitable 'research' findings even though the author(s) may not have set out to present the material in that formal academic light, or in such a manner that it could be easily identified as 'research'. This is a particularly acute problem with 'quality' journalism. The use of journalistic sources can be valuable in research but also must be treated with caution.
- How was the information collected and how easy is it to identify criteria for establishing the reliability and validity of any conclusions or findings? Is it of the 'Cabinet leak', 'spokesperson near to the Princess' type of information, or are there hard facts, references to specific named sources, attributed quotes, statistical data collected through correctly designed samples, surveys and questionnaires?

The other key question you have to answer when manipulating secondary data is how do you make it 'work' for you. How can you make use of information which has been collected and collated by someone for quite different purposes, based on quite different theoretical considerations, or analysed and presented with results which bear little relation to that which you are studying? You have made the creative or imaginative mental leap in recognizing the possibilities, but what paths, or lines of thought, will enable you to process what you have in front of you? If the data is the result of statistical analysis, then one of the well-known statistical computer packages, for example, SPSS (Statistical Package for the Social Sciences), can be enormously helpful, and, additionally, qualitative data analysis programs like NUD.IST offer the same facility for reorganizing and re-evaluating concepts and variables. But computers only regurgitate what is fed into them and there are some initial steps to be gone through.

- Does the original material use concepts and variables which have some affinity with your research? It is easier to identify that affinity if the words and ideas are quantitative in some way, measurable, observable; less easy when they are about perceptions, emotions, attitudes, values. There may well be a legal definition of a building society but many former building societies, now effectively banks, manage to convey the view that they are the same as building societies which have not become banks. It could be argued that secondary data analysis is virtually impossible with observational data.
- Is the hypothesis the research is based upon at least in some way one which bears relation to your hypothesis(es)? This may not be immediately obvious in the case of sources which are not overtly, or do not claim to be, academic, but any piece of

investigation starts from some understanding as to what is to be investigated and why.

• When was the information collected? Is what you want to draw out of it appropriate to the timescale or period within which you are working? An academic article studying employment patterns in banking at the turn of the century could be of limited use if you are undertaking a similar exercise today, not simply because of changes in banking since that time, but because of the quite different cultural and social factors and expectations of banking at that time.

Finally, can you be sure that, as in all social research, there are no ethical issues raised by your using data which has been collected by someone else, who presumably, if there are ethical issues like that of invasion of privacy, will have obtained the consent of those involved? This is particularly important in the area of explanatory research which often purports to investigate feelings and emotions, rather than in descriptive or 'number-crunching' research which collects the factual characteristics of individuals or groups. Those researchers whose work you are using expect you, even if they do not know you, to respect the same guarantees of confidentiality and anonymity they have given.

Recording qualitative data

We now turn to some elementary issues on the management of qualitative data, with a particular emphasis on primary data. Although you may not be able to record your observations and impressions immediately, you must have planned out a systematic approach to the recording of information (see Chapter 7). Your 'field' notes must be structured, updated as often as possible, and as detailed as your hearing, sight and memory allows. Additionally, as soon as possible after the event, try to assess the significance of what you have recorded and how it relates to the concepts, theories and hypotheses you feel are relevant to your study. It is essential to undertake this exercise with urgency after collecting chunks of data because you have to avoid the trap of reporting 'everything' and thus creating a horrendous burden for yourself when you come to analyse your data. Even although there are now computer packages which do this, at least feed in the data as quickly as possible. As Woolcott (1990: 152) pithily states 'the critical task in qualitative research is not to accumulate all the data you can, but to "can" most of the data you accumulate.'

Organizing data

It is of crucial importance that you organize your data as efficiently as possible. Initially remember that you must have some formal data base not only for your own purposes but also so that, if required, it could be available to other researchers, one of the tests of 'scientific' research being that the research methods and findings should be accessible to anyone who is interested. As Yin (1984: 309) notes, you must, just as in a court case, 'maintain a chain of evidence'.

Qualitative research has been described as 'intellectual craftsmanship' as there is no one standard way to go about analysing your data. Imagination and creativity (within limits, of course!) will determine how you frame the original questions you wanted answered, how you identify categories, where you assign data, what patterns you identify, and imagination and creativity is in action when you try to relate your findings to concepts and theories already in use. Do not be afraid to articulate a new theory which seems to be suggested by your analysis after all others seem to be exhausted – that's why genius is defined as '99 per cent perspiration and 1 per cent inspiration!' Remember too that in organizing and assessing qualitative data you may find yourself requiring to use quantitative data to verify or cast a new light on qualitative findings. For example, your initial exploration through observational methods may be supplemented by a questionnaire which draws out a generality about specific findings, or prevents you from jumping to general conclusions too easily or quickly.

The handling of data, whether it be from observation, conversational or textual analysis, requires self-discipline, an organized mind and perseverance. To emphasize, good qualitative research must get beyond the merely anecdotal; the data you collect ought at some stage to be able to be fitted into, and have some significance for some theory or model. You must be constantly on the lookout for new insights into the data, and assessing where a particular action or setting being observed can offer a complex statement of necessary and sufficient conditions which suggest that, given these, a similar situation might be observed or repeated elsewhere. The analysis should end only when you begin to see the data fit into some more general and conceptual framework, and you have 'squeezed it dry'. That is, you can no longer generate or extract new insights from it (this is where an up-to-date computer program on qualitative analysis can help; it won't 'tire' of looking for new connections and correlations, even if it cannot make the truly creative leaps in thinking the human mind is capable of).

You do not, indeed must not, wait until you have collected all your data before starting to analyse it. By its very nature, observational research is at its most effective when the process of collection and the process of analysis run parallel and 'feed' on each other. This means that you have to write up or somehow record your field notes as soon as possible, recognizing that you may find yourself writing up for as much time as you were observing! As you evaluate each new set of notes, you will be involved in a continual process of reflection. New avenues may open up, interesting or surprising findings may be apparent, as may inconsistencies or contradictions.

At the outset you must have broad descriptive codes which relate, say, to particular people or types of people, activities, topics of interest or concern. These broad codes are then examined in terms of what are the smallest pieces or segments of information about something which can stand up by themselves, and then finally each segment becomes a category. The purpose is to aggregate all data about the same topic or theme so that each category can be studied individually. It may be useful to assign data to more than one category in order to maximize the range of relationships which can be generated. Imagine that you are investigating the factors that have an impact on where someone would choose to open a bank account. Of course, you would have been using statistical or quantitative techniques to identify your initial sample, but then you want to use unstructured interviews to collect your data, because what you are really interested in is the 'image' of a certain type of bank for someone. To do this you have to listen to respondents' perceptions, beliefs, values, attitudes, declared motives, and to search for the 'meaning' behind statements, for key words and phrases which suggest rather than clearly articulate. Then you build up your raw data under a 'family tree' of headings or concepts which initially might look like the following:

social – political – economic – environmental

Under 'social' you sub-divide into sociological and psychological. Then you might further divide sociological into class – gender – occupation – status, then class into socio-economic grouping 1, 2, 3, etc., and status into married, single, widowed, divorced. And so on, constantly looking for how these general categories may be further split if necessary as your data-collection continues. For example, some way through your collecting of data, you feel that age is a factor in the equation, so you re-assess your 'tree' and make age a new sub-category because you want that to sub-divide into 18–25, 26–44, 45–60, and 60 upwards. Then perhaps you feel education is a factor, which is not necessarily correlated with age, or even socio-economic status. Of course, this 'family tree' is both horizontal and vertical ('brothers and sisters' as well as 'mothers and children') and it may be that you decide one direction deserves more emphasis than another. There is a large element of imagination and creativity in categorizing, as the range of variables you might use are far less restricted and less 'tidy' than those which are appropriate for 'number-crunching' so it is not surprising that this type of research is felt to be more challenging – and more exhausting. But at the end of the day, after cross-referencing and analysing responses, you find that those who are aged between 21 and 35, who are single, whose socio-economic classification is groups 1 or 2 , feel that the appropriate choice of bank for them on account of the image they have of themselves is one which practises ethical investment. They have not actually said that, and perhaps would not even consciously think of themselves in that category, but your data analysis strongly suggests it. The development of the psychological 'family tree' (the concepts of perception, personality, motivation) would help us find answers to important marketing questions like product and destination-positioning, advertising and promotion. One example of such research, quoted in Plog (1994: 211) looks at the significant personality differences between golfers and tennis players (who are demographically very alike) but in fact turn out to have major differences in personality structures. That research strongly suggested that any major resort development which planned to construct an integrated clubhouse had better think again – that was most certainly not the best route to go down!

If it possible for you to have access to software for analysing qualitative data, it is actually a very good idea not just to run through the demonstration program but also to try a mock exercise just to give you the flavour of the thinking required. The important thing to is to ensure that your categories, sub-categories and groups are appropriate (a) in terms of the data you feel you need for your research and (b) in terms of that which you can intelligently and justifiably use to classify your data. And always remember that what you have collected is not something objective, 'out there', which exists independent of you. The data has been affected by your perception from the very outset through the decisions you have made as to what to observe, record and process. It is recognition of this fact that persuades some researchers that qualitative data is somehow not so 'respectable' unless it is turned somehow into numbers. To try and avoid this positivist stance, the analysis of qualitative data must be systematic and demonstrably logical in its execution and presentation.

In conclusion, if we try and summarize what it is that makes for good qualitative research, we would see that the 'core' qualities which are required – awareness of strengths and limitations of a range of methods of collecting and analysing data, awareness of different research designs, clarity of thought, flexibility and creativity – are not any different from the standards one would set for good quantitative research. At the rise of caricature, there is something in the view that quantitative methods are primarily linked towards the need for 'speedy and 'solid' results', whereas qualitative methods are more time-consuming and require different kinds of research skill. Certainly, qualitative methods come into their own particularly where small samples exist, and where the research focus is more on behavioural or people issues. It serves no useful purpose to regard quantitative and qualitative methods as inherently mutually excusive, however. The use of each (and both) in research enriches the other and a basic command of all such methods is a prerequisite for the most simply effective researcher.

■ □ ▨ ■ 11

Measuring attitudes

Of all the psychological characteristics, attitudes are possibly the most conspicuous. Attitudes reveal themselves because they have a quality of being positive or negative. This quality can be observed. It is also a quality that attitudes share with another aspect of human behaviour – the opinion. Consequently one leads to judgement of the other and more often than not the two concepts become coterminus. True, people's opinions on matters often betray their attitudes but that does not mean that attitudes and opinions are the same thing. They are two distinguishable concepts. Mistaking the two often leads to confusion in survey work and research when it is not clear whether attitudes or opinions are being measured. Although close cousins they are different and must be measured differently. Whilst this problem is sometimes awkward it is reasonably easy to solve. The real problem for attitudes is their relationship to behaviour.

It would not be unreasonable to suppose that, as attitudes have a positive/negative quality, then such a quality might be translated into some form of behaviour. In other words, there should be some consistency between people's verbal expressions of their attitudes towards an object and their behaviour towards it. Although such a connection is notoriously complicated it is an assumption of the advertising industry that such a relationship exists.

Importance of attitudes in business and management

Whether they are aware of it or not decision-makers in business are always making assumptions about how people will behave. The people in question could be customers, employees, suppliers, fellow managers or superiors. Whoever they are and whatever the subject of the decision, that decision will assume some desired or anticipated behaviour as an outcome. Introduce a new product, alter a control system, contemplate an incentive – almost all strategic, tactical and contingency decisions have behaviour outcomes. The analytical perspective asks 'what caused this behaviour?' and 'what are its consequences?' This is the realm of psychology but it is also the concern of decision-makers who at one level can 'best guess' from experience but could improve on that guess with some measurement. In this respect the concept of the attitude is most helpful. For whenever attitudes exist they are conspicuous to measurement by their positive or negative characteristic. It is this quality that, in the business context, makes attitudes useful in themselves, notwithstanding the indications they give out of possible behaviour.

What is an attitude?

Of the many definitions of attitudes, perhaps one of the most famous is that an attitude constitutes 'A mental state of readiness, organized through experience, exerting a directive or dynamic influence upon individual's response to all objects and situations which it is related' (Allport 1935). The key words here are 'organized', 'experience' and 'influence'. Attitudes are formed by experience and organized in a coherent way within the self. They are also involved in action. Exactly how they get involved in action is complicated but the connection is nevertheless there. The idea of attitudes as states of readiness is shown by another definition (Riley 1996: 75):

> A predisposed response to situations, objects, people, other self defined
> areas of life. It has both a *perceptual* and an *affective* component. The latter
> produces a direction in the attitude – positive or negative. This, in turn,
> can influence the perceptual element – we see what we want to see!

Unlike the first definition this one draws out the elements of feeling and evaluation attached to attitudes and invests them with the power to influence how we see things; the 'love is blind syndrome' (for further perspectives on the nature of attitude measurement, see Hogg and Vaughan 1995, and Oppenheim 1982).

Neither of these definitions gets across those characteristics of an attitude that distinguishes it from other aspects of human psychology, particularly opinions. The key characteristics of an attitude are, first, *focus and fixity*. In other words, attitudes tend to be focused on an object, a person, groups, specific behaviour, particular ideas. They also tend to be fairly fixed over time. This is not to say that they are permanent or that they cannot be changed – they can. However, evidence suggests that they are fairly stable in the short and medium run. Second, attitudes are closely *related to feelings* whereas opinions may or may not carry connotations of feeling. Third, attitudes 'live' in groups. What this means is that some aspects of being human are organized in a coherent way within the self. To carry positive and negative components which may be contradictory, for example, to be liberal and conservative about some issue, is inconsistent and will cause dissonance. The more likely pattern, within the self, would be that someone with say, a positive attitude towards personal fitness, would also be positive about healthy eating, clean environment, no smoking and so on. In other words, there are rope bridges between specific attitudes which join them together in a coherent way. The sense of wholeness and identity depends on our inner coherence.

If anything is 'fixed' in life we tend to assume it is anchored to something. This is true of attitudes. The fixity we associate with attitudes comes from anchors and reinforcers. Obviously a person does not go around thinking of a particular object. No object is in constant focus, therefore if the attitude is anchored, the anchor must be broader, deeper and wider than a fleeting focus on an object. We can therefore ask, 'To what is an attitude anchored?'. There are four main responses to this question:

- to values – what is desirable and meaningful across a range of life situations and over time;
- to culture – shared values, shared norms, shared understanding of symbols;
- to habitual behaviour; and
- to approved behaviour.

If values, culture and behaviour anchor and reinforce attitudes, the question that arises is, 'Where is an attitude anchored?'. Tied to a tree like a horse? In a way, yes. The clue comes from the second definition quoted earlier. The perceptual element of attitudes suggests that the attitude is anchored in perceptual categories. If, for one moment, the mind can be envisaged as a set of lock-up garages with some we have forgotten we own, some whose contents we cannot remember and some we find useful, it is likely then we put stuff we like in some lock-ups and stuff we do not like in others.

In other words, our perceptual categories have already been evaluated – things we like/things we do not like. It is this quality of positive-negative within our 'way of seeing' that transfers itself to the attitude and is itself reaffirmed by the positive-negative character of the attitude – 'mutual reinforcement-hard to change'. The message from the attitude–perception relationship is that to change an attitude you have to change the way the object is seen which is the same thing as saying change the way the object is categorized, move it to another lock-up. What, then, is the character of attitudes? Four aspects are important, namely:

- they are related to an object, a person, an idea, a piece of behaviour within the individual's environment;
- they influence perception by influencing the way the individual collects information. In turn this relationship becomes reciprocal. They influence the formation of goals;
- they are learnt and enduring; and
- they imply both evaluation and feeling.

The interior components of an attitude

There are three components within an attitude. These are as follows:

(1) Cognitive: this component is concerned with the object in terms of attention to it, awareness of it, learning about it, understanding it, placing it in relation to other things. The words we associate with this component are concerned with understanding the object's origins, location and consequences. For example:

will lead to	causes
goes with	yields
comes from	produces
results in	costs
prevents	

The flavour is 'the way we see it'.

(2) Behavioural: this component is concerned with the action implicit in the perception of the object and sees the object in terms of behaviour, intention and action. The words we associate with this component are verbs, for example: buy, sell, hit, vote for, kill, rent to, endorse, hire, fire, choose, reject. The flavour is one of action.

(3) Affective: this component is concerned with the object in terms of interest in, evaluation of, feelings towards, belief in and so on. The words we associate with this component are, for example: like, dislike, love, hate, want, fear, happy, sad, angry, bored. The flavour is, like it/do not like it.

Clearly, the relationship between these components is not one of constant equal influence. The relative dominance of each will change according to circumstances, most notably:

- how much the person already knows about the object;
- whether or not the person can clearly identify the object; and
- how much interest the person has in the object.

Forming and maintaining attitudes

Attitudes are learnt – babies don't have attitudes! They are learnt by absorbing the culture of which we are a part, through experiences and through our own behaviour. Although they are personal they are not determined entirely by the individual. Not only are attitudes learnt they are also conditioned by the acceptance or rejection of other people the individual regards as important. This may be society itself, a group or simply 'people we like'. This conditioning of attitudes is known as the influence of 'social norm'.

Because they are personal, attitudes perform certain functions for the individual such as:

- direct people, moving from the undesirable to the desirable;
- help to define who we are; and
- give direction to experience: we have learnt something and our attitudes tell us what to do when the experience is repeated.

Attitudes have two distinct relationships with behaviour. It would be wonderful if we could predict behaviour from attitudes but alas this is not really possible. However, if the notion of intention to behave is placed between attitudes and behaviour then careful measurement can produce some predictions.

The theory of reasoned action

Through its wide application in the advertising industry this theory carries considerable weight in the world of management. It is used as the basis of studying the relationship between attitudes and behaviour and offers the opportunity to predict the latter from the former. Hence its application in advertising. The theory states the relationship between belief, attitudes, intentions and behaviour. At the heart of the theory is the notion of 'intention to behave'. Whilst we do not always act upon our intentions, we often do so when they are focused on some specific piece of behaviour rather than generalized goals or broadly defined areas of behaviour. Note the differences between 'I'd like to be fitter' (generalized goal), 'I should play more sport' (broad category of behaviour) and 'I'm going to play squash' (focused behaviour). The latter is more predictable as a form of behaviour than the others.

The application of this theory is based on measuring two aspects of the attitudes. These are:

- the attitude towards the intention to the behaviour; and
- the attitude towards the social norm associated with the behaviour.

By 'social norm' is meant the approval of other people, which may be society as a whole or specific others, on whether the behaviour should or should not be activated. In other words, a person's intention to do something is founded on whether they are positive or negative towards the behaviour and whether or not that behaviour is approved of by people who the person likes or feels they ought to refer to. This reference to the approval or otherwise of other people has an expectancy-value dimension. This expectancy-value consists of two dimensions, namely (a) a belief that they will or will not approve the behaviour; and (b) an evaluation as to how far the person cares about the approval of others. A degree of predictability can be obtained from measuring attitudes and social norm expectancy – values in relation to the intention to take an action.

A more intimate bond between attitudes and behaviour can be expressed in the conundrum – do I behave a certain way because of my attitudes or is my attitude an after-the-fact justification for my behaviour? Both are true. If we habitually perform certain behaviour then we take on the appropriate attitude. On the other hand, if we hold an attitude rooted in some personal value and are confronted with the need to respond to some stimulus then we are likely to follow our attitude and behave accordingly.

Attitudes live in groups

The psychological conditions of attitudes are that, within us, guiding concepts are organized and are consistent with each other. The need to be consistent within ourselves is the organizing principle. It is this need for consistency that is so helpful because the discovery of one attitude may lead to the discovery of others.

In fact, this relationship between attitudes is one of ever greater parameters so that each attitude is subsumed within a larger one. In other words, each attitude group belongs to a larger attitude group or construct thus forming a hierarchical basis for 'internal organization'. For example the attitude 'I hate sport' may be associated with physical laziness, a preference for artistic pursuits, and be subsumed within some larger constraints such as 'a dislike of competition', or 'strong individualism' or 'a dislike of being in teams'. There are many ways in which one attitude can be interpreted and it is the task of attitude measurement to find the attitude under investigation through the manipulation of assumed known associates and assumed larger constructs.

Attitude measurement

Some fundamental concepts and problems

Before the technical detail is outlined, it would be appropriate to discuss some of the fundamental problems that are inherent to scaling in general and attitude measurement in particular. An appreciation of these problems will aid understanding of the techniques.

Attitudes are measured by scales because they are relative concepts. They are also subjective. If these two characteristics are taken together the clear implication is that there are no absolute values in this domain. This lack of a universal standard or norm is problematic but solutions adopt one of two approaches. On the one hand the absence of a standard can be overcome by setting up an artificial absolute standard by creating a template then seeing how far people agree with this template or on the other hand, the researcher can take advantage of the 'groupness' of attitudes and trawl for a set of dimensions which indicate the attitude.

Despite these inherent problems with attitudes, the process of scaling has its fundamental complications. To illustrate the problems of scales let us assume an arbitrary seven-point scale without saying what it is supposed to be measuring. For the purposes of illustration we have two people as subjects A and B. How do we know that when A marks 2 on one statement and 2 on another statement he or she is using the scale in the same way? In other words is the relative weight of 2 the same in each application? How do we know that when A ticks 2 on one statement and 4 on the next he or she implies the same difference as when they tick 5 and 7? This is an oblique way of asking whether the assumption of the scale is one of equal intervals.

These two problems are not mutually exclusive; subjectivity and relativity come as a pair in scaling methods. These inherent problems of intra-subject judgement are extended to inter-subject judgements. How do we know that when person A ticks 2 on the first statement and person B ticks 2 on the same statement, that they mean the same thing or similarly, when A ticks 3 and 6 on two statements and B ticks 1 and 3 on the same statements that the same difference is implied? The truth is that if we could be so sure of people's judgements as to be able to guarantee the answers to these questions we would not need scales at all! In one sense, we use scales because judgements are subjective and relative and because the objects of judgement are themselves subjectively perceived, defined, and categorized. In the case of psychological phenomena such as attitudes, perceptions of the objects are unseen and can only be inferred.

The problems outlined above are handled in two ways. The assumption of equal intervals would solve many of our basic problems. Yet this cannot be assumed. If, however, the scale has been constructed so that from pilot studies the distance between points on the scale represents the mean judgements of the pilot sample and that the sample itself displays normal distribution (see Chapter 16), then the assumption of equal intervals can be made with greater confidence. The second approach is to test for inter-coherence. In this approach the problem of equal intervals is side-stepped by the assumption that if the subjects are using the scale as if the intervals were equal, then the results will contain a coherent structure which can be tested.

The general principles of scale measurement

The assumption of scaling is that there is an object to which degrees can be applied. In other words, there are relative values attached to that object. It follows from this that for the researcher the task of describing the object is one of describing it by degrees, that is, capturing the relative nature of the object. From this assertion comes the logic that a set of relative values might best be illustrated by being expressed as a range within the parameters of contrasting poles, for example agree-disagree, like-don't like, favourable-unfavourable, acceptable-unacceptable, good-bad and so on. To complicate matters further, it is unlikely that the object can be described by just one dimension therefore scaling has to be applied across a number of dimensions.

To put it in practical terms, the task of the researcher is, first, to identify the appropriate dimensions then, second, to find statements which describe those dimensions in relative terms, in other words, by degree. Once dimensions are introduced it is necessary to revisit the fundamentals again. Now a trio of concepts need to be integrated. These are, first, the alternative approaches of setting up an artificial standard or using the groupness of attitudes, second, the assumption or not of equal intervals in the scale and third, the assumption that the dimensions that are being sought are either independent of each other or dependent. Attitude measurement falls into two broad camps; one which starts from an artificial standard (created from pilot studies) which assumes equal intervals and which assumes no relationship between dimensions and one which uses the groupness of attitudes, makes no prior assumption of equal intervals, but does assume that the dimensions it is seeking are related. The implications for interpreting the scores are different in each case. In the first case, individual subject scores count as well as the sample score but in the second case, only the total scores can be interpreted.

The general procedure for designing attitude surveys

The descriptions which follow are simplified illustrations of the process. Normally each stage of the procedure is required to be done several times and the final survey questionnaire piloted several times before it is used. The intention here is merely to give an insight into the process.

The procedure for designing an attitude survey is in five parts:

- developing and refining attitude statements;
- scaling;
- administering the questionnaire;
- scoring procedures; and
- validation of the test.

The application of this procedure will be illustrated through an outline of the three main types of constructed scales.

The Likert scale

This scale assumes the groupness of attitudes so that dimensions are said to be related and therefore only total sample scores can be interpreted. To put it simply, the objective of an attitude survey is to find this positive-negative tendency towards the object. We do this by developing an equal number of positive and negative statements about the object then invite the subjects to say to what extent they agree or disagree with the statement. If we are measuring a tendency then there must be some dividing line between positive and negative. The mid-point in the scale fulfils this function. The measurement principle is to find a total score and see if the subjects are above or below the mid-point score: above means positive, and below negative.

The first task is to develop an equal number of positive and negative statements in relation to the object. First, brainstorm as many statements as you can, then, refine them into the most likely candidates. To get the imagination going it is often useful to envisage two 'ideal type' opposites. The sort of person who would be positive about the object and the sort of person who would be negative. The statements should be carefully worded so as to elicit from the respondent a real feeling towards the object. The statements should create different responses from those who are for the object and those who are against it. In other words statements should differentiate respondents. Statements should be expressions of behaviour rather than matters of fact. The problem with fact is that both those favourable and those not favourable can agree about facts. The skill is to avoid ambiguity but also avoid being obvious: 'dogs are friendly' and 'dogs smell' are far too obviously directed statements.

The approach of Likert is to recognize that attitudes are not held independently within a person but exist in a coherent whole and therefore to capture an attitude it is necessary to find a batch of attitudes and then to isolate the one which is the interest of the research. As there is an assumption that the dimensions being sought are related, the statements which represent them should correlate. In the Likert scale subjects are asked to choose between five degrees of relative agreement as follows:

- strongly agree;
- agree;
- uncertain;
- disagree; and
- strongly disagree.

Given these statements' scale values, the usual practice is to make Strongly Agree = 5, Agree = 4, Uncertain = 3, Disagree = 2, and Strongly Disagree = 1.

At this point it is worth restating that we have two modes of statement – positive and negative. If we say we *strongly agree* with a *positive* statement we are saying the same thing as *strongly disagree* with a *negative* statement. If we leave the scale as it is we would get a score of 5 for the first case and 1 for the second. As the subject would have to answer both the negative and positive statements the total scores for two subjects responding in this way would be 6 and 6. In other words, they cancel each other out. Therefore *in scoring* we reverse the values on the negative statements. As an example, suppose we were trying to find out about attitudes to dogs. Take two statements: 'positive = Dogs are friendly' and 'negative = Dogs are smelly'. If we keep the scale values the same then a person with a positive attitude to dogs might respond:

	Score
I strongly agree dogs are friendly	5
I strongly disagree that dogs are smelly	1
Total	6

A person with a negative attitude to dogs might respond:

I strongly disagree that dogs are friendly	1
I strongly agree that dogs are smelly	5
Total	6

As we can see, in both examples, respondents score the same! If we reverse the scale values of the negative statements then a person with a positive attitude to dogs might respond:

I strongly agree that dogs are friendly	5
I strongly disagree that dogs are smelly	5
Total	10

A person with a negative attitude to dogs might respond:

I strongly disagree that dogs are friendly	1
I strongly agree that dogs smell	1
Total	2

By reversing the negative values we have shown a clear difference in the scores. When the questionnaire has been completed by the appropriate sample it is then a case of scoring the whole test. If, for example the questionnaire had 10 statements the maximum score would be 50 and the minimum would be 10. The midpoint is $10 \times 3 = 30$ (3 is the mid-point of the scale). A score of, say, 35 is just above the mid-point and is therefore a measure of a mildly positive attitude. A score of 40 would be strongly positive. If you have 30 questionnaires with 20 statements (10 +, 10 −) the procedure is to create a matrix of 30 subjects × 20 statements as shown in the matrix below. Here, the columns would be the scores of each subject on a particular statement. The rows would be the scores of an individual subject on all the statements.

Subject	Statement						
	1	2	3	4	5	n.....	Total Score
01							
02							
03							
04							
05							
06							
07							
08							
n							

Average per statement

The important column is the total score for each subject – you will have 30 such scores. Now as you have 20 items the maximum score would be 100 (20 × 5) and the minimum score would be 20 (20 × 1). The important figure is the mid-point which would be 60 (20 × 3). You then *count* the number of subject total scores that exceed 60 and the number that score below 60. If, for example, the result is 25 positive scores and 5 negative you might conclude that the sample was positive towards your object.

This is not the end of the procedure. The statements are supposed to illustrate the dimensions which convey the direction of the attitude. If none of them were related then the assumption of groups would be invalid. The relatedness between the statements is represented mathematically by the concept of correlation (see Chapter 18). The principle is that a statement is likely to be valid if it is strongly related to all the other statements (the groupness principle). Therefore the process is one of correlation of each statement score with the total score minus the statement score itself as in the following example.

Subjects	Total Score	Score on Item 5	Total – Item 5
1	45	5	40
2	42	5	37
3	35	4	31
4	35	4	31
5	20	1	19
6	39	4	35
7	33	3	30
8	40	4	36
9	22	1	21
0	27	2	25

This correlated at $r = +0.96$. This is a very high level of correlation therefore the item is retained. If items do not reach a level of $r = +0.3$ then they are normally rejected from the pool.

To do an item analysis test, take the matrix, then correlate each item column with the total score minus the score on that item. See how many scores are above $+0.3$. This test may well devastate your original results. Those which make the $+0.3$ re-enter the survey. If sufficient items pass the test then an attitude may be measured from this remaining data. However, it is more likely that a new questionnaire will emerge using the validated items with more statements and the process run again.

The Thurstone scale

This approach follows the 'template' case in which 'absolute values' are constructed. The scale is a 'mother' scale which represents some absolute scale values to which subjects are asked to approve through a self-rating technique. The basis of this scale is that subjects are asked to express how far they favour a defined item or topic. The poles of the scale are strongly approve – strongly disapprove separated by a (usually) seven-point scale in which point 4 is deemed neutral. The assumption of the scale is that the intervals between the numbers are equal. The basis of this important assertion is that the scale is derived from a set of eleven categories represented by statements that have an independent relationship to the topic. Because these eleven statements are not correlated they can be assumed to have the same relationship to the topic and therefore it follows that, if the template scale has been produced correctly, then the same assumptions about equal distance can be applied to the self-rating scale. The equal interval property stems from the method scale construct which may be outlined as follows.

First, the researcher generates a large number of statements about the topic under investigation.

Second, a large number of judges (at least 100 and drawn from the target population) are asked to sort these statements into categories which progress from unfavourable to favourable opinions on the topic.

Third, the judges allocate each statement to one of eleven categories. In this way the researcher is left with a distribution of statements from all the judges. The next task is to measure the degree of agreement between the judges. The researcher forms a matrix of 'judges × categories'. Two measures stem from this matrix; the average numerical scale position per statement and the extent of inter-judge agreement.

Fourth, the statements which are used in the final scale are those which display high inter-judge agreement and are placed at relatively equal intervals. Two statements represent each of the eleven categories.

The application of the scale proceeds as follows. Subjects are asked to express their degree of approval for each scale item The expectation is that subjects will agree with only one or at least very few statements and that if this were the case, then the statements would be adjacent, for example a subject might indicate approval by agreeing with statements 6, 7, 8. The subjects score are computed on the median which in this example would be 7. However, the scale is subject to some criticism because the scoring can be idiosyncratic, for example a subject might choose 3 and 11 which would come out also as 7.

The Guttman scale

Another scale within the template approach is the Guttman scale which assumes that an attitude can be measured along a single continuum represented by a set of statements which are ordered in terms of degrees of acceptability. In other words the scale moves in one direction towards greater acceptability and in the opposite direction in terms of greater unacceptability. If the statement order is valid then the acceptance of one statement implies endorsement of all those below it and rejection of those above. It is, therefore, a cumulative scale.

To devise the scale the researcher begins with a set of statements ordered by assumed acceptability. The subjects may accept none of them, i.e. score = 0. Each item in the order carries a higher number based on the cumulative principle thus, Statement A = 1 statement A and B = 2, Statements A, B and C = 3 cumulating at 5. Subjects can choose any statements they wish. The scale is created by errors in the sense that if a subject chooses C but not A and B then the statements are not cumulative and are eliminated. Only when tests show a tendency for subjects to choose in a cumulative way does the scale and the dimension it is measuring, enter the survey. Once the scale is ready the scoring is relatively easy. An example of a Guttman scale might be in terms of attitudes to individual development. Consider the following five statements.

Least acceptable

(A)   industrial development should be discouraged because it is unsightly, pollutes the local environment and brings benefits only to those outside the locality;
(B)   industrial development causes problems and brings benefits to only a few in the locality;
(C)   as long as the new plants take precautions and make good damage they cause that's fine;
(D)   the benefits will spill over to the residents in the locality which will outweigh the problems; and
(E)   industrial development will mean extra amenities in the locality to the benefit of everybody.

Most acceptable

As the above illustrates, if a subject chose B and E they would be inconsistent because they have, in choosing B subsumed C and D. Whereas, if they chose A and B or D and E they are being consistent because A and E subsume all the others. An item enters the scale only when trials show that people use the item consistently.

Osgood's semantic differential

The assumption of this type of scale is that attitudes can be measured by the meaning of words or, more specifically, by the cognitive meaning of words which is a meaning the word suggests apart from the explicit meaning. What makes this idea so useful is that words often carry evaluative concepts. Sometimes we say 'good friend' to express emphasis but even the word friend on its own infers 'good'. In such a fashion enemy implies 'bad'. In this type of scale evaluative concepts are expressed by opposite words along a seven-point continuum, e.g. good/bad, strong/weak, fast/slow and so on. Osgood's approach assumes that this semantic dimension corresponds to an attitude. It is an important part of this approach that the scale is not numbered. Numbers are implied. Care has to be taken at the initial stage of design to find words that apply to the attitude object. In reality, many of the words we use to evaluate objects are fairly obvious, such as, good/bad. However, some of the words are specific to the object or object class. For example, in the evaluation of personal service, general concepts like good/bad might apply but in addition, specifics like informed /uninformed apply. In this instance, general concepts like fast/slow become a specific.

The concepts of reliability and validity

It is essential that the researcher understands the principles that lie behind the measurement of reliability and validity (see Chapter 2). Any attitude research method has to display its reliability and validity. A scale is reliable to the extent to which repeated applications of the scale produce the same results given that the attitudes under investigation remain the same. In a sense, reliability is about replication (being able to repeat or reproduce results). Validity, on the other hand, is about whether your measuring instrument actually measures what you intend it to measure. A valid attitude measurement actually measures the specific attitudes you set out to find and not some alternative attitudes however closely they may be related. Even casual analysis indicates that the two concepts are related. An unreliable scale has no validity, but a reliable one does not guarantee validity. It does, however, go some way to support a claim for validity.

At the heart of all 'methods' of calculating reliability lies the relationship between the number of item statements in the survey and the strength of the correlations between them. In any field of endeavour the more items used the more room there is for error and therefore the more unreliable the results. However, if the items were homogenous, the actual number would count for less. In other words, the degree to which the items correlate offsets the influence of the number of items. Reliability would increase with a smaller number of items that were strongly correlated and decrease with a larger number of items that were weakly correlated. Although the focus of attention here is the measurement of reliability it should be noted that the principles involved are in fact principles of scale construction. If the item statements are poorly designed and the attitude in question not clearly defined in the mind of the researcher then the outcome will be an unreliable test.

The two main approaches to the measurement of reliability are the 'split half method' and the internal consistency approach. The split half method simply involves the researcher splitting the results of the survey into two parts. The normal practice is to take even-numbered item statements into one sample and odd-numbered statements into the other. The sample's scores on each of these two artificial groups are then correlated. If the survey is reliable then the two parts should correlate fairly strongly. What is being assumed here is that a person completing the attitude questionnaire would be consistent throughout. Here the internal consistency of the results is being inferred by consistency in application. Given the nature of attitudes this would appear to be a reasonable assumption.

Internal consistency methods are the purest form of reliability and work solely on the two dimensions of number of item statements and the correlation between test items. The actual measure is a coefficient. The Spearman-Brown formula expresses the relationship between these two dimensions as follows:

$$Rxx = \frac{k(r\ y)}{1 + (k-1)r\acute{y}}$$

Here, k is the number of items in the survey and $r\acute{y}$ is the average correlation amongst the survey items. It is essential to see what is at stake here, instead of the item statements being split into odd and even numbers, the whole data set is correlated and the average intercorrelation used. In a sense this formula is simply an extension of the split half method. The only difference is the use of a finer measure of interrelatedness. Indeed it is possible to use the formula for the split half method as follows:

$$Rxx = \frac{2\ roe}{1 + roe}$$

where the number of items is 2 (column of scores on odd numbered and even numbered statements) and where roe is the correlation between the odd and even columns.

If it is relatively easy to secure a measure of the reliability of a survey, it is somewhat harder to do the same for validity. In a way high reliability represents 'face validity' but it is not enough. Put simply, the problem of validity is that attitudes are inferred phenomena, that is, because we see a positive or negative direction towards an attitude object we infer that we have found a dimension which measures attitudes to the object. It is circular logic. What this means is that the best approach to validity is through what is called content validity. It might just as well be called 'proof of the pudding' validity. Within this approach there are directions which are (a) predictive validity and (b) concurrent validity. Both work on the principle of comparing the performance of the survey with some measured variable external to the survey. The important stricture here is that there must be some theoretical justification for the comparison. An example of the predictive type might be a comparison of attitudes to religious tourism and the frequence of communal worship. This carries the important limitation of the problematic relationship between attitudes and behaviour. An example of the concurrent type might be a comparison of the results of an attitude survey with those obtained by interviews on the same subject and with the same sample. Validity always comes down to a matter of judgement and the purpose of using external measures such as expected behaviour, alternative tests, established facts, previous research findings is to reinforce the judgement of validity. It goes without saying that there has to be a theoretical or empirical justification for the choice of external comparison.

How to interview

The interview, along with the questionnaire, are the most commonly used forms of data collection in social science. In a sense, they 'represent' the qualitative and quantitative approaches respectively and as such are often viewed as alternatives. It is frequently suggested that qualitative approaches provide a 'richness' of data that is not possible with a questionnaire approach. Whilst true, this is slightly unfair to questionnaire approaches but does serve to contrast the special merits of both. The case for interviewing rests on two conditions. First, that the researcher is seeking, at the level of 'meaning', 'feeling' and 'value', insight into how individuals or groups think about their world and how they construct the 'reality' of that world. Second, if the researcher is uncertain as to how the target population actually thinks about the topic under examination – if it is not known how they conceptualize the area, how sure they are of it, or how much they actually know about it, then the interview serves the purpose of giving explanatory insights.

It is important that the researcher thinks about these two conditions carefully before deciding upon an interview approach because an interview is not an easy option: it actually requires as much planning and forethought as questionnaire design. In addition, if the researcher takes the interview option then the benefit of 'richness' only occurs if *all* the data collected is sensitively interpreted. As much of the data generated by interviews cannot be anticipated, readiness to receive it requires considerable forethought. In other words, to get the real benefit of interviewing, detailed planning is essential. At a fundamental level, If the very nature of the material under scrutiny is subjective, then the researcher has to get to grips with what this actually means in terms of data collection. In qualitative research it is always a case of 'know thy enemy' – namely, subjectivity.

The problem of subjectivity

Subjectivity stems from the individual nature of cognitive classification systems. The way we form categories in our mind and associate particular characteristics and properties with those categories is individual, personal and unknown at the level of behaviour and social intercourse. What we see in social terms is a subjective view. The depth we seek in an in-depth interview is some insight into the effect of an individual's categorization system. It is the province of cognitive science methodology to seek directly what an individual's categorization system actually contains. Notwithstanding the problems of psychology, subjectivity produces certain problems for the interviewer. These can be reflected in a series of questions as follows.

- Is the subject talking about the topic or variables they are supposed to be concerned with?
- Is the subject's definition of the topic or variable in line with normal definitions or the researcher's operational definition?
- From what perspective is the subject thinking about the variable? Self, role in the organization, organization, social norm?
- Is the subject talking about the topic or variable in terms of what it is or what it does?

There are problems of focus, meaning and perspective. During an interview the focus can slip and the researcher must be aware of this and either try to draw the subject back into focus or take advantage of the slip to explore and widen the field of data collection. An example would be helpful here. Let us suppose that the researcher is interested in 'price branding'. The subject may appear to define 'price branding' in terms of a pricing strategy rather than as a marketing concept. If the subject appears to be generally in favour of price branding this may be attributed to a personal view based on knowledge and evaluation of other branding properties or stem from the fact that it makes life less complicated for the incumbent in the role. It would be simply a matter of conformity to the organization's policy, or the accepted norm amongst marketing professionals that price branding is a 'good thing'. In one sense these issues of focus, perspective and definition are problematic but the researcher must accept them as such and take advantage of them to explore 'meanings'. Querying definitions 'could you clarify that?' and checking perspectives 'when you say that, where are you coming from?' are the initial keys that get the researcher into deeper levels.

However, diverting into fruitful areas of questions can only happen if the interviewer has a degree of control over the process. This control comes from having a well-thought-out set of *objectives* for the interview and a firm idea of the range of answers or general parameters of the topic under scrutiny. This is not to impose restrictions on the subject but to keep the objective in broad focus.

Tackling subjectivity

Awareness of what problems subjectivity presents should help the interviewer to 'use and explore' subjectivity during the interview. The challenge however, comes at the interpretation stage when the researcher is faced with tape recordings or transcripts of the interview. Three useful questions can be applied to interview data to get a grip on its inherent subjectivity.

- What relative comparisons (RC) are being made directly or by inference?
- From what point of view (POV) is the subject speaking?
- What is the context or background – stated or implied?

Relativity

When people make statements they often make relative judgements and thus comparisons, either directly or by inference. Locating the subject of the comparison 'compared to what?', 'relative to what?', often creates an important insight. Comparisons can be seen on two dimensions – subject and time. Where the subject is making a comparison with the past or future is salient to understanding the meaning they attribute to what they are describing.

Point of view

There are three aspects to point of view, which again may be expressed as questions.

- Is the subject's perspective the self, a role they play, e.g. a manager?
- What area of knowledge is the subject using when making a statement?
- How expert is the subject? The level of knowledge or ignorance that lies behind a statement plays a part in its interpretation.

Context

When people speak there is always an implied background or situation even if it is not mentioned specifically. This background is important to understanding what is being said. Here again, an example would be helpful. The following conversational data is from an interview with a retail manager and is first stated then reiterated with interpreted markings.

> In my opinion, labour turnover is high in this industry. I used to work in engineering and it wasn't like this. Mind you, I shouldn't complain about my staff moving on because I've moved about a bit myself but in this industry that's normal ...

The same quotation (with interpretation markings; POV=point-of-view):

> In my opinion, labour turnover is **high** in this industry (subjective-relativity). I **used** to work in **engineering** and it wasn't like this (relatively=past POV=self). Mind you, I shouldn't complain about my staff moving on (POV=role) because I've moved about a bit myself but in **this industry** that's normal (context) ...

Being on the look out for implied comparisons, changes in point of view and implied contexts as in the above example is part of good research interviewing practice.

Development of an interview

The research interview may usefully be conceived of in a number of stages as follows.

Pre-planning stage

Five core activities are essential here.

- Clarify what you are seeking. Be secure in the concept you are examining and have operational definitions from which to work.
- Turn your research objectives into specific methodological objectives.
- Visualize the possible outcomes.
- Think carefully about how data can be aggregated.
- Think carefully about what your subjects know of your topic because their responses will, in part, be differentiated by their level of knowledge and awareness.

Planning the interview

There are two important questions which must be answered at this stage – what type of interview is appropriate and does the interview need 'interventions' to enhance it? The interview as an instrument is very versatile and can be formulated in a number of ways. Fundamentally these approaches fall into three categories.

- *The structured interview* is where the researcher has a plan of sequenced questions to take the interviewee through. Good structuring usually means not just one route through the sequence but a proposed set of alternative ways of getting to the objectives. The form is that of an algorithm with branches dependent on the actual answers to the questions.
- *The guided discussion* is similar to the structured interview but simpler in concept and execution. Particularly suited to research involving 'issues'.
- *The open discussion* is just that. Here, the interviewer 'takes part' in the interview – introducing issues, putting a point of view and generally debating with the interviewee.

The case for interventions is often overlooked at the researcher's cost. The term interventions is a catch-all expression that includes any prepared information brought into the interview at a pre-arranged point. The need for intervention occurs in circumstances where:

- it is necessary to clarify a meaning by choosing a definition from a range;
- it is necessary to indicate a meaning by positioning the subject's meaning in terms of polar extremes or an ideal type profile;
- it would be helpful to obtain preferences.

An example of intervention is useful here. Figure 12.1 shows a nominal typology of managers and information and can be used as self-orientation or as a means to categorize others under discussion. It would be introduced at an appropriate point

Would rather not get involved with data. Stresses limitation before understanding is even attempted. Pigeon holes a problem before from the start. Finds large quantities of data frightening. Personalizes too much and makes wild assumptions. Best guesses situations and trusts instinct rather than information.

Always uses a set of good housekeeping rules. Implants subjective opinion on information. When faced with complex data takes time to 'worry out' the meaning of it. Uses the past to interpret data and gets deterred from thinking through problems by early implications. Looks at data to confirm what is already known or what current opinion is.

Calculates the risks of action and hold post mortems on problems to learn lessons. Can distinguish fact from opinion. Takes time and effort to understand large quantities of complex data. Can see when a principle is at stake. Struggles to resolve incomplete and ambiguous data and seeks more information to do so.

Sees the value of information in predicting long-term consequences. Can recognize what is important and can synthesize incomplete and ambiguous data into a conclusion. Can quickly grasp the meaning of large quantities of data. Can see the principle at stake and understands the policy and the context simultaneously.

FIGURE 12.1 Typology of managers and information

in the interview. Basically sort cards, labels, profiles and so on are 'props' that make the interview more illuminating and more enjoyable and interesting for the interviewee.

Conducting the interview: principles of good technique

However formal or informal the interview, there are parameters you would wish to lay down to guide the discussion and to ensure that you draw out information of use to you. The principles of good interviewing technique can be easily summarized but in practice require researchers to be alert to a wide range of possibilities and contingencies. The key techniques may be usefully summarized as follows.

- In your initial contact with, or introduction to, the interviewee, whether it be personally or through a formal channel such as your tutor, it is good psychology to state initially to the interviewee roughly how much of their time you require, your broad objectives, and a willingness to be flexible about dates and times in order to fit in with the interviewee's schedule. Give some thought to the location of the interview. At the most basic level the most desirable environment is one free from interruptions such as telephone calls, knocks on the door and other interruptions. This is difficult to achieve in many interviews which will take place at the interviewee's place of work so other skills have to be developed, for example prompting skills that return the interviewee on a subject after an interruption.

- Attempt to keep the interview as relaxed as possible, ensuring that a rhythm is established between you as interviewer and the interviewee.
- Seek to ensure that you keep to the objectives and agreed timescale of your interview.
- Maintain awareness of the signs which suggest that the interviewee is losing interest or becoming impatient, or alternatively appears to be quite happy to respond and can thus be probed further than originally planned. This applies equally to telephone interviews where observation of 'body language' is not possible but much can be read from the tone of voice used, the use of silences and the para-language of 'humphs' and 'grunts'.
- If you have obtained permission to tape the interview (this should always be established prior to the interview itself), ensure you have enough tapes and know how to operate your recording device. At the same time, ensure that you do not use the tape as a complete substitute for writing down key points. Noting comments of major importance serves not only as a useful aide-memoire, but guards against failure of the tape machine.
- Be careful not to 'lead' the interviewee in such a manner as to put words into his or her mouth, or by suggesting your own view on a subject (unless the latter is integral to the methodology), or by casting judgement upon an issue under discussion. These tendencies, often called 'interviewer bias', can be overcome by using open questions or 'probes'. The following examples of technique illustrate this point.
- Repeat the initial question in order to remind the interviewee of the point.
- Develop or clarify a vague or inadequate answer by asking 'could you explain further?' or 'why do you say that?'.
- Use silence – saying nothing and leaving the interviewee to decide when to continue whilst noting the point or question at which the interviewee seemed hesitant could be important to the interpretation of your data.
- Repeat the last few words, statement, views or ideas of the interviewee and then say something like 'that sounds interesting/exciting/provocative – tell me more about it'.
- Offer an idea which is interesting/exciting/provocative, either to get the interviewee thinking generally or to get them back to the line of questioning you are pursuing.

Evidence from an interview

At the most elementary level an interview must provide evidence for the researcher. A minimal requirement of an interview is that it reveals to the researcher the following about the interviewees:

- how they perceive the topic;
- how they feel about the topic;
- how much they know about the topic;
- what preconceived ideas and images they have about the topic;
- what were their expectations of the topic; and
- what they are comparing the topic with: another subject, the past, their personal circumstances?

This evidence comes in various forms, for instance:

- what they say;
- the structure of what they say;
- what they leave out;
- what settings or context they use;
- what reference points they use; and
- an orientation towards the subject (i.e. positive or negative).

If interviews have been recorded, they will have to be transcribed. It can take many hours to transcribe an interview accurately. Attention has to be paid, even in transcribing the interview, to those signals, the 'ums' and 'ers', that though not meaningful in themselves may have meaning in the wider context of the interview. For extensive interview data, computer software such as NUD.IST can be helpful to analysis. The form of analysis of interviews has much in common with content analysis (see Chapter 10), the process whereby you formally organize the content of the interviewee's statements and classify the meanings and interpretations you have attached to them. If you have not recorded the interview, it will have been necessary to keep as verbatim a record of the exchange as possible.

Telephone interviewing

Telephone interviewing requires much the same planning as face-to-face contact. It is likely that you will require a more structured approach than you might consider necessary for a face-to-face interview, because without the useful cues apparent in face-to-face contact it is less easy to monitor responses which suggest misunderstandings or inconsistencies, and it is not very good practice to ring back a second time for clarification! If you feel that it will not prevent an essential 'surprise element' in the interview, it is obviously helpful to the respondent to have a list of the questions to which you hope to obtain responses, especially given the expense involved in extensive interviewing by telephone.

Focus group interviewing

This is a highly sophisticated technique for drawing out information, particularly about attitudes and motives. It is thus very popular in the world of marketing – whether it is the marketing of consumer goods or of politics! It requires interpersonal skills of a rare order, because a group of people is interviewed simultaneously and the group management skills required are both varied and complex. Unless you are sure you possess such skills, it therefore should not be attempted, otherwise the information that you require for your research may never surface, or there may be so much of it you cannot control both it and the group!

The technique is supposed to encourage not only an exchange of views and ideas, but also the production of new ideas as a consequence of the public sharing and assessing of the ideas of others. Each member of the group is free to argue, disagree, question and discuss the issues with others in the room. One can see its use in a real-life management situation where staff responses are required relative to a new policy or a tricky problem. It is perhaps of less value for collecting 'hard' data about motives and feelings because social pressures can condition responses, and despite the efforts of the 'leader' some individuals may dominate a discussion, leading to questions as to whether evidence is biased or prejudiced as a consequence of the group's dynamics. However, again, for the perceptive researcher it can be a way of, say, testing the responses to a questionnaire, of offering new lines of thought on a topic, and, of course, in applied market research. For instance, in establishing a new product or analysing alternative packaging of an established product.

Effective focus group research depends, as always, upon careful preparation. You have to ensure you:

- thoroughly work out the parameters of the topic you wish discussed;
- try if possible to bring together groups who already have something in common, e.g. gender, experience of the product and its alternatives – this will create an initial psychological 'comfort' for the group and thus make it easier for members to speak their mind;
- plan how to keep the discussion focused without obviously leading it;
- try to anticipate and be sensitive to the emergence of unexpected information, or information which could be threatening in some way to some members of the group;
- build a good rapport with the group, that they will speak freely with one another;
- seek to ensure that everyone has an equal opportunity to contribute to the discussion; and
- in your evaluation of the success of a session, the key criterion for success is just how useful your results are in guiding and informing further steps in the research process.

The most important factor in the success of any form of face-to-face discussion or interviewing as a form of research is that of the relationship between the parties involved. This is not only a matter of practicalities – the elucidation of valuable data. It is also a matter of ethics. Access to information which is highly confidential, emotive or personal may be essential to the research project; whether one gets it and then how it is used, depends very much on the trust built up between the interviewer and interviewee. Even if those interviewed are not fully aware of the true objective of the research (often the case because one would not get the information required) you must still be fully aware of your social responsibility if you use this technique.

■ □ ▨ ■ 13

So just what is ethnography?

Ethnography, which may be defined as the systematic observation of social groups, grew out of anthropological studies. If we aim to truly understand what makes a group of people 'tick', then we have to engage ourselves in an extended period of observation. Modern ethnography grew out of the work of the 'Chicago School' of sociology in the 1930s.

If ethnography is about observation, there are two principal types of such observation – overt and covert. As these rather grand terms suggest, overt observation is where the researcher declares their identity to the group being studied and covert observation is where they do not reveal their true identity or purpose. Both overt and covert observation come in two forms – participant and non-participant observation. These ideal types may be defined as follows.

- Overt, non-participant observation is where the researcher's identity and purpose is declared and he or she does not participate in the activities of the group under scrutiny but stands on the periphery.
- Covert, non-participant observation is where the researcher's identity and purpose is undeclared and he or she does not participate in the activities of the group under scrutiny – this is perhaps the least satisfactory ethnographic form in ethical terms as it may court accusations of parallels to spying.
- Overt, participant observation is where the researcher's identity and purpose is declared and where he or she participates in the activities of the group as a member of that group.
- Covert, participant observation is where the researcher's identity and purpose is not declared and where he or she participates in the activities of the group as a member of that group.

All four forms of observational method are 'grey at the edges' in that, in the real world, overt and covert approaches merge into each other. However, all ethnographic research – whatever the methods of observation – have certain things in common. To paraphrase Fielding (1993) and Bryman (1988), the main characteristics of ethnographic research are as follows.

- Ethnography entails the study of behaviour in 'natural settings' – the ethnographic researcher goes to the scene of the action.
- Ethnographic research seeks to view the social world of its subjects through their own eyes and thus entails researchers gaining access to, and an understanding of, the 'symbolic world' of those being studied. By symbolic, we allude to the *meanings* that subjects attach to their own behaviour, experiences and attitudes and which differentiate them as a group from other groups. To adequately achieve this, the researcher has to acquire an understanding of the communications conventions of the group under study – not simply dialect or jargon, but the special meanings attached to ordinary words and terms plus all forms of non-verbal communication.
- Ethnography usually involves very detailed description in order to give clues to what is happening in a particular situation and to suggest further ideas as to what is happening and why.
- Despite focusing on a particular situation or context ethnography enables us to understand events observed within a wider social context, emphasizing the interrelationship between a series of events.
- Ethnography benefits from a generally unstructured research design as the observer must be open to observing, evaluating and interpreting quite unexpected behaviour and events and thus should not or cannot have preconceived frames of reference.

How do we set about observational or ethnographic research?

We assume that a topic has been chosen, and that you are assessing its feasibility, as has been suggested, against the criteria in Chapters 2, 3, 4 and 5. If these criteria are looked at again, one can see why ethnographic research really does test you! That is not to say that you should avoid it – it can be the most exciting, most satisfying and most 'real' of all research methods, but it does require that you know exactly what you are setting out to do; it does not start from a nice neat hypothesis which then sends you out to collect statistics to be 'number-crunched' by the computer! In terms of complexity and difficulty the points made above about the nature of observational research show that it is not just about standing and watching. The rules that govern human behaviour and 'everyday' life are often so familiar, appear so 'natural', that we take them for granted. These are not laboratory experiments, which test hypotheses about human behaviour under highly controlled conditions, often the way psychologists in the fields of perception and cognition go about their business.

Assuming you have settled your topic, chosen your particular area of focus (identified the group you wish to study) then the first decision to be made is whether you will observe covertly or overtly. A second decision, coterminous with the first, is whether you can gain access to the group of your choice. The particular importance of this latter topic is discussed in detail later in the chapter. From the standpoint of the overt/covert decision, the following points are worth bearing in mind.

- The 'open' ethnographer can avoid observing (if also a non-participant) or engaging in (if a participant) distasteful or illegal behaviour. By the same token, of course, such behaviour may be the very stuff of the research and avoiding it may render the research pointless or at least less effective. In their study of the hotel industry, Mars and Nicod (1984) (see Chapter 2) one of the researchers, Nicod, was, as we noted, a covert participant observer, undertaking his researches in the guise of a waiter and was privy to, and became involved in, acts of petty theft.
- The 'open' ethnographer can generally regulate their degree of involvement in the group under study with greater precision. By way of contrast, the 'covert' researcher can find themselves 'sucked in' to certain activities and behaviours because refusal would risk rejection by the group or even the compromising of an assumed identity: this is, in effect, a corollary of the first point.
- The 'open' ethnographer runs the risk of changing the behaviour of members of the group under study by virtue of his or her openness. This was a key problem with Whyte's study of youth gangs, *Street Corner Society* (1943).

The next decision to make is, of course, whether to be participant or non-participant. To a very large degree, this decision will be determined by the nature of the group(s), the wider study and the problems of access to such groups. Two other guidelines are important, however. If you choose to be a non-participant, it may be very difficult to actually appreciate or have access to how the individuals you are observing define 'reality', and to discern the motives and perceptions behind the behaviour you are observing or the conversations you are listening to. Conversely, if you are a participant, then you may become over-involved with the group, become institutionalized into their culture and thus be no longer able to stand outside it objectively (known, somewhat insensitively, as 'going native').

The next issue to be considered is how your data will be recorded and marshalled into a coherent whole. Ethnographic research is extremely time consuming and generates (or can generate if performed properly) huge amounts of data. While a central tenet of ethnographic research is to 'describe things as they are', it is important to remember that facts 'do not speak for themselves' but must be interpreted by the researcher in the light of his or her understanding of the group's own perceptions and conventions. Indeed, one of the major criticisms of ethnographic research based on observation is that it is 'unscientific', as the researcher's interpretation of data cannot be regarded as objective or reliable. This emphasizes the importance of adequate methods of data recording. You have to have some question or questions you want to answer, which you can formulate, however generally, from what interested you in the topic in the first place. It is not necessary to make watertight operational definitions of variables at this stage, just to be able to identify which observations will be most useful to you as indicators of the presence of certain social phenomena or social relationships. 'What is going on here? Why are these people behaving the way they are? Why are they feeling the way they are?' But note that your aim is to get beyond good descriptive journalism. You have to learn to make a critical assessment of reality, you have to develop a 'tough-minded suspicion' about what you see and hear. As your observations develop, you may have to reassess the questions you want answered, reject some, refine others. If your particular observations are to be of real scientific value, you should at the end of the day be able to produce complex statements which may lead to generalizations, perhaps about the necessary and sufficient conditions for a pattern of action and behaviour, drawn from your observations of a particular situation. The important thing to establish at the outset, however, is that you must have a clear focus, which has come about as a consequence of your reading around the subject and how you went about initially establishing your research aims. If you do not, you will not be able to judge which particular aspects or features of a situation or interaction you want to include and which to leave out.

We said above that you have to have some question or questions you want to answer. More often than not you will not be able to ask these questions in the manner of an interview (but may be able to work them into any number of conversations). Thus, many of the questions/issues in which you are interested may have to be answered by observation alone, *and inferences based on that observation.* In reporting such observations, inferences must be made explicit.

The main method of recording data in ethnographic research is by pen and pencil – the fieldnote. Tape or video-recording may be possible in certain circumstances but their usefulness is constrained not simply by the context of the research but by ethical considerations. The use of fieldnotes can be sufficiently problematic to absorb much of the researcher's time, especially if the research is covert and participant. Here, the recording of notes can at best be done in a rough and ready fashion. Indeed, Fielding (1993: 161) notes that a stock in trade of the ethnographer 'is to develop the reputation of having a weak bladder, enabling frequent retirements to scribble notes'. In covert research, developing the skill of acquiring and retaining mental notes is useful and the most effective way of doing this is to restrict the number of mental notes one seeks to memorize and develop a system for 'jogging' the memory later. Whether 'jotting' or taking mental notes, the key tactic is to record meaningful key words and phrases that can be converted quickly into fuller notes at a later point. This 'later point' is important: the general recommendation is that the writing up of full fieldnotes should take place no later than the morning after the shorter form has been recorded. Several copies of such notes will be required for analysis – at least one to stand as the 'file' copy, another for 'cutting and pasting' in seeking to organize data into categories and a third for working on prior to the 'cutting and pasting' stage. Similarly, within the fieldnotes it will be necessary to develop a number of conventions for denoting such things as who the note(s) relate to, timing, the use of direct quotations, the use of précis and so forth.

Access to your subject matter

As indicated earlier in the chapter (see also Chapters 3 and 4) gaining access to subjects is an especially important aspect of ethnographic research. If the situation you wish to observe is already open to the public, you have less of a problem, whether you are intending to observe overtly or covertly. However, it is always advisable and indeed ethical, to make a formal approach if you can identify who has ultimate responsibility for the group or activity. Perhaps you wish to observe the interaction between chainstore sales assistants and foreign customers, or the way in which customers in a chainstore respond to sales assistants from minority ethnic groups, or the way in which bar staff treat businesswomen on their own (a particular gripe of one of the authors!). Then, however insignificant you feel you could make yourself in the store or bar, it is still both ethical and good policy to seek the support of management, even though you may merely say you are a student 'doing a project'.

Obtaining access can be very time-consuming, and this must be taken into account when you are determining what you are going to do. Perhaps you are planning to observe in an informal context, such as a staff room, or in a 'private' setting, such as the boardroom, or a staff training session. Even if the observation is overt, developing relationships with people and gaining their confidence is essential in order that they lose the sensation of being observed and thus behave more naturally, and in order that they feel they are not going to be 'set up' in any way that reflects negatively on them. Given the time constraints on a student project, it makes sense that you only select groups or a situation for this type of study if you are already, to some extent, an 'insider' – say, an office or retail outlet where you have had some industrial placement or a part-time job.

As part of your deliberations on how you obtain access, however, you will have to consider two factors. First, it is not just access you require, but access to key informants (see Chapters 3 and 4). In other words, you have identified exactly who is to be useful or the most useful for your purposes. Second, you have to appreciate that there may be 'gatekeepers' who interfere with your attempts to get the most meaningful information. You may have to get permission at the outset from a certain key individual like the general manager of a store or from someone who does *not* have a position of formal authority (Whyte's study of street corner life was only possible after one of the members of the gang invited him to join). Alternatively, the most formal authority given you may now allow you access to what you really need to know if you are not able to identify the *real* gatekeeper, the individual (or key informant) who actually does hold the information you feel you need. Again, the time allowed you for writing an undergraduate dissertation is insufficient to build up the knowledge and relationships required to ensure you get around the 'gatekeeper' phenomenon.

References for Part Two

Allport, G. (1935) 'Attitudes', in Murchison, C. A. (ed.), *A Handbook of Social Psychology*, Worcester: Clark University Press, 798–844.

Arber, S. (1993) 'The research process', in Gilbert, N. (ed.) *Researching Social Life*, London: Sage, pp. 32–50.

Bryman, A. (1988) *Quantity and Quality in Social Research*, London: Unwin Hyman.

Chisnall, P. M. (1991) *The Essence of Marketing Research*, London: Prentice-Hall.

Clark, M. A. (1994) 'Communications and Social Skills: perceptions of hospitality managers', *Employee Relations*, 15, 2, 51–60.

Collins, H. M. (1984) 'Concepts and methods of participatory fieldwork', in Bell, C. and Roberts, H. (eds) *Social Researching*, London: Routledge and Kegan Paul.

Cunningham, S. (1991) *Data Analysis in Hotel and Catering Management*, Oxford: Butterworth-Heinemann.

Easterby-Smith, M. Thorpe, R. and Lowe, A. (1991) *Management Research: An Introduction*, London: Sage Publications.

Fielding, N. (1993) 'Qualitative interviewing', in Gilbert, N. (ed.), *Researching Social Life*, London: Sage, 135–153.

Foxall, G. and Hackett, P. (1994) 'Consumer satisfaction with Birmingham's International Conference Centre', *The Service Industries Journal*, 14, 3, 369–380.

Gilbert, N. (ed.) (1993) *Researching Social Life*, London: Sage.

Hakim, C. (1982) *Secondary Analysis in Social Research: A Guide to Data Sources and Methods with Examples*, London: Allen and Unwin.

Hogg, M. and Vaughan, G. (1995) *Social Psychology: an Introduction*, London: Prentice-Hall.

McClelland, D. A. (1961) *The Achieving Society*, Princeton: Van Nostrand.

Mars, G. and Nicod, M. (1984) *The World of Waiters*, London: George Allen and Unwin.

Moeller, G. and Shafer, E. (1994) 'The Delphi technique: a tool for long-range travel and tourism planning', in Ritchie, J. B. and Geoldner, C. (eds), *Travel, Tourism and Hospitality Research: A Handbook for Managers and Researchers*, New York: John Wiley, 2nd edition, 473–479.

Moser, C. and Kalton, G. (1993), *Survey Methods in Social Investigation*, London: Heinemann, 2nd edition.

Murdoch, J. and Barnes, J. A. (1986) *Statistical Tables for Science, Engineering, Management and Business Studies*, Basingstoke: Macmillan, 3rd edition.

Oakshott, L. (1994) *Essential Elements of Business Statistics*, London: DP Publications Ltd.

Oppenheim, B. (1982) 'An exercise in attitude measurement', in Breakwell, G., Foot, I. and Gilmour, R. (eds), *Social Psychology: a Practical Manual*, London: Macmillan, 38–53.

Plog, S. (1994) 'Developing and using psychographics in tourism research', in Ritchie, J. B. and Goeldner, C. (eds), *Travel, Tourism and Hospitality Research: A Handbook for Managers and Researchers*, New York: John Wiley, 2nd edition, 209–217.

Procter, M., Arber, S. and Dale, A. (1988) *Doing Secondary Analysis*, London: Allen and Unwin.

Richter, L. K. (1994) 'The political dimensions of tourism', in Ritchie, J. B. and Geoldner, C. (eds), *Travel, Tourism and Hospitality Research: A Handbook for Managers and Researchers*, New York: John Wiley, 2nd edition, 219–231.

Riley, M. (1996) *Human Resource Management in the Hospitality and Tourism Industry*, Oxford: Butterworth-Heinemann, 2nd edition.

Rosenfeld, P., Edwards, J. and Thomas, M. (eds) (1993) 'Improving organisational surveys: new directions and methods', *American Behavioural Scientist*, 36, 4, 414–418.

Slater, R. (1982) 'Questionnaire Design', in Breakwell, G., Foot, I. and Gilmour, R. (eds), *Social Psychology: A Practical Manual*, London: Macmillan, 1–13.

Stewart, R. (1985) *The Reality of Management*, London: Heinemann, 2nd edition.

Stewart, R. (1988) *Managers and their Jobs*, London: Macmillan, 2nd edition.

Van Maanen, J. (1983) *Qualitative Methodology*, London: Sage.

Weber, D. (1990) *Basic Content Analysis*, London: Sage.

Whyte, W. F. (1943) *Street Corner Society: The Social Structure of an Italian Slum*. 1993 edition, Chicago: University of Chicago Press.

Woolcott, H. (1990) *Writing up Qualitative Research*, London: Sage.

Yin, R. K. (1989) *Case Study Research, Design and Methods*, London: Sage.

■ □ ▨ ■ Part Three

Key Statistical and Quantitative Techniques

Chapters

An introduction to statistical terms and concepts

The chapters in this section discuss basic statistical terms and their application to data analysis. The discussion is not intended to be either exhaustive or a substitute for introductory statistics texts since the commentary is highly selective. Rather, the intention is to outline a simple foundation that can be developed through the use of specialist texts.

To begin on a note of caution, it is important to recognize that the ability to understand basic terms and the conditions for the manipulation of elementary statistical techniques is a must for any competent researcher. Yet many people – and especially students – are frightened by numbers and quantitative research is consequently a turn-off for many. This is particularly true where statistical analysis is concerned which is a pity. Not only can statistical techniques and methods play an important role in demonstrating the likely validity of research claims, but competence in them at even a basic level is a useful skill in its own right.

This chapter is concerned with definitions of some principal terms and is a reference point for what follows in Chapters 15–18. It is also more than this. Most of the definitions considered are, in fact, part of the foundations of statistical analysis. Thus, reading through this chapter could save you a lot of 'page-turning' later on. The reader will find the following discussion is developmental, proceeding from the foundations of statistical analysis to the more sophisticated conceptual architecture of statistical ideas. At a pinch, the headings may also be used for handy reference, whether or not you read what follows before proceeding to later chapters.

Census, populations and samples

The term *population* refers to the total number of people, objects, or events that are relevant to the research aspect being studied. Thus, if we were interested in the characteristics of Americans visiting London, the population would include all Americans falling within this category. Similarly, a study of British public libraries would include the population of all public libraries within Britain.

A *census* is a survey which collects information on all members of a population. A *sample* survey is a survey which covers only part of a population and the term 'sample' usually refers to that part of the population studied for some research process. Furthermore, samples are often used to draw inferences about the populations of which they are a part. Usually it is impractical to study a whole population, that is, to take a census of every member or item in a population. The techniques used in selecting a sample are thus very important and may usefully be revisited by studying Chapter 8 once again.

Descriptive and inferential statistics

A major distinction is frequently drawn in the study of statistics and statistical methods between descriptive and inferential statistics. Rowntree (1981) makes the very useful point that the distinction between descriptive and inferential statistics is to a large extent dependent on that between a *sample* and a *population*. Thus, you will find the two terms arising particularly in texts dealing with sampling theory. *Descriptive* statistics are quite literally those methods and techniques used to describe or summarize data: more usually they describe a group of people or things in terms of numbers, tables and charts. For instance, a researcher might describe the characteristics of a group of public library users according to their age, gender and ethnic group based on observed data. *Inferential* statistics, on the other hand, are techniques used for extrapolating from a set of observations aspects concerning the population as a whole. Thus, they attempt to predict the qualities and behaviour of a phenomenon which cannot be wholly observed. Inferential statistics bring into play probability theory and the reliability of making certain estimates and predictions.

Parameters and statistics

The term *statistic* is often thrown around a little too lightly. In statistical analysis the term 'statistic' has a very precise meaning. A 'statistic' is a numerical value or measure which summarizes or describes some aspect of a sample. For example, an average based on a set of sample data is a statistic. In this case it is technically called a sample statistic and more precisely the sample average. However, when the numerical value represents a summary measure relating to a population it is called a *parameter*. Thus, the calculation of an average age based on the ages of all people in a population would constitute a 'parameter'. In a strict sense, the term 'statistic' applies only to sample values whereas, when dealing with populations, the term 'parameter(s)' is used.

It will be shown later that sample statistics can be used to estimate population parameters. Thus, we can attempt to estimate the average age of a population of tourists from appropriately drawn sample data. In Chapter 17, in the discussion on significance tests, attention is drawn to the differences between parametric and non-parametric tests. It will be found that the former can only be applied when the parameters relating to a population adhere to certain laid-down conditions.

Variables

Constant reference is also made in statistical texts to the term *variable* and to a lesser extent to the distinction between quantitative and qualitative variables. A *quantitative* variable simply refers to an item of information a researcher is interested in evaluating or monitoring which can be described through one or more words and which assumes different numerical values. For example, we may be interested in evaluating peoples' ages, heights or weights or the number of patients admitted to a hospital accident and emergency department. Each item constitutes a variable. In each case the nature of the variable can be described in textual terms and appropriate values assigned or observed. Thus, in a study of people visiting a public library we might define one of the variables as 'age' and then record numerically the ages of each library visitor included in the study.

By contrast, there are situations where information relating to a particular characteristic or phenomenon naturally assumes a non-numerical value. For instance, eye colours might be categorized as blue, brown, green, grey and hazel. These types of variables are qualitative in nature (see Chapter 9). Other qualitative variables include gender, nationality or hair colouring. There are many other examples. In practice, qualitative variables may be converted into numerical form by assigning a numerical value to each option. Eye colourings can be numbered to cover the full range of possibilities, i.e. blue = 1, brown = 2, green = 3, and so on. Another example, would be to code the gender characteristic as male = 1 and female = 2. The reason for making the conversion is largely one of convenience for the purposes of statistical analysis. In effect, the information is coded to permit easier manipulation of the information. It does not mean, of course, the information suddenly assumes some 'real' quantitative value.

Discrete and continuous variables

Another distinction that is drawn between different types of variables is that drawn between 'discrete' and 'continuous' variables. This applies particularly to quantitative variables. A *discrete* variable is a variable whose numerical value varies in steps or, put another way, where the values are integer numbers. Normally, we associate such variables with counts of things. For example, we may make a count of the number of firms, products or employees when conducting a particular study. A *continuous* variable, on the other hand, is a variable which assumes a value that can be denoted on a continuous scale. Examples are weights, heights and age. Such variables may be for convenience or, because of the way data is requested on a questionnaire, be recorded in rounded terms or even according to groups. But in reality, the value relates to a more specific value that lies at a point on a continuum. For example, a person's age may be recorded in rounded or 'discrete' form as being so many years, but in reality their age can be placed at a point on a continuum which reflects not only the number of years but also the number of days, minutes and even seconds passed since the moment of their birth. The relevance of distinguishing between 'discrete' and 'continuous' variables becomes more apparent in subsequent chapters where it is shown how different types of data can be presented. The distinction also has implications in the calculation and evaluation of certain statistics.

Dependent and independent variables

One other distinction which is drawn between different types of variables is worth noting here. It is the distinction between dependent and independent variables. A *dependent* variable is, as its name suggests, a variable which is identified as having a relationship or dependence on the value of one or more *independent* variables. The term has particular relevance in predictive studies where the focus is on determining the value of the dependent variable when other phenomenon, as measured in terms of one or more independent variables, is allowed to change.

For example, it may be relevant for planning purposes to predict the number of cups of coffee sold per day by a student canteen. In practice, many factors are likely to come into play such as the drinking habits of different groups of students. But one key factor will undoubtedly be the number of hours the canteen is open. If it is shut all day, then obviously no cups of coffee will be sold. Once open, however, the number can be expected to increase according to some measured flow. Thus, the dependent variable represents the number of cups of coffee sold and the independent variable the number of hours the canteen is open. In such a study, sales would be observed over a sample period and from this data the researcher could set up a predictive model to estimate the sales of coffee at other times.

If the aim is then to produce a more refined model, other independent variables might be introduced. These might distinguish between disproportionate flows occurring at different times during the day. Thus, one independent variable might reflect the number of peak hours the canteen is open, while a second the number of off-peak hours it is open. Other models might take account of the proportion of students with different drinking habits. Following this approach, models can be built-up where the value of the dependent variable is predicted from the values of one or more independent variables.

Scales of measurement

Another essential aspect to appreciate prior to embarking on any kind of statistical analysis is that variables assume different levels or scales. These are generally referred to in order of importance as nominal, ordinal, interval and ratio scales. Nominal is the least sophisticated while interval and ratio are the highest. Depending on the level a particular set of data assumes so different types of statistical tests and measures are applicable.

Nominal and ordinal data

The essential point about nominal data is that the data assumes no natural ordering. Nominal data is largely allied to measuring qualitative characteristics such as eye colour, hair colour, gender, nationality or even lifestyle groups, i.e. singles, young married, retired. In compiling the data we may derive a count of the number of people in a sample with blue eyes and the number with brown, but we do not necessarily list the number with blue eyes first. The point is that no particular ordering suggests itself (see Table 14.1).

In contrast, ordinal data, as its name suggests, does assume an ordering. A good example of ordinal data is 'Rating Scales' (see Chapter 11). These are widely used in business and management research and may be used to describe customers' opinions regarding some product or service. For example, rail travellers might be asked to give their views on the quality of their local train service according to a scale of 1–5 where:

1= very poor
2 = poor
3 = acceptable
4 = good
5 = very good

When tabulating the results, the number stating 'very poor' will be placed before the second group and so on. Hence, a definite sequence presents itself (see Table 14.2).

The point to note is that nominal and ordinal data are essentially categorical in nature and compared with interval data, which is discussed next, they lend themselves to less statistical manipulation. For example, with nominal data, because it follows no particular ordering, it is only possible to show the proportion of people or items falling within each category. It is also possible to state which category includes the highest number of counts. The same is true of ordinal data. However, because the categories also follow a natural ordering it is possible to define a 'middle' or specific interval point. Thus, in the rail traveller example, we could state at what point on the rating scale people split into different levels of opinion. Using the data given in Table 14.2, we might highlight the fact that 40 per cent of the sample thought the service 'good' or 'very good', while 73.3 per cent (nearly three-quarters) thought it 'adequate'

TABLE 14.1 Eye colour of a sample of men (sample size = 200)

Eye colour	Number of men	%
Blue	60	30
Brown	80	40
Green	30	15
Grey	20	10
Hazel	10	5
Total	200	100

TABLE 14.2 Views of rail travellers on the service quality of their local train service (sample size = 300)

Rating	Number of rail travellers	%
1 Very poor	30	10
2 Poor	50	16.7
3 Adequate	100	33.3
4 Good	80	26.7
5 Very good	40	13.3
Total	300	100

or more than adequate. In contrast, 26.7 per cent, or just over one-quarter, rated the service as 'poor' or 'very poor'. In reality, this latter aspect might be of considerable importance to the railway company and closer inspection might help to identify the reason why these customers were dissatisfied.

Interval and ratio data

The great strength of interval data is that the values progress both in order and according to a series of equal steps. There are many examples. They include the number of babies born to different families (i.e. 1, 2, 3 ...), or the number of people pre-purchasing theatre tickets at a particular venue over different periods (say 20, 40, 60, 100 ...), or the age, weight and height of a sample of human beings. Interval data may be discrete or continuous and it will be found in nearly all cases that it displays ratio properties. For instance, a man who is 6ft tall can be described as being twice the height of a child who is 3ft. The other advantage of interval data over nominal and ordinal data is that it permits a much wider range of statistical evaluations and tests to be carried out. This is discussed in later chapters.

A final note on rating scales

Before leaving this chapter, it is important to note one aspect concerning rating scales. Although ordinal in nature, rating scales are often viewed by researchers as having interval data properties. One reason for this is that researchers like to calculate average scores. For example, from the data in Table 14.2, an average score might be calculated by multiplying each code value by the number of counts in each cell, aggregating the results, and dividing by the total sample size. The result is a score of 3.17, i.e. $(1 \times 30 + 2 \times 50 + 3 \times 100 + 4 \times 80 + 5 \times 40)/ 300$. The attraction in making this calculation is to try and show where the centre of opinion lies. However, the procedure is statistically fraught with problems and caution should be applied when manipulating data in this way. Chapter 11 included some guidance on specialized techniques that may be used to overcome some of the difficulties associated with rating scales, especially where they are used to measure attitudes. The point made both here and earlier is that in their basic form, rating scales do not display the properties of interval data. Thus, taking the simple example in Table 14.2, the distance between 3 = good and 4 = very good is not necessarily the same as the distance between 1 = very poor and 2 = poor. Indeed, peoples' perceptions of what constitutes 'very good' service may also differ from one person to another depending on their expectations and experience of dining out. This is a major problem associated with scaling methods and it may be advisable to review the discussion on scales as contained in Chapter 11.

■ □ ▨ ■ 15

The concept of probability theory

It is now appropriate to give some attention to the concept of probability. It is a concept of which we are all aware and use, almost subconsciously, in everyday speech or activities. For example, depending on whether or not we are prolific correspondents, we may or may not anticipate the probability of the postman calling every day. Busy people with many friends, a business to run, or a range of professional associates may expect the postman to call at least once every day, while those leading very quiet lives may never expect him to call, or hardly ever. Thus, most of us make subconscious judgements of how often certain events will occur although we may not attempt to quantify their likelihood.

Relevance to business and management research

In business and management studies the concept of probability theory arises in several ways. It arises in the selection of samples for study and in making inferences about the relationships between sample statistics and population parameters. Probability theory also assists researchers with making deductions about differences between groups and the effect of influences such as new marketing practices on people's behaviour. Probability theory also assists with predictive studies where the aim might be to determine the probable level of demand for a particular product or service. For instance, it may be important to assess the demand for certain kinds of hospital in-patient treatments taking account of the characteristics and needs of people in a given area. Utilizing probability theory, the researcher is able to put some measure on the likelihood that certain levels of demand will be reached for particular treatments.

The aim of this chapter is to introduce the reader to situations where probability theory can assist with making deductions relevant to business and management studies. It provides a 'lead-in' to the explanation of specific statistical techniques as contained in Chapters 16–18. There is no attempt to provide a detailed mathematical explanation of probability theory. There are many textbooks covering these aspects to which the reader can refer, where the laws of chance are explained through examples based on tossing coins or casting die.

Probability and non-probability sampling

When drawing samples, cases may be selected from a population of people or things according to an equal probability of selection. This procedure forms the foundation of *random* sampling theory. It permits deductions and inferences to be made from the sample results about the overall population parameters. Chapter 8 describes ways in which such random selection procedures may be carried out. The alternative option is to select samples on a judgemental basis. Most qualitative studies follow this pattern. Such samples are known as *non-probability* samples because there is an intervention by the interviewer or survey planner which impinges on the random selection process.

In the case of qualitative studies where the aim is to conduct a series of in-depth interviews or 'brainstorm' for ideas among a panel of people, i.e. focus groups, the latter procedure of sample selection is more common. The reason is usually due to limitations on resources. To transcribe notes from a one-hour in-depth interview can involve several hours of work. Thus, only a small number of respondents may be selected. Moreover, these respondents are likely to be virtually hand-picked in order to ensure they represent a reasonable cross-section of views. They may also be selected for their willingness to identify with the aims of the survey.

A good example of a qualitative panel survey is one of the many group discussions shown on television. A selected group of people are brought into the studio. The intention is they will represent a range of opinion concerning a particular issue. Theoretically, it may be difficult to select sufficient people to ensure every possible opinion is expressed, especially if the issue is highly controversial. Furthermore, it is not always easy from such discussions to detect which are the majority or minority points of view, or how views weigh proportionately against the range of opinions held by the community at large. Thus, although such discussions may act as useful 'sounding-boards', and that may in itself be sufficient reason for conducting the survey, the resultant data lacks the inferential properties of data drawn from surveys based on random sampling procedures.

Another example of non-probability sample surveys are many of the street surveys conducted by market researchers, particularly those using quota selection procedures (see Chapter 8). In the case of quota samples certain numbers of people are selected according to predetermined characteristics such as age or sex. In both general street surveys and quota sample surveys arguments arise over the extent to which interviewers exert an influence over the sample selection process. Clearly, some people are more approachable than others! Also, there is a real danger with such surveys that certain groups of people who do not frequent the streets or shopping areas at particular times of day, e.g. schoolchildren or businessmen, may be excluded from the survey. Steps can be taken to overcome some of the difficulties which arise with street surveys and thus minimize potential bias in survey results. It is, however, extremely important when presenting the results of your work to explain clearly the basis upon which samples are drawn. In this way, the reader can be alerted to the potential limitations of the data and the inferences which can be drawn.

Inferring population parameters from sample statistics

It was stated in Chapter 14 that sample statistics are often used to predict population parameters. For example, we might calculate from a randomly drawn sample of 1,000 American businessmen visiting the UK in any one year, that the average age for the sample is 35 years. We might then ask whether or not we can state with some degree of certainty what the average age is of all American businessmen visiting the UK in that year? Given certain information regarding the variance in ages for the sample such estimations are possible. The procedures for doing this are explained in Chapter 16.

Distinguishing between groups

Another situation involving probability theory is where a researcher wishes to assess whether or not differences between groups as measured according to some observed characteristic or phenomenon are distinct. For example, having determined the average age of American businessmen visiting the UK from a randomly selected sample, we might ask whether or not it is possible to state, again with some degree of certainty, whether or not this age is markedly different from the average age of a sample of Canadian businessmen on similar visits? Another, but rather different, circumstance would be to see whether or not some experience such as viewing a promotional video showcasing a new model of car influenced people's opinions in respect of their willingness to purchase that vehicle. Again, procedures for making such evaluations utilizing probability theory exist. These are discussed in Chapter 17 with regard to significance tests.

Predictive studies

The final range of situations to be discussed involving probability theory is that concerning studies of a predictive nature. As business and management students you may become involved with studies of this type and want to make statements about the likelihood of certain outcomes.

For example, you may be interested in predicting the demand for instant coffee sales. You may want to set up a model which predicts, for instance, the number of jars of instant coffee a supermarket might be expected to sell over a given period, or the number of times customers choose certain types of coffee. Should you anticipate a heavier demand for caffeinated rather than decaffeinated coffee? In setting up your model you will need to take into account past experiences concerning the behavioural patterns of different groups. You may define groups according to key characteristics known to affect coffee drinking habits. You may want to take into account the age, social class, sex, nationality or religion of each person. In effect, you are introducing 'control' variables and these will help refine your model. Over and above this, you will also want to put some probability measure on the likelihood of certain outcomes.

Whatever the situation, final predictions will be based on past observations. If it has been shown from past studies that on average 5 in 100 people over the age of 50 buy a new car each year (the figures are hypothetical) and the number entering this group, based on past birth patterns, has been increasing or decreasing at a certain rate per annum then, assuming we know the current size of the population for this group, we can begin to make some predictions about future demand. Moreover, if it has been found that the proportion of people over 50 buying a new car each year has varied over the last 10 years from say 3 in 100 to 6 in 100, we can build these aspects into our model. We can make judgements concerning the likelihood of different levels of demand. In other words, we can assign probability values which indicate the accuracy of different statements.

In theory, the more refined a model is, the greater the chance that an outcome can be predicted to a reasonable degree of accuracy. Thus, in the example relating to new car purchase we might decide to segment the sample and examine buying patterns among different groups aged 50 and over. If it is observed that people aged 60–70 have an even greater propensity to buy a new car each year compared with those aged 50–60 or 70 and over, a more refined model taking into account these variations could be devised.

However, there are situations where further refinements are not possible. In some instances, the data required to expedite refinements do not exist. There are also situations where further refinement results in little or no increased accuracy. For example, if the new car purchasing patterns for those aged 50 and over differ little when segmented by age then the effort involved in producing a more refined model is not worthwhile.

Moving on, there are situations where an outcome cannot be predicted with any degree of certainty. This may occur in situations where the data is too unreliable or where there are just too many imponderables involved. There may also be situations where there are unknown or, perhaps, unexpected factors at play. For example, in 1995 no one could have foreseen the enormous fall in the sales of British beef that subsequently occurred in the spring of 1996. The effect of the BSE health scare suddenly rendered any models predicting the consumption of British beef invalid.

Thus, probability measures can only reflect aspects of known situations where a degree of reliability in past patterns exists. There will always be imponderables or unexpected events which throw predictions off course. In general, however, the more we know about the behavioural pattern of different groups of people or things, the more accurately we can predict the likelihood of certain outcomes. The point is taken up again in later chapters and in particular in Chapter 18 where an initial introduction to certain predictive techniques are explored through the mechanisms of correlation coefficients.

Ways of expressing probability levels

Returning to the example of the postman, we can say there are two extreme possibilities either: (a) the postman will call every day from Monday–Saturday; or (b) he will never call on these days (note: we exclude Sundays when no mail service operates in the UK to avoid undue complexity).

These outcomes can be expressed as percentages reflecting different probability levels. That is, at one extreme there is a 100 per cent chance the postman will call and at the other a 0 per cent chance he will call. Between these values there is a range of options. If, for example, it has been shown over an observed period of time the postman tends to call at a particular address every other day, then we can say there is a 50 per cent chance he will call on any one day from Monday–Saturday. Similarly, if it is observed from past experience he tends to call only every third day then the probability is 33.3 per cent and so on. Taken a stage further, we can go on to express such probability levels in other ways. They may be stated in ratio or fractional terms, or as decimal values on a scale ranging from 1 to 0 as shown in Table 15. 1

Direction of hypothesis or underlying statement

The term 'hypothesis' is an important one. It forms the foundation of all statistical tests. The term has already been referred to in earlier chapters and is enlarged upon in Chapter 17. Nevertheless, it is useful to examine aspects of the concept here in the context of the postman example. This is because the way in which a hypothesis is posed affects the way in which probability levels are expressed. *The Oxford English Dictionary* defines the term 'hypothesis' as 'a supposition made as the basis for reasoning without reference to its truth, or as a starting point for investigation'. Put another way, we can say that in many aspects of statistical evaluation, we start by making an assumption or posing some question. We then put probability measures on whether or not that assumption or statement is true or false. For example, we posed the question 'What is the probability the postman *will* call at a given address on any one day?' Note, we stated, 'will call' and then gave a range of probability levels from 100 per cent to 0 per cent.

TABLE 15.1 Probability the postman will call on any one day as based on past patterns, illustrating different ways in which probabilities may be expressed

Observed patterns Normally calls:	Probability values %	Ratio	Decimal
(a) Every day	100	1 in 1	1
(b) Every other day	50	1 in 2	0.5
(c) Every third day	33.3	1 in 3	0.33
(d) Never	0	0	0

We might, however, have posed the question differently. For instance, we might have asked 'What is the probability the postman will *not* call at a particular address?' In this case, the probability level would be the reciprocal of those values shown in Table 15.1. In effect, putting the question this way means that in the situation where the postman does call every day the probability he will *not* call is 0 per cent. Conversely, at the other extreme we would say the probability that he does not call when in fact he never does is 100 per cent.

Conditional probabilities

When calculating the probability of a particular outcome, it may be necessary to take account of whether or not other events have already occurred. This is because the probability of certain outcomes are conditional on prior events taking place. For example, an addressee cannot receive a bill if the postman never calls! Or you cannot get wet if it never rains! Taken in another context, we might say an American businessman visiting the UK will never experience the wonders of Edinburgh if his schedule does not include visits to Scotland and, indeed, Edinburgh.

Let us assume in each case the initial event does take place, how might we then describe the probability of the final outcome? Taking the example relating to our American businessman, statistics derived from the International Passenger Survey (IPS), the major source of information on international visitors to the UK, show that in 1994 just under 3 million Americans visited the UK and of these 15.8 per cent (approximately 1 in 6) visited Scotland. Furthermore, of those Americans visiting Scotland 55.1 per cent (approximately 1 in 2) visited Edinburgh. From these statistics, we can broadly state there was a 1 in 12 chance that any American visiting the UK in 1994 would have visited Edinburgh. This probability is arrived at by multiplying together the two components, i.e. $1/6 \times 1/2 = 1/12$. In mathematical terms this can be generally expressed as $P(\text{outcome}) = P(A) \times P(B|A)$ where:

- $P(\text{outcome})$ = Probability American businessman visiting UK visited Edinburgh.
- $P(A)$ = Probability American businessman visiting UK visited Scotland.
- $P(B|A)$ = Probability American businessman visited Edinburgh given he visited Scotland.

Rules of probability

The above example demonstrates an aspect of one of the basic two rules of probability. These are the rules of multiplication and addition. The above example shows how to calculate the probability of an occurrence where the second or subsequent event is conditional upon a previous event taking place. There are, however, situations where the second or subsequent event is independent of a previous event. The outcome may then be expressed as $P(\text{outcome}) = P(A) \times P(B)$. For example, if a Michelin-starred chef found from continued past experience that 1 in 5 of his customers chose coq au vin as their main course and 1 in 3 crème brûlée for dessert then he can generally expect $1/5 \times 1/3 = 1/15$ of his customers to choose this combination from his menu. This outcome assumes customers eating coq au vin have no special predelection towards eating crème brûlée compared with other customers. It also assumes the proportions represent reliable indicators. Thus, out of a sample of 600 diners around 40 might be expected to choose this combination. In this case the interest was in knowing whether both events A *and* B occurred.

The rule of addition applies where the interest is in knowing whether events A *or* B have occurred. For example, our chef may be interested in determining how many diners can be expected to choose chicken or fish as their main course compared with the number choosing an alternative, such as lamb. If in this case he observes that 1 in 5 choose his chicken dish and 1 in 6 his fish dish, then the proportion choosing chicken or fish is $1/5 + 1/6$ or $6/30 + 5/30$ (introducing a common denominator). Thus the result is $(6 + 5)/30 = 11/30$. In this instance the probabilities are regarded as being mutually exclusive since it is assumed one choice precludes any other. If certain choices are not mutually exclusive then the probability of both options occurring must be deleted in order to avoid double counting. In this case the generalized formula is $P(\text{outcome}) = P(A) + P(B) - P(A \text{ and } B)$. This can best be described by reference to a simple diagram (see Figure 15.1). The left-hand side demonstrates two mutually exclusive events and the right-hand side events which are not mutually exclusive.

To summarize, where the probability of an outcome is dependent on more than one event occurring the individual probabilities relevant to each event are multiplied together. If, on the other hand, the requirement is satisfied regardless of whether event A, B or C occurs then the individual probabilities are added together.

Conclusion

This chapter has attempted to provide the reader with a brief, general background to the concept of probability theory. The aim has been to show how considerations concerning probability theory arise in the context of business and management studies. Subsequent chapters deal with practical examples and the more important aspects of distribution theory which underly the concepts and calculation of probability measures in different situations.

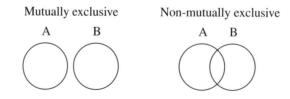

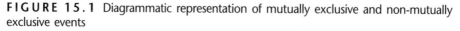

FIGURE 15.1 Diagrammatic representation of mutually exclusive and non-mutually exclusive events

16

Descriptive statistics

In this chapter, we shall examine some of the key concepts of descriptive statistics using for the most part a case study based on *continuous interval* data (refresh your memory as to the meaning of the terms by reading back to Chapter 14). The scenario is as follows. The Style Hairdressing Salons Group, a medium-sized chain, has decided to investigate the age profile of its clientele. To do this, all salons in the group are to undertake data collection during the same week in May. Originally, the company had intended that during this week, all units in the group would undertake a *census* of its customers but on the advice of the consultants conducting the research, decided against this as it was felt that this would be too time consuming and costly and, indeed, not all customers would be prepared to reveal their age adding to the complexity of dealing with a larger number of cases. Instead, it has been decided to *sample* the customer *population* in each salon during the appropriate week.

The Style Hairdressing Salon in London has, at the commencement of the 'sampling week', bookings for 280 customers over the next seven days. Typically, there is around a 10 per cent 'no show' so the salon is expecting around 250 guests during the course of the week. It has been decided to obtain a *systematic sample* of 20 per cent of the population – in the case of this salon that is some 50 of the expected 250 customers. Receptionists in all salons have been trained to ask guests as they arrive to fill in a special registration card which in addition to the usual information provides for recording the ages of customers. Those customers selected as part of the sample will have the nature of the research exercise explained to them. The company understands that even using this method, it is possible that some customers chosen as part of the sampling process will refuse to comply. Thus it is not expected that every salon will achieve a 20 per cent sample of its customer population for the week.

In order to implement the systematic sampling procedure, each salon in the group has been asked to commence with the fourth customer registration of the week and proceed by selecting every fifth customer thereafter (since a 20 per cent sample is required, this is one in five of the given population: thus in the case of the London salon, the first customer to be included will be the fourth to register and thereafter every fifth customer will be chosen. Thus, it will be the fourth, ninth, fourteenth, nineteenth registering customer and so on that will be approached with a view to obtaining a 20 per cent sample, i.e. some 50 customers in all, with the last customer approached being the 249th).

The nature and preliminary handling of data

Raw and grouped data

With great good luck, the Style Hairdressing Salon in London is successful in obtaining its data – the ages of 50 persons, some 20 per cent of the salon's customer population of the week in question. This *raw data* is presented in Table 16.1.

While a useful first stage, the recording of data in this way reveals little about the customer profile. A useful next step is therefore to arrange the data in the form of an *array*, where the raw data is reordered in ascending order of numerical value – i.e. the lowest value to the highest. This is shown in Table 16.2.

TABLE 16.1 Raw data of customers in sample from the Style Hairdressing Salon, London

10	35	10	23	17
22	39	29	29	14
27	37	29	37	43
42	62	36	43	23
41	62	36	54	47
55	54	39	58	28
61	47	53	36	63
64	43	64	36	25
50	16	19	34	21
34	11	18	36	49

TABLE 16.2 Array of customers' ages in sample from the Style Hairdressing Salon, London

10	23	35	41	54
10	23	36	42	54
11	25	36	43	55
14	27	36	43	58
16	28	36	43	61
17	29	36	47	62
18	29	37	47	62
19	29	37	49	63
21	34	39	50	64
22	34	39	53	64

The array allows a much more systematic view of the raw data but is still unwieldy. It is therefore often useful to group the data in some way – usually into classes – and thereby reduce the number of observations to more manageable proportions. The disadvantages in doing this, however, should be noted. Although grouped data may be easier to handle, the greater degree of accuracy or processes described by the raw data is lost. This is one of the reasons why the way in which classes are constructed and described should be treated with care, including any statistics computed from grouped data. As stated, the purpose of this grouping is to generate more manageable descriptions of the data. This also leads us to usefully dealing with other terms including those concerning the construction of *frequency distributions*. To construct a frequency distribution in tabular form, it is first necessary to grasp two related concepts, those of *class frequencies* and *relative class frequencies*.

Class data

In this context, the term 'class' refers to a number of pairs of upper and lower boundaries that divide the data set. Table 16.3 illustrates this point. Table 16.3 also shows the frequency – written in statistical notation as 'f'. This is the number of observations that fall into each category or, more precisely, fall within each pair of class boundaries. The final column in Table 16.3 shows the relative frequency for each class, which is the percentage of the total number of observations (n) represented by the number of observations in that class.

Number of classes

A word on determining the number of classes that should be used in arranging data in this way is appropriate here. The number of classes should be neither overly small or overly large. Between 5 and 20 classes is the number usually recommended depending on the nature of the data. Among others, Clark (1993: 9) offers a formula for determining the appropriate number of classes for any given data set which involves finding the first power of two that is greater than, or equal to, the number of

TABLE 16.3 Grouped frequency distribution of customers' ages in the Style Hairdressing Salon, London

Class	Nos persons in each category (f)	Relative frequency $(f/n \times 100)$ %
10 and under 20	8	16
20 and under 30	10	20
30 and under 40	12	24
40 and under 50	8	16
50 and under 60	6	12
60 and under 70	6	12

observations being tabulated. Thus, two to the power of one is two, two to the power of two is four (2×2), and two to the power of three is eight $(2 \times 2 \times 2)$ and so on:

2^2	4	2^5	32
2^3	8	2^6	64
2^4	16	2^7	128

On this basis, in a sample of 50 observations, six classes would be appropriate and this is indeed the view that has been taken in the present example as is shown in Table 16.3. While the formula described above has its uses, the creation of classes adequate to the tasks of statistical analysis should not be a dogmatic affair and there is no substitute, given the nature of any data set, for considered judgement.

This can be clearly seen when considering certain other desirable and actual properties of classes. First, no class should overlap with another one. A common error found in the work of inexperienced student researchers is the presence of overlapping classes, e.g. 10–20, 20–30, 30–40 and so on. This clearly risks assigning individual observations to more than one class thus confusing subsequent analysis of data. Second, the upper and lower limits of each class are referred to as the *class limits* or *class boundaries*. In describing these boundaries, it is important to show how certain marginal data values have been assigned to individual classes. There is also an important distinction to be drawn between the nature of these limits as they refer to continuous as opposed to discrete data. In our case (see Table 16.3) we are measuring ages and our data is continuous, although for practical purposes individual ages have been recorded in Table 16.1 in terms of whole years. In fact, by stating our first grouping as 10 but under 20 years, we are assigning anyone who is over 19 but not yet 20 to this group. Thus, the *true limit* of the class is 10 years exactly and up to 19 years and 364 days and covers a 10-year class interval. The wording makes this clear.

Another system would have been to adopt a rounding procedure based on the mid-point between years. Arithmetic convention is such that anything which is 0.5 and above is normally rounded up while anything which is less than 0.5 is rounded down. A class described with an interval running from 10–19 years could then, in fact, include all customers with ages from 9.5–19.49 years. Obviously, it is important in presenting your results to state clearly how the data values have been assigned to individual classes.

In the case of discrete data another concept also emerges – that of setting *mathematical limits*. It is purely a convention necessary for undertaking mathematical calculations, but can result in certain values which need to be treated with understanding and common sense. Let us assume, for example, the data represented by Table 16.3 refers instead to the number of times people visited the London salon over a given period. This would be discrete data since one cannot visit a hairdressing salon for 0.5 or 1.5 times. We might then present the groupings in Table 16.3 more sensibly as: 1–5 times, 6–10 times and so on. However, for certain computational and presentational purposes which will become evident as the chapter progresses, the gaps must, in certain circumstances, be regarded as being 'closed' by extending each class half a unit in each direction such that each class touches the class(es) adjacent to it.

These extended limits are known as *mathematical limits*. There is further discussion on this aspect in the sections relating to the construction of histograms and frequency polygons.

Class widths

Third in this discussion of the nature of classes is the need to give some consideration to the concept of the *class width* or *class interval*. The class width or class interval is quite literally the difference between the class limits (boundaries) and whether these are the true or mathematical boundaries will depend upon whether the data is discrete or continuous. In Table 16.3 all classes are of the same width but this does not have to be the case for all representations of data in this manner. Most non-statisticians feel more confident about handling data that is organized into classes of similar width, but this should not prevent experimentation with classes of different widths, if appropriate. The determination of class width can be a relatively arbitrary process. It is certainly one requiring some personal judgement. Nowhere is this more evident than in the case of *open-ended classes* which are often used at the extremes of distributions – for example 'less than x' or 'more than y'. The use of open-ended classes is generally appropriate where the closing of 'beginning-and end-classes' would be inappropriate because too few observations would fall into such classes. Alternatively, they could be used where observations extend to extreme values relative to the distribution as a whole. In other words, 'open-ended' classes are used where the introduction of closed classes would unnecessarily fragment the data.

A final point to emphasize here is that once an observation has been assigned to a particular class, its individual value is submerged, its new value lying between the limits or boundaries of the class to which it has been assigned. In effect, a refinement in the data is lost which has implications for the computation of certain descriptive statistics. Accordingly, it is usual in situations where grouped data is being used to take a *class mark* as the representative value for each class. The class mark is the mid-point of each class and is made to represent all values for that class. Of course, the class mark might not be representative of the values in the class. To a very large degree the class mark will perform this role reasonably well however if classes have been constructed with care and accuracy. The class mark is also useful for performing a variety of computations and operations as we shall see later.

Pictorial and diagrammatic representation of data

Students are fond of presenting data in graphic, diagrammatic and pictorial form and such methods can be helpful providing only a representation appropriate to the data is used and described with the necessary clarity. There are situations where certain diagrammatic forms are totally inappropriate. For example, where a question offers the opportunity for multiple response, pie charts are not a good idea (see below). In short, the presentation of data by diagrammatic means should be considered carefully. Ask yourself first, does the diagram, graph or pictorial representation help the reader to understand a particular point or aspect of the data? Sometimes it does but, on the other hand, there are situations where a point can be more easily assimilated by an audience via a simple verbal description.

Most pictorial and diagrammatic methods of presenting data are well known and include graphs, pictograms, bar charts and pie charts. Accordingly, the principle of constructing these devices will not be dwelt upon here. Rather, observations will be made concerning points to bear in mind when using each means of illustration.

Graphs

A graph plots two variables against each other – the *dependent* and the *independent* variable. These concepts might usefully be reviewed at this point by referring back to Chapter 14.

Pictograms

These come in two principal forms. One kind is where the total value of all data is expressed by the number of pictures shown, where each picture represents a uniform unit of value and where a fractional picture shows a correspondingly fractional proportion of that value (see Figure 16.1). The other type of pictogram, to be avoided, is where the size of the picture changes to represent changes in value. The problem with this method is that expanding the size of the picture can mislead viewers because it often involves increasing the 'volume' of the picture (see the later discussion on histograms).

Bar charts

Bar charts represent values in the length or height of their bars depending on whether they are presented using a horizontal or vertical axis. In business applications, bar

January	ΔΔΔΔΔ	50
February	ΔΔ∠	25
March	Δ	10

Note: One Δ triangle = 10 triangles sold

FIGURE 16.1 Pictogram showing number of triangles sold by 'The Music Shop', January–March 1996

charts can take several forms, one is to present data in the form of a simple array of bars. The height of each bar represents an appropriate number or proportional value as in Figure 16.2(a). *Component bar charts* sub-divide individual bars to reflect more detail about the data in question. Thus, if a shop offers three products, books, CDs and videos, then sales of each of these products may be represented in a single bar indicating total sales each day but also showing the contribution of each product to the total sales value as in Figure 16.2(b).

There are several physical representational variations on this theme, just as there are also arithmetic variations. The most obvious in the case of the latter is where bars are used to represent proportional values rather than raw numeric data. When constructing bar charts and indeed other charts, it is worth taking time to consider which form of measurement and diagrammatic representation is most useful and meaningful in the context of the study and data aspect being reviewed. If, for example, the aim is to compare the sales of two shops would you be more interested in comparing actual value of sales analysed between books, CDs and videos as in Figure 16.3(a), or would you want to know how the sales compared proportionately between these three options as in Figure 16.3(b)? There is an argument for both depending on the aspect to be highlighted.

Note also another point. With bar charts there are distinct spaces between bars representing the different categories of interest. Where bar charts are being used to make a comparison it is also advisable to limit the number of groups being compared in order to avoid undue complexity. Certain writers suggest no more than one comparison should be made at a time (Emden and Easteal 1987: 58). Figure 16.3a provides a relevant example where only the sales of Shop A and Shop B are being compared at one time. Clearly it is also important to ensure shadings are distinct in order to indicate differences in the data.

Thus, although bar charts are a highly versatile diagrammatic way of representing data of a categorical nature, care should be taken when using them to avoid sloppy and confusing representations that do little to enhance or draw out the meaning of what is really important. Note also simple bar charts of the type described in Figure 16.2(a) and 16.3(a) are often the most appropriate when dealing with diagrammatic representations of the results of multiple choice questions. This is because each bar is independent of the others. With such bar charts it is also not necessary to detail the results of responses to all categories included in a question. In certain circumstances it may be pertinent to present results relating to selected categories only. For example, in Figure 16.3(a) the comparison could be limited to showing sales for two products only.

Pie charts

Pie charts represent raw or percentage data as a series of categories (classes). The whole of the data is presented such that the relative proportions of all categories or classes of data represented can be easily compared. Typically, a pie chart will nearly always represent data in percentage terms as this is the pie chart's unique pictographic facility (see Figure 16.4).

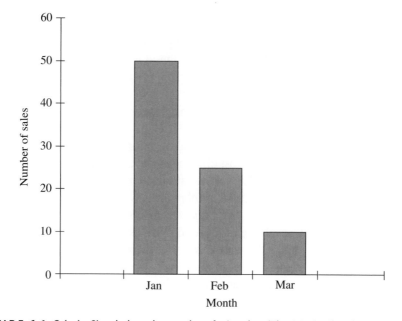

FIGURE 16.2(a) Simple bar chart: sales of triangles, 'The Music Shop', January–March

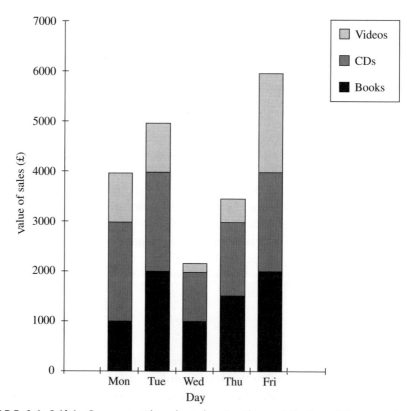

FIGURE 16.2(b) Component bar chart showing the contribution of three products to total daily sales at Shop A, Monday–Friday

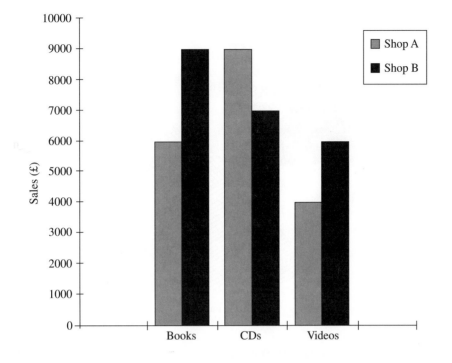

FIGURE 16.3(a) Comparative bar charts: total sales values over one week in Shops A and B by product

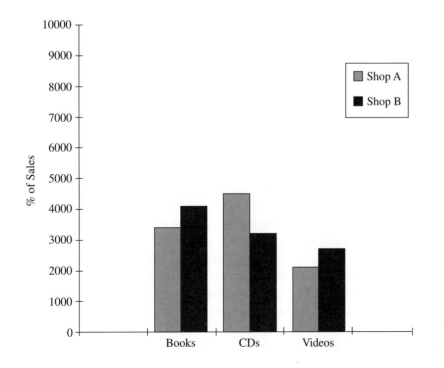

FIGURE 16.3(b) Proportional sales by type of product

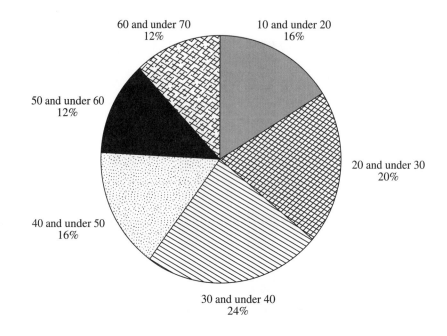

FIGURE 16.4 Pie chart showing proportion of customers in each age group (data from sample taken at the Style Hairdressing Salon, London – see Table 16.3)

Note that it is recommended the number of segments should not be too large. Five segments is suggested as a reasonable maximum and segments representing less than 7 per cent of the total number of cases in the sample or population should be avoided where possible by regrouping the data (Emden and Easteal 1987: 60). Violations of the number and size of individual segments can make charts too detailed and confusing to read, although, as with other situations described, there are no hard and fast rules and the researcher must make their own reasoned judgements.

The overall total number of cases represented by the pie should equal the sample size, or aggregate to 100 per cent where segments denote proportional frequencies. This is important and may seem obvious, but such errors do occur particularly when attempts are made to use pie charts to represent the results of multiple choice questions. In such cases, bar charts are often more suitable. Another consideration concerns the ordering of the segments. They should follow a logical sequence as in Figure 16.4. Another aspect concerns the choice of shading. If your report is to be photocopied into black and white, avoid shadings that involve colours as the distinctions will clearly be lost. Clear labelling of charts is essential and can help the reader to quickly interpret a diagram's meaning. Note how each segment is clearly labelled and the percentage values have been added to indicate quickly which are the principal groups and by how much. Chart titles should accurately describe the data being presented.

Histograms

All the aforementioned ways of visually depicting data are of little use if it is a frequency distribution relating to a continuous variable that is to be presented. A histogram is a means of visually presenting a frequency distribution. Histograms are like bar charts in appearance but they are not bar charts. They differ in a number of respects, the most important of which is that with a histogram, it is the area represented by the bars and not the height of the bars that is important.

In a histogram the areas described by the bars represent proportional values or visual or spatial perspectives. This is a concept or representation that is not altogether easy to understand. The easiest situation to interpret is where the class intervals as shown in Figure 16.5 are the same. In this case, the number of customers aged 50 and under 60 are half the number aged 30 and under 40. Hence, the height of the 5th bar and the area described by it, is half that for the 3rd bar. Numerically, the area can be said to be described by 10 (units of age) × the frequency (nos. of people). In this case the sums are for the 5th bar are: $10 \times 6 = 60$, and for the 3rd bar: $10 \times 12 = 120$.

The construction of a histogram needs to be treated with considerably more caution, however, where the class intervals are not the same. In such situations there is a very real danger of producing a highly distorted and incorrect visual representation. This can be illustrated by reference to the sales of two car companies A and B. Company A, which is based in a highly dense conurbation, regards its catchment, or distribution, area as being confined to people residing or working within a 10-mile radius of its showroom. Moreover, sales over the peak period of August–October amounted last year to 100 cars. Company B, on the other hand, is located in a semi-rural area and therefore has a wider catchment area of a 25-mile radius. Let us suppose the number of cars sold by Company B during the months of August–October is still the same as for Company A. Representing these situations graphically in the form of a histogram, we may be tempted to present the results as overleaf:

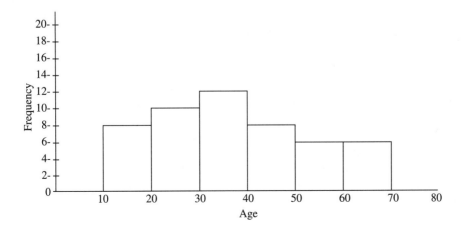

FIGURE 16.5 Equal class interval distribution histogram of data in Table 16.3

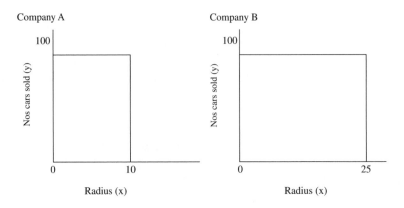

The representation for Company B would however be wrong as visually it appears as though they have more sales rather than equal sales spread over a wider catchment area and the area described by the bars would also be incorrect, i.e. A = 10×100 = 1,000 and B = 25×100 = 2,500. The correct representations would therefore be:

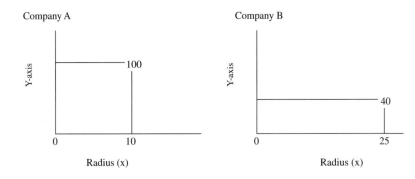

In other words we must adjust the frequency axis (y) to reflect the wider spread (x). In this case, since the sales radius for Company B is two and a half times that for Company A we adjust the height of the bar by a factor of 2.5 to give a value on the (y) axis of 40. The area of the bar is thus $40 \times 25 = 1,000$ or the same as for Company A. This is the underlying principle for the construction of histograms and where the class intervals are unequal the (y) axis is referred to as the frequency density. The point is underlined by Cunningham (1991: 9–10) who also offers one of the clearest explanations of why it is the area and not the height that is important in the bars of a histogram. He asks us to consider two hotels, Hotel A and Hotel B, where the turnover of Hotel A is twice that of Hotel B. If this relationship is represented as two vertical lines, the first twice the 'height' of the second, this relationship can be viewed quite clearly as follows:

Hotel A   Hotel B

The above representation is known as a line chart. If , however, we take each line as the left side of a square and draw in the rest of the lines of this square in each case, then the area of Square A will be four times greater than that for Square B, yet the relationship that it is purported to represent is one where A is twice the size of B Thus the diagram below is incorrect. It is as well to consider the nature of these problems relative to the use of pictograms as discussed above.

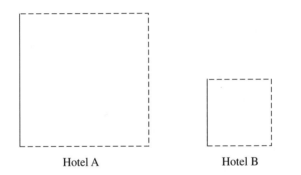

Hotel A   Hotel B

As has been noted, with an equal class interval distribution these problems of distorted representation do not arise and it may be best for the inexperienced student to confine themselves to such diagrams whenever possible.

Another concern is when the frequency distribution involves open-ended classes, and again, problems may arise in the representation of data since the existence of open-ended classes implies a distribution that includes unequal class intervals (i.e. where some classes have a larger – or sometimes smaller – width than others). It has been shown that in a histogram utilizing an *unequal class interval distribution* the y axis representing the frequency density must be adjusted or the use of data will lead to a distortion in the histogram. Before proceeding to consider further how adjustments are made in the case of distributions with open-ended classes, it is necessary to first make a number of other fundamental observations about the nature of histograms.

First, a histogram is in essence a graph of a given frequency distribution. The horizontal axis (x) uses a continuous scale running from one extreme of the distribution to the other. It is thus labelled with the name of the variable together with the units of measurement being employed. The vertical axis shows the frequency values (y) against which the variable is set. Second, each bar in the histogram is drawn with its base on the horizontal axis. The extremities of each bar, the distance between the left- and right-hand 'walls', are class limits (boundaries) of the class. Third, unlike a bar chart, a histogram's bars are continuous, that is, there are no spaces between the bars. The reason for this is simple. The class limits (boundaries) represent either the true or mathematical limits in the case of, respectively, continuous or discrete data. Finally, for reasons that will be elaborated upon shortly, it follows that if each 'bar' on a histogram runs from its lower to its upper class limit, then each bar is itself centred on the class mark.

Returning now to the histogram itself, consider the data contained in Table 16.3. The resulting histogram of this equal class interval distribution is shown in Figure 16.5. Note that in this instance, where class intervals (widths) are the same, the vertical axis is labelled 'frequency'. This is because the heights of the rectangular bars are proportional to the frequencies, so the height of each bar does indeed correspond to the actual frequencies.

But what happens when we have an unequal class interval distribution? Let us say, for the sake of argument, that some of the observations in our original array of values (Table 16.2) fall beneath 10 and above 70. Let us make the first two under 10s children of six and eight years old, and the last two over 70s, as 72 and 78. Now, we could suggest introducing two new classes (under 10 years and 70 and under 80 years) but because of the small number of observations at the extremes of the distribution and the relatively small number of observations now contained in the classes from which they have been robbed, it might make more sense for the purposes of the table to use two open-ended classes, 'less than 20' and '60 and over' (see Table 16.4).

This presents a problem, however, when we come to draw a histogram. The first thing we must do is to arbitrarily close these open-ended classes at some value and the first logical step is to close the class at the lower end at zero since nobody can be less than this age. For the higher class, any closure decision must ensure that all observations are included and since the new 'high' value is 78, so under 80 years would seem a reasonable cut-off point. These discussions have the advantage of maintaining an equal class width for each of the arbitrarily closed classes. It should

TABLE 16.4 Grouped frequency distribution of customers' ages in the Style Hairdressing Salon, London, sample using unequal class intervals and open-ended classes.

Class	Nos of persons in each category (f)	Relative frequency (f/n × 100) %
Less than 20	8 (two customers aged less than 10)	16
20 and under 30	10	20
30 and under 40	12	24
40 and under 50	8	16
50 and under 60	6	12
60 and over	6 (two customers older than 70)	12

also be, once again, noted that while common sense is a good guide to how open-ended classes should be closed, any such decisions are, to a degree, always arbitrary.

Now we could draw the histogram of our revised data as shown in Figure 16.6. The combined frequency of the 'less than 20' class is still eight although two observations now fall below 10. Similarly, the combined frequency of '60 and more' is still six although two observations now exceed 70 and a closure at 80 is defined.

Unfortunately, as in the example of the car sales and hotel turnovers the histogram shown in Figure 16.6 is gravely in error since the 'less than 20' category bar is clearly greater in area than it should be i.e. $20 \times 8 = 160$ rather than $[(2 \times 10) + (6 \times 10) = 80)]$ had the distribution been represented according to equal class intervals of 'under 10 years' and '10 and under 20'. A similar problem exists with the '60 and over' class. Again, in order to draw the histogram correctly so that each bar represents accurately its area, it is necessary to adjust the heights of all the non-standard classes to that of a base class, the base class being chosen on the criterion of selecting the most common class width (interval). The formula is:

$$\text{Height} = \text{Class Frequency} \times \frac{\text{Width of Base (most common) Class}}{\text{Actual Width of (non-standard) Class}}$$

In our data set, the most commonly occurring class width is 10 and there are only two non-standard classes, that is, the 'less than 20' and '60 and more' categories. To calculate the appropriate heights we apply the formula thus:

$$\text{Height (for less than 20 category) is } 8 \times \frac{10}{20} = 4$$

$$\text{Height (for 60 and more category) is } 6 \times \frac{10}{20} = 3$$

Redrawing the histogram we arrive at Figure 16.7, with the area of the non-standard classes in this unequal class interval distribution now accurately reflecting visually the frequency distribution. Note, however, that the vertical axis is now labelled 'Frequency Density'. This is because the adjustment to the areas of the non-standard

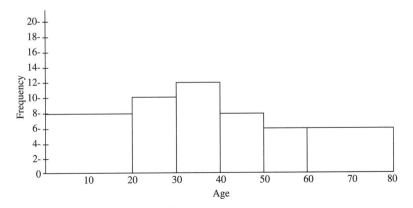

FIGURE 16.6 Incorrect histogram of the data shown in Table 16.4

classes means that the heights of the bars now measure how closely packed observations are within each class. Thus, although the class of 'under 20 years' embraces eight observations, these are spread over 20 years at an average density of four observations per 10 years.

The frequency polygon

The next development to the histogram is the construction of a frequency polygon. In Figures 16.5–16.7, it will be noted that the histogram is, as it should be, based on the horizontal axis. To construct a frequency polygon we now add at each end of the distribution, an additional class of zero frequency. In practical terms this means no bars have been added. The reason for doing this is to satisfy the mathematical properties concerning frequency polygons. The point becomes clearer as the procedures for constructing polygons progress. In all cases these additional 'invisible' classes must be of the same width as those immediately adjacent, but, as the frequency is zero, no bar is drawn. This means in the case of Figure 16.5 that the first 'invisible' class extends from zero to 10 at the lower end, and from 70 to 80 at the upper end. This is because in each case the category class interval is 10 and, in fact, the chart represents an equal class interval distribution. The frequency polygon is then constructed by drawing a straight line that joins up the class marks (mid-points) of each of the bars including the mid-point of the 'invisible' bars (see Figure 16.8).

The important point to note is that the area represented by the polygon is equal to the area described by the histogram. In other words, the shaded areas correspond.

Advantages of histograms

The advantage of histograms and frequency polygons is that they allow us to visually compare the distribution of different sets of data. For example, we might compare the age distributions of customers at two different hairdressing salons in the Style Group via this method. The ultimate situation in terms of diagrammatic representation of a frequency distribution can be regarded as the frequency curve when the edges of the

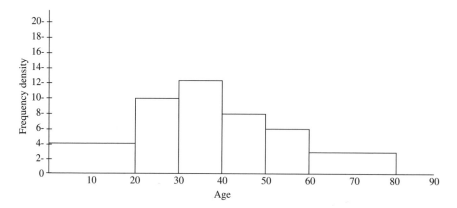

FIGURE 16.7 Correct histogram of the data shown in Table 16.4

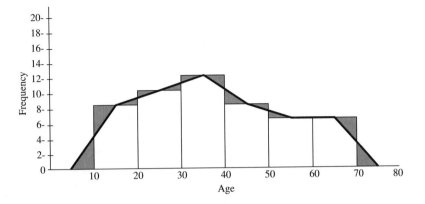

FIGURE 16.8 Histogram of the data shown in Table 16.3, together with the derived frequency polygon

polygon are effectively smoothed out. This occurs where the class intervals are small and there are a large number of observations resulting in a dense pattern.

Measures of central tendency

The most commonly used measures of central tendency are the 'averages' known as the *arithmetic mean*, the *median*, and the *mode*. Known also as measures of central location, they indicate in a literal sense key points around which a data set is located.

Arithmetic mean

The arithmetic mean is the most commonly used average (indeed it is usually referred to simply as *the* average) and is computed by adding together the values for all observations in a data set and then dividing by the number of items. The computation formula is:

$$\bar{x} = \sum_{i=1}^{n} x_i \Big/ n$$

The symbols may be explained as follows:

$\bar{x}$ pronounced 'x-bar' denotes the arithmetic mean of a sample;

$\sum$ pronounced 'sigma' means the 'the sum of';

x_i means all values of x where $x_1, x_2, x_3 \ldots, x_n$, represent the values of each observation in a data set. Thus i assumes, in turn, the values 1, 2, 3 and so on; and

n is the total number of observations in the data set.

So our formula reads 'The arithmetic mean is the sum of all values in the data set divided by the total number of observations in that set'.

Consider once again the array of data in Table 16.2. Adding together all the ages of the customers in the sample and dividing by the total number of observations, i.e. 50, the formula for the arithmetic mean is operationalized thus:

$$\bar{x} = \frac{(10 + 10 + 11 + 14 \ldots + 64)}{50}, \text{thus}$$

$$\bar{x} = \frac{1861}{50} = 37.22 \text{ (when given to two decimal places)}$$

So the arithmetic mean of the sample is 37.22, but remember, the 0.22 does not refer to months or days in respect of the customers' ages but to 0.22 of one year. That is, it represents just under one quarter (0.25) of a year, or just under three months. Another way of expressing this even more accurately would be to say 0.22 of a year represents some 80 days (i.e. $0.22 \times 365 = 80.3$ days). In point of fact we would more often than not simply express the average age as 37 years, since for general purposes a rounded figure is often sufficient and easier for the reader to grasp thus avoiding undue confusion or complexity. The decision on how to present values and the number of decimal places to give is a matter of judgement. In presenting results it is important to consider the form of presentation that is most helpful to the reader and appropriate in the context of the material being described. In many cases a rounded figure is sufficient although not so accurate. Where decimal values need to be given one decimal place is often sufficient.

Weighted arithmetic mean

Sometimes it is necessary to find the arithmetic mean of a number of means. Suppose our London salon conducted its research exercise each week for three weeks and the mean ages for each resulting sample were 37.22, 44.64 and 51.27. If the number of ages observed in each sample is the same (50) then computing the average of the means will be:

$$\bar{x} = \frac{37.22 + 44.64 + 51.27}{3} = \frac{133.13}{3} = 44.38$$

While this computation yields the correct answer on this occasion, the computation method itself is inappropriate and in error. If the original data sets from which each of the means was calculated were drawn from samples of a different size the application of this formula would produce an incorrect value. Instead, to find the 'mean of means', properly known as the *weighted arithmetic mean*, it is appropriate to follow the undernoted procedure.

Step 1 Multiply the mean for each sample (data set) by the number of observations in that data set (the frequency) and add these values together to obtain a grand total.

Step 2 Divide this grand total by the grand total of observations aggregated over all the data sets.

Following this formula through for our existing data we get:

Step 1 $(37.22 \times 50) + (44.64 \times 50) + (51.27 \times 50) = 1861 + 2232 + 2563.5 = 6656.5$

Step 2 $\dfrac{6656.5}{150} = 44.38$

Thus the correct weighted mean value covering the ages of guests at all three hairdressing salons is 44.38 years but we have taken into account the size of each individual sample in our calculations. Note that if we write our formula in statistical notation rather than simply describe it, it looks like this:

$$\bar{x}\left(\sum_{i=1}^{r} f_i \bar{x}_i\right) \bigg/ \sum_{i=1}^{r} f_i$$

Where:

f_i is the frequency, or number of observations, in sample i;

i denotes the sample number running from 1 to r. In this case 'i' runs from 1 to 3 as there are three samples in all;

$\bar{x}_i$ is the mean value for sample i; and

$\sum_{i=1}^{r} f_i$ is the total number of observations across all samples.

To understand this formula more clearly, it is useful to show how the method works for calculating the weighted mean for data sets comprising different numbers of observations. Let us, therefore, assume that:

- 37.22 is the mean of the original data set of 50 observations (which of course it is);
- 44.64 is the mean of a data set of 40 observations; and
- 51.27 is the mean of a data set of 30 observations.

Obviously to add these numbers together and simply divide by three would be incorrect as the weighted mean must reflect the different balance in the size of the three groups. Thus, we must use the formula for the weighted arithmetic mean described above. In this case there are three samples. Therefore, 'i' assumes the values 1, 2 and 3 and the three frequency values (f_1, f_2 and f_3) = 50, 40 and 30 respectively. The mean ages of customers for each sample are also stated, i.e. $\bar{x}_1 = 37.22$, $\bar{x}_2 = 44.64$ and $\bar{x}_3 = 51.27$. Thus, we can construct the formula for the weighted mean as follows:

$$\sum_{i=1}^{3} f_i \bar{x}_i = (50 \times 37.22) + (40 \times 44.64) + (30 \times 51.27)$$

$$\text{or } 1861 + 1785.6 + 1538.1 = 5184.7$$

$$\sum_{i=1}^{3} f_i = 50 + 40 + 30 = 120$$

Thus, the weighted mean value:

$$\bar{x} = \frac{5184.7}{120} = 43.21 \text{ years}$$

Note in this situation we have retained the decimal places during the calculation to ensure a greater degree of accuracy in the final result. Developing the notational aspects further we can introduce the symbol 'w' to denote the weight given to each mean value where:

$$w_i = \frac{f_i}{\sum\limits_{i=1}^{r} f_i}$$

In other words, in our example we have utilized three weights, w_1, w_2 and w_3 to obtain a weighted mean and these weights assumed the values 50/120, 40/120 and 30/120, or 5/12, 1/3, and 1/4. Thus another way of presenting the generalized formula is to say the weighted mean value can be expressed by :

$$\bar{x} = \sum\limits_{i=1}^{r} w_i \bar{x}_i$$

The weighted arithmetic mean is important because a common error made by students when handling statistics in dissertation and project work is to find they have calculated an overall mean from the means of different samples (or sub-samples of a larger sample) using only the simple arithmetic mean formula when the weighted arithmetic mean procedure should have been used.

Calculating means relating to grouped data

Often it is necessary to calculate means for grouped data, that is from data contained in a frequency distribution table rather than an ungrouped array. Consider our data in Table 16.3. To calculate the arithmetic mean for such data it is necessary to know the class marks (mid-points) for each class as was the case in the construction of the frequency polygon. These are shown in the modified Table 16.5. Again, eschewing complex notations, we can follow the undernoted steps to calculate the arithmetic mean of grouped data as may be presented in a frequency distribution table.

Step 1 Multiply the class mark by the frequency for each class and add together the products of these calculations to arrive at a grand total.
Step 2 Divide this total by the total number of observations in the overall data set.

Following this procedure, Table 16.5 shows the outcome of the first stage to be 1870 which, divided by 50 (the result of the second stage), yields an arithmetic mean of 37.4 years . This varies slightly from the arithmetic mean derived from the ungrouped array of data and indicates one of the weaknesses of grouped data. Inevitably, the grouping of data and the use of class marks to represent all values in a class leads to a certain loss in accuracy. In the case of our salon example the loss of accuracy is not too great. Reference to the raw data shows the individual values are fairly well spread among each of the classes. Also each class interval is not overly wide. A greater distortion will occur where class intervals are wide and where data values are unevenly

TABLE 16.5 Grouped frequency distribution of customers' ages in the Style Hairdressing Salon, London, sample with the addition of class marks

Class	f	R(f)%	Class marks	f × CM
10 and under 20	8	16	15	120
20 and under 30	10	20	25	250
30 and under 40	12	24	35	420
40 and under 50	8	16	45	360
50 and under 60	6	12	55	330
60 and under 70	6	12	65	390
				1870

distributed within each class. Clearly, the class mark will then only be an approximation to the true mean of the data values within each class.

It is important to dwell on this aspect of data presentation for a moment as it has implications for the way data is collected in many questionnaires. Often it is easier for practical reasons to ask a respondent to indicate personal characteristics such as age or income according to broad groupings. For instance, it may be easier and less sensitive to ask people to indicate which age groups they fall into rather than ask for their exact age. In respect of income groups not only may people be shy about stating their exact income, but they may find it difficult to be totally precise. In the latter case the question should always state whether it is 'net' or 'gross' income which is required and whether such aspects as interest on investments or bonus payments should be included. Setting aside these definitional points, it clearly may be considerably easier for a respondent to indicate their income group rather than give a precise income amount. The problem is that the resultant information will be less accurate than if raw data had been obtained. Thus subsequent calculations will be less exact. In many cases, the researcher will accept this situation in the interest of obtaining information from respondents. If, however, it is important to have more precise continuous data for the purpose of obtaining more accurate measures, or for conducting certain statistical tests as described in the next chapter, then this must be borne in mind when designing the questionnaire.

The median

The median is the value of the observation in a data set that divides that data set in half. To find the median, observations must be ordered in an array of ascending values, for example:

4, 4, 5, 6, 6, 6, 7, 8, 9, 10, 10, 11, 11, 12, 12

In this case, the median is 8 because there are an equal number of observations above and below it. It will be noted, however, that the list above contains an odd number of items making location of the median an easy task. For an array of data where the total number of observations is even, as is our case (Table 16.2), there is no single observation which can be chosen such that half the data set is above and half below the median. In such circumstances, it is usual to take the mean value of the two central observations in the data set, in this case the twenty-fifth and twenty-sixth observations. Note an effective 'shorthand' way of calculating the observations in a data array which identify the median is to divide the total number of observations plus one by two. In this case the result, is 25.5. Furthermore, since the values of the twenty-fifth and twenty-sixth observations are the same (36), the median is computed as 36. If, on the other hand, the numbers had been different say 36 and 37, then the median would have been 36.5. In practice the median is only quoted on limited occasions. It may usefully be quoted alongside quartile values or where a distribution is skewed (as discussed later in the chapter). Otherwise, the arithmetic mean is more frequently used.

Medians in respect of grouped data

Should it be necessary to find the median of grouped data, then it is first necessary to construct a table showing cumulative frequencies. Table 16.6 shows such a table using the data on the ages of our London salon customers. The cumulative frequency (column 3) indicates in each case the frequency with which observations fall *under* a particular value – thus in terms of actual values there are 30 people aged less than 40 years in our data set. In contrast, the 'relative cumulative frequency' is an expression of the cumulative frequency shown in percentage terms. So 60 per cent of people in our sample are aged less than 40 years.

Returning to the shorthand method of calculating the location of a median we know that for our data the median is located between the twenty-fifth and twenty-sixth observation. The median must therefore lie in the 30 and under 40 age class. The cumulative frequency shows that the 18th observation lies on the border of the 20 and under 30 class, thus we need to determine where on the scale the succeeding 7th and 8th points lie (i.e. $25 - 18 = 7$ and $26 - 18 = 8$). Making the assumption that

TABLE 16.6 Grouped frequency distribution of customers' ages at the Style Hairdressing Salon, London, showing 'cumulative frequency' and 'relative cumulative frequency' data

Class	f	Cumulative frequency	Relative cumulative frequency %
(1)	(2)	(3)	(4)
10 and under 20	8	8	16
20 and under 30	10	18	36
30 and under 40	12	30	60
40 and under 50	8	38	76
50 and under 60	6	44	88
60 and under 70	6	50	100

observations in the median class 30 and under 40 are evenly spread, which is again a substantial but necessary assumption, we find the 25th observation must lie 7/12 (seven-twelfths) of the way into the median class and the 26th, 8/12 (eight-twelfths) given there are 12 observations in the class. Since the class interval represents an incremental addition of 10 years, the 25th point is $7/12 \times 10 = 5.83$, and the 26th point $8/12 \times 10 = 6.67$. Thus the mid-point between these two is at $(5.83 + 6.67)/2 = 6.25$. Adding this to the lower limit of the median class, i.e. 30 years, we determine the median to be at 36.25 (30 + 6.25) years. We can write this, somewhat crudely as follows:

$$\text{Median} = \text{LCL (median)} + \left[\frac{(n+1)/2 - \text{cf}(LC)}{\text{f(median)}} \times \text{w(median)} \right]$$

The notation is as follows:

LCL (median)   is the lower class limit of the median class (in our case 30);
$(n + 1)/2$ is the number of observations plus one divided by two (i.e. 51/2 = 25.5);
cf (LC) is the cumulative frequency of the class immediately below the median class (in our case 18);
f (median)   is the frequency of the median class (in our case 12); and
w (median)   is the width of the median class (10 years).

By substitution we therefore obtain the median of our grouped data to be equal to:

$$30 + \left[\frac{(25.5 - 18)}{12} \times 10 \right] \text{ or } (30 + 6.25) = 36.25$$

The accuracy of this measure will, once again, be dependent on how individual values are distributed within the classes. In practice, it may be more meaningful and less onerous to refer to the cumulative frequencies and point out in the case of our example that just over one third (36 per cent) of the customers were aged under 30 and 60 per cent were aged under 40. This point is taken up again in the discussion on inter-quartile ranges later in the chapter.

The mode

With ungrouped data, the mode is simply the observation that occurs most frequently in any data set and where two values occur equally often the distribution is said to be bi-modal as opposed to unimodal. For our ungrouped data set, there is only one mode and this is equal to 36 years (see Tables 16.1 and 16.2). As Cunningham (1991: 27) notes, with ungrouped data, the mode may be atypical of the whole data set. Modes are therefore most useful with grouped data. To ascertain the mode of a grouped data set we may review the structure of a histogram as described by Figure 16.9 or we may progress through to other computational methods. In respect of the histogram method, the modal class is the one with the greatest frequency or frequency density (the tallest class once all classes have been standardized, where necessary, to a base class). To calculate the actual value of the mode in such cases two lines must be drawn which run, respectively, from:

(a) the top right of the modal class to top right of the preceding class; and
(b) the top left of the modal class to top left of the succeeding class.

Figure 16.9 shows how this geometric method operates. The result suggests the mode for our grouped data to be around 33 (in fact, it was found to be 33.33), i.e. some distance from the ungrouped mode of 36. This situation might be explained by recalling that in grouping data, we submerge individual values in classes with a concomitant loss of accuracy. In fact, it is often more useful and meaningful to simply indicate the boundaries of the modal class rather than attempt to calculate a mode in respect of grouped data. In other words, rather than attempting to say the most common age is around 33, which is not entirely accurate or representative of the situation, it would be more meaningful to say that more people fell within the 30 and under 40 age group than any other group described by Figure 16.9. Should you wish, however, to calculate the mode of grouped data by computational methods there are several variations of a basic formula (e.g. Cunningham 1991: 28; Harper 1991: 121–122) and students interested in the mathematical rationale underlying these variations should consult these and similar sources.

To conclude, while all measures of central tendency discussed in this section are useful to some degree, the arithmetic mean is the most widely used statistic as it is the only one to possess further mathematical properties. For certain lower level data it is not, however, possible to calculate arithmetic means. This aspect was referred to in Chapter 14 and includes the calculation of arithmetic means in respect of nominal and ordinal data (see below). It has also been shown that the calculation of averages in respect of grouped data should be treated with caution where considerations involving loss in accuracy are regarded as important.

Limitations in respect of lower level data

It will be recalled that nominal data indicates no ordering but simply the number of observations falling into categories described generally according to some descriptive

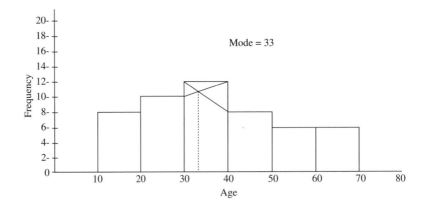

FIGURE 16.9 Calculation of the mode from the histogram shown in Figure 16.5

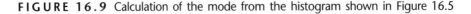

label such as the number of students in a statistics class with blue eyes, blonde hair and so on. Consider therefore the following example.

Eye colour of students in a statistics class (sample size = 50)

Eye colour	Number of students	%
Blue	20	40
Brown	30	60
Green	10	20
	50	100

Clearly there is no way of calculating an arithmetic mean in respect of such data since the variable 'eye colour' assumes no numerical value. Thus, although we might assign numerical codes to each of the three groups, i.e. blue =1, brown = 2, green = 3 for ease of recording, the calculation of an arithmetic mean would have no meaning. Similarly, it was stated in Chapter 14 that the calculation of an arithmetic mean in respect of ordinal data represented in the form of rating scales should be handled with care.

Skew and the relationship of mean, median and mode

Skew is the term used to denote the shape of data represented by a frequency distribution or frequency curve. In many instances the data builds up slowly from the left to a central peak or modal point and then declines to the right. If the peak is at the centre and the slopes of the graph to either side are equal then the distribution is said to be symmetrical. If the peak or modal point lies to one side or other of centre, the distribution is said to be *skewed* and the direction of the skew can be described as having a positive or negative value. A *positive skew* is when the peak lies to the left and a *negative skew* when it lies to the right. The further the peak lies from the centre of the horizontal axis, the more the distribution is said to be skewed. Figure 16.10 represents these concepts graphically.

It can also be seen that the three principal measures of location; the arithmetic mean, median and mode, vary in their position according to whether a distribution is

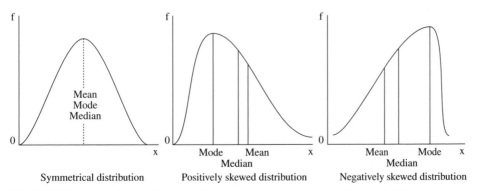

FIGURE 16.10 Symmetrical, positively and negatively skewed data distribution

symmetrical or positively or negatively skewed and, in particular, in symmetrical distributions all three measures of central tendency coincide. On the other hand, where the distribution is positively skewed then the mean and median are pulled to the right of the mode and where it is negatively skewed, the mean and median are pulled to its left. In a positively skewed distribution, the mean will have the greatest value, the mode the lowest value and the median will fall between the two. In a negatively skewed distribution, the mean will have a lower value than both median and mode, whereas the mode will have the highest value. Consider values for our grouped data as computed earlier. These are:

$$\text{Mean} = 37.40 \qquad \text{Median} = 36.25 \qquad \text{Mode} = 33.33$$

From this, we can see as would be expected from external visual inspection of the histogram on Figure 16.9 the distribution is slightly positively skewed and the mean therefore has the greatest value, the mode the lowest and the median is between the two and, in fact, based on the raw data, the median and mode are identical with a value of 36 years meaning the distribution is not too far from being symmetrical.

Measures of dispersion

As well as describing aspects of distributions in terms of measures of central location, as above, we can describe distributions in terms of their spread. Sometimes known as measures of variation, measures of dispersion describe how scattered or dispersed the data values are. The simplest indicators are known as quartiles and effectively show how the sample values are spread across quarterly intervals. They are therefore not dissimilar in concept to the median which divides the sample values in half. For this reason quartile and median values are often quoted together. In contrast, other more sophisticated measures of dispersion reveal how extensive or not the clustering of the data is, particularly around the arithmetic mean. The two most important measures of this nature are the standard deviation and variance – these, together with a measure known as the 'mean deviation', identify the extent to which any set of observations deviate from the arithmetic mean. In this section we shall focus on quartiles first and then proceed to the other more sophisticated measures of dispersion.

Quartiles

As the term indicates, the quartiles indicate at which points the data falls into quarterly intervals. The lower point is known as the 'lower quartile' (Q1) and the upper as the 'upper quartile' (Q3). The area in between is known as the 'inter-quartile range' and includes the median, which as stated earlier reflects the mid-point of the data values. In the case of continuous data, the lower quartile value (Q1) is determined by first ranking the data in order as in Table 16.2, and then dividing the total sample size by 4. The result, in this case, where the sample size equals 50 is 12.5.

This means the lower quartile lies between the ages of the 12th and 13th customers. Thus the lower quartile value is 24 years, i.e. $(23 + 25)/2$. The upper quartile value is computed in a similar way but by dividing the sample size by three-quarters. Thus the upper quartile value falls at the 37.5 point or between the ages of the 37th and 38th customer. Thus the value is 48 years, i.e. $(47 + 49)/2$. To summarize, we can state one quarter of the customers were aged 24 years or under, while one quarter were aged 48 years or more. In addition, we can quote the inter-quartile range by stating that 50 per cent of the customers were aged between 25 and 47 years of age.

To calculate the quartile values for grouped data, it is first necessary to calculate the cumulative frequencies as in column three of Table 16.6. The lower quartile value still lies between the ages of the 12th and 13th customer since the sample size remains unchanged. However, because the data is now arrayed in classes, it is not possible to be so precise in the calculations. It can be seen the value must lie in the class aged 20 and under 30 but to calculate a value it is necessary once again to make assumptions about how the ages of the customers are distributed within this class. It is assumed the distribution is even and the lower quartile is calculated as follows:

$$Q1 = 20 + \frac{(12.5 - 8)}{10} \times 10 = 24.5$$

More generally, the formula is:

$$Q1 = \text{LCL}(Q1) + \left[\frac{n/4 - cf(LC)}{f(Q1)} \right] \times w(Q1)$$

Where:

Q1	is the lower quartile value;
LCL (Q1)	is the lower class limit of the class containing the lower quartile (in this case, 20);
n	is the sample size (in this case, 50, hence $n/4 = 12.5$);
$cf(LC)$	is the cumulative frequency of the class immediately below that containing the lower quartile (in this case, 8);
w(Q1)	is the width of the class interval containing the lower quartile (in this case, 10); and
$f(Q1)$	is the frequency of the class interval containing the lower quartile (also 10)

To calculate the upper quartile, we follow a similar procedure. As noted earlier the upper quartile (Q3) fell at the 37.5 point or between the 37th and 38th observations. It therefore follows from looking at the cumulative frequencies that the upper quartile value is in the class denoted by the ages 40 and under 50 and is 7.5 points above the cumulative frequency calculated for the immediately preceding class. Thus, the calculation for the upper quartile is:

$$Q3 = 40 + \frac{(37.5 - 30)}{8} \times 10 = 49.4 \text{ years}$$

or expressed in more general terms:

$$Q3 = \mathrm{LCL}(Q3) + \left[\frac{3n/4 - cf(\mathrm{LC})}{f(Q3)}\right] \times \mathrm{w}(Q3)$$

Where Q3 reflects the relevant upper quartile values and can be substituted in the description of terms stated for calculating Q1.

Mean deviation

The mean deviation is the simplest measures of dispersion which uses all the observations in a data set. In short, it indicates by how much *on average* the observations in a data set differ from their arithmetic mean. Think about this. What the mean deviation tells us is the average distance by which all items in a data set differ from their mean. Consider the numbers 2, 3, 4, 5 and 6. The *range* of these values (i.e. the difference between the highest and lowest) is 4 and the mean is also 4. The numbers 2 and 6 are each two points away from the mean while the numbers 3 and 5 are both one point away. The remaining number is the mean (4). If we average these absolute differences, that is the signs are ignored, we obtain the values $2 + 1 + 0 + 1 + 2 = 6$. Since there are five values in the data set dividing 6 by 5 results in a mean deviation of 1.2.

To summarize, the mean deviation is found by summing the absolute deviations of all values from the mean and dividing by the total number of items. The formula may be written:

$$\text{Mean deviation} = \frac{\sum_{i=1}^{n} |x_i - \bar{x}|}{n}$$

Note the vertical lines to either side of the expression $|x_i - \bar{x}|$ do not mean divide but are an instruction to find the absolute difference between the values enclosed by the lines. Thus positive and negative signs are ignored. If this was not done the result of the summation would be zero.

To calculate the mean deviation of the ungrouped data in Table 16.2, we first recall that the arithmetic mean was earlier calculated as 37.22 years. The next step is to calculate by how much each value deviates from the mean of 37.22. The results are shown in column 2 of Table 16.7. These values are then summed across all observations and divided by 50, the total sample size. Thus, the mean deviation of the sample is: $628.32/50 = 12.57$ years.

The procedure for finding the mean deviation of grouped data is rather more complex. First, if the mean is not known, it must be found in the prescribed manner stated above for calculating the mean of grouped data. Second, the absolute difference between the class mark (the class mid-point) and the mean is calculated for each class and multiplied by the frequency for that class (see column 5 of Table 16.8). The resultant figures are then summed and divided by the total frequency for the data set. Table 16.8 shows the outcome of this process and reveals the mean deviation for the grouped data on ages to be $664/50 = 13.28$. Note the result is an approximation to the result obtained from calculations based on the raw data.

TABLE 16.7 Mean deviations of values in Table 16.2

Ages	Absolute deviation from the mean	f	Total	Cumulative total
(1)	(2)	(3)	(4)	(5)
10	27.22	2	54.44	54.44
11	26.22	1	26.22	80.66
14	23.22	1	23.22	103.88
16	21.22	1	21.22	125.10
17	20.22	1	20.22	145.32
18	19.22	1	19.22	164.54
19	18.22	1	18.22	182.76
21	16.22	1	16.22	198.98
22	15.22	1	15.22	214.20
23	14.22	2	28.44	242.64
25	12.22	1	12.22	254.86
27	10.22	1	10.22	265.08
28	9.22	1	9.22	274.30
29	8.22	3	24.66	298.96
34	3.22	2	6.44	305.40
35	2.22	1	2.22	307.62
36	1.22	5	6.10	313.72
37	0.22	2	0.44	314.16
39	1.78	2	3.56	317.72
41	3.78	1	3.78	321.50
42	4.78	1	4.78	326.28
43	5.78	3	17.34	343.62
47	9.78	2	19.56	363.18
49	11.78	1	11.78	374.96
50	12.78	1	12.78	387.74
53	15.78	1	15.78	403.52
54	16.78	2	33.56	437.08
55	17.78	1	17.78	454.86
58	20.78	1	20.78	475.64
61	23.78	1	23.78	499.42
62	24.78	2	49.56	548.98
63	25.78	1	25.78	574.76
64	26.78	2	53.56	628.32

Note: The arithmetic mean $\bar{x}$ is 37.22 and the sum of the absolute deviations where n equals 50 (see column 5) is $\sum_{i=1}^{n} \left| x_i - \bar{x} \right| = 628.32$

TABLE 16.8 Data required for the computation of the mean deviation using grouped data where the mean based on grouped data is 37.4 years

Class	Class mark	f	$|cm - \bar{x}|$	$f|cm - \bar{x}|$
(1)	(2)	(3)	(4)	(5)
10 and under 20	15	8	22.4	179.2
20 and under 30	25	10	12.4	124.0
30 and under 40	35	12	2.4	28.8
40 and under 50	45	8	7.6	60.8
50 and under 60	55	6	17.6	105.6
60+	65	6	27.6	165.6
TOTALS		50		664.0

Note: in the table, the notation 'cm' represents the value of the class marks and $|cm - \bar{x}|$ donotes the absolute deviation of each class mark from the mean of the grouped data, which is then multiplied by the frequency relative to each class as shown in column 5.

Standard deviation and variance

The standard deviation and the associated concept of variance are together by far the most important measures of dispersion encountered in statistics. In the calculation of the mean deviation, the signs (positive or negative) of the differences were ignored. This is because in any data set, the positive and negative deviations from the mean will always cancel each other out, leaving a value of zero. Whereas the mean deviation gets around this problem of signs by taking absolute values, the calculation of the standard deviation achieves this by squaring the deviations, thereby removing all negative signs. Note, in mathematics multiplying two negative values together produces a positive value. Thus, by summing the squares of the deviations, the *sum of squares* or *sum of squared differences* is arrived at and the mean of the 'sum of squares' is known as the *variance*. The square root of the variance is the *standard deviation*.

The sample variance is normally denoted as s^2 whereas the population variance is denoted by the Greek letter σ^2 (pronounced 'sigma squared'). Likewise the standard deviation of a sample is denoted by 's ' or sometimes 'SD' and the standard deviation for the population as 'σ'. In inferential statistics the sample statistic 's ' may be used as an estimator of the population parameter 'σ'. In this case, to calculate the variance of the sample the sum of squares is divided by (n−1) rather than 'n' in the formula shown below. This produces what is known as an unbiased estimate of 'σ'. To go further into the reasons for this is beyond the scope of this text and, in fact, the division by (n−1) rather than by 'n' makes little difference where the sample size is large.

It is also worth noting that the variance is a value which is based on the aggregation of squared units. Thus, the standard deviation, which is the square root of the variance, returns the measurement to ordinary units compatible with the original data. As we saw with the calculation of the mean deviation above, the calculations involved in deriving these statistics or population parameters can be a laborious process when calculated manually. Therefore, the use of programmable calculators with a built-in statistical function, or the use of an appropriate computer package such as Minitab or SPSS, are necessary aids to conducting such analyses. For those interested in the mathematics, there are ways of introducing modifications to the formulae that lessen the number of steps in the calculation procedures, although even these are no substitute for computer packages or a calculator's statistical function. In the discussion that follows, the variance and standard deviation for our grouped and ungrouped data are calculated using the full, laborious, 'pencil and paper' approach in order to explain the processes.

Taking first the calculation of the variance and standard deviation for ungrouped data, the figures in Table 16.9 are derived from those given in Table 16.2.

From Table 16.9 it can be seen that the sum of squares $\sum f_i(x - \bar{x})^2$ (presented in simplified notational form) equals 11,832.7. Given the observations are from a sample, the sample variance is calculated using the formulae:

$$s^2 = \frac{\sum f(x - \bar{x})^2}{n - 1} = 11832.7/49 = 241.5$$

Therefore the standard deviation (s) is:

$$s = \sqrt{\frac{\sum f(x - \bar{x})^2}{n - 1}} = \sqrt{241.5} = 15.54$$

Notice that an obvious alternative to calculating the standard deviation where the variance is known is simply to find the square root of the variance.

To calculate the variance and standard deviation of grouped data, the following shortened procedure is appropriate. It represents a modified series of steps to the fuller approach based on the formula:

$$s^2 = \frac{\sum f_i(cm_i - \bar{x})^2}{\sum f_i} \quad \text{(for grouped data)}$$

In practice this formula can be reduced to the following:

$$\frac{\sum f_i(cm_i)^2}{\sum f_i} - \bar{x}^2$$

where:

cm_i equals the class mark for class i;
f_i is the frequency for class i;
$\bar{x}$ is the mean of the grouped data

Thus the simplified steps for calculating the variance are:

Step 1 First, the mean is calculated in the appropriate manner. For our salon example it will be recalled the mean was calculated as 37.4 years. This value is then squared.

TABLE 16.9 Raw calculations for use in computing variance and standard deviation of ungrouped data in Table 16.2

x	f	$(x - \bar{x})$	$(x - \bar{x})^2$	$f(x - \bar{x})^2$
10	2	−27.22	740.93	1481.86
11	1	−26.22	687.49	687.49
14	1	−23.22	539.17	539.17
16	1	−21.22	450.29	450.29
17	1	−20.22	408.85	408.85
18	1	−19.22	369.41	369.41
19	1	−18.22	331.97	331.97
21	1	−16.22	263.09	263.09
22	1	−15.22	231.65	231.65
23	2	−14.22	202.21	404.41
25	1	−12.22	149.33	149.33
27	1	−10.22	104.45	104.45
28	1	−9.22	85.01	85.01
29	3	−8.22	67.57	202.71
34	2	−3.22	10.37	20.74
35	1	−2.22	4.93	4.93
36	5	−1.22	1.49	7.45
37	2	−0.22	0.05	0.10
39	2	+1.78	3.17	6.34
41	1	+3.78	14.29	14.29
42	1	+4.78	22.85	22.85
43	3	+5.78	33.41	100.23
47	2	+9.78	95.65	191.30
49	1	+11.78	138.77	138.77
50	1	+12.78	163.33	163.33
53	1	+15.78	249.01	249.01
54	2	+16.78	281.57	563.14
55	1	+17.78	316.13	316.13
58	1	+20.78	431.81	431.81
61	1	+23.78	565.49	565.49
62	2	+24.78	614.05	1228.10
63	1	+25.78	664.61	664.61
64	2	+26.78	717.17	1434.34

Note: The mean ($\bar{x}$) of the ungrouped data equals 37.22 years, thus $\sum f(x - \bar{x})^2 = 11832.7$.

Step 2 The class mark (mid-point) for each class is squared and multiplied by the relevant class frequency.

Step 3 The values obtained from Step 2 are then added and divided by the total number of observations.

Step 4 The results of Step 1 are subtracted from the result of Step 3.

To obtain the standard deviation the square root of the variance is taken. A brief examination of Table 16.10 should be sufficient to explain how the four instructions outlined above relate to the formula and the example based on the grouped data of the London salon's customers.

Definition of a standard deviation

It has been said that the standard deviation is a measure of dispersion, which indicates the spread of the data values around the arithmetic mean. But what is the standard deviation exactly? A useful way of conceptualizing this most important measure of dispersion is given by Rowntree (1981: 54):

> Quoting the standard deviation of a distribution is a way of indicating a kind of 'average' amount by which all the values deviate from the mean. The greater the dispersion, the bigger the deviations and the bigger the standard ('average') deviation.

Thus if it were found for two different samples of hairdressing salon customers that the average age was 37 years in both instances but the standard deviation was 12 years in one case and 18 years in the other, then the second sample would include customers covering a wider age span.

TABLE 16.10 Calculations for use in computing variance and standard deviation of grouped data in Table 16.3

Class	cm	f	fcm	cm^2	$f(cm^2)$
10 and under 20	15	8	120	225	1800
20 and under 30	25	10	250	625	6250
30 and under 40	35	12	420	1225	14700
40 and under 50	45	8	360	2025	16200
50 and under 60	55	6	330	3025	18150
60 and under 70	65	6	390	4225	25350
TOTALS		50	1870	–	82450

Step 1 $\quad \bar{x} = \dfrac{\sum fcm}{\sum f} = \dfrac{1870}{50} = 37.4$ Hence $\bar{x}^2 = 1398.76$

Step 2 & 3 $\quad \dfrac{\sum f(cm^2)}{\sum f} = \dfrac{82450}{50} = 1649$

Step 4 $\quad$ Variance $= 1649 - 1398.76 = 250.24$

Standard deviation $= \sqrt{250.24} = 15.82$

Normal distributions

The standard deviation is a particularly important and useful statistic in all instances where the distribution of the data conforms to a symmetrical, or almost symmetrical, pattern and is unimodal. In short, it is particularly useful where the distribution conforms to the familiar 'bell-shaped' curve known as the *normal distribution*. In this case the arithmetic mean, median and mode have the same value and the standard deviation can usefully be used to describe the spread of the data around the mean according to given percentage values. In the case where data follows a perfect normal distribution curve, it will be found that approximately 68 per cent of the data values fall within plus or minus one standard deviation of the mean, 95 per cent within plus or minus two standard deviations, and 99 per cent, or virtually all the data values, lie within plus or minus three standard deviations of the mean (Hannagan 1988: 184). Other percentage values can also be calculated by reference to statistical tables describing percentage values under the normal curve (see Appendix A for this and subsequent statistical values).

Figure 16.11 describes the classic bell-shape for a normal distribution. In practice, many variables have frequency distributions which conform, or almost conform, to this general type. They include variables relating to such basic biological characteristics as age, weight, and height of the population.

Based on our sample of the ages of London salon customers the value of various statistics have now been computed using raw and grouped data. These are listed in Table 16.11.

It will be seen that the arithmetic mean, mode, and median of the data are close together and, as stated before, the distribution is slightly positively skewed with a standard deviation of 15.54 years. Reference to Table 16.2 shows, in fact, 60 per cent of the values fall within plus or minus one standard deviation of the mean, that is, between 21.68 and 52.76 years (i.e. 37.22 ± 15.34) and all the values (100 per cent) fall within plus or minus two standard deviations. It can therefore be seen that the

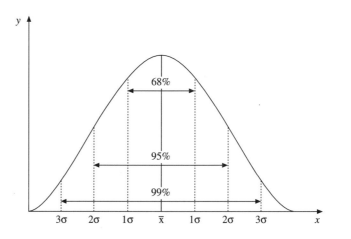

FIGURE 16.11 The standard normal distribution

distribution tends towards normality although, in practice, the researcher may wish to apply certain tests which examine the degree of skewness and peakedness (known as kurtosis) before making final judgements. To describe the nature of these concepts is beyond the scope of this text and the interested reader is referred to texts by Milewski (1994: 65–67) and Kanji (1993: 42–43). For the purposes of subsequent illustration, it is assumed the ages of our sample of salon customers are drawn from a normally distributed population.

Inferences based on the normal curve

We have now discussed aspects of the *normal distribution* and, in Chapter 15, the *concept of probability*. These two important aspects of statistical theory are now brought together as they have particular implications for what follows in the subsequent chapters relating to statistical tests and for the development of the discussions contained in Chapter 8 concerning sampling.

   In fact, all the examples given in this section of the book are based on theoretical samples drawn from wider populations and T. J. Hannagan, in his useful text *Mastering Statistics* (1988: 184), points out that, although we cannot expect a sample to be an exact replica of the population from which it is drawn, the best estimate of both the population mean and standard deviation are the corresponding sample statistics. This assumes, of course, that the sample has been drawn appropriately at random from a normally distributed population. Moreover, in general, the larger the sample the more representative it will be of the population from which it has been drawn (see again Chapter 8).

   Taking the discussion a stage further, it is possible to utilize these concepts to great advantage when making predictions about population parameters based on sample data or when drawing inferences about differences between samples. These aspects will be developed further in the next two chapters, but it is useful to touch

TABLE 16.11 Statistics relating to sample of customers of the Style Hairdressing Salon, London, based on raw and grouped data

	Raw data	Grouped data
Mode	36	33.33
Median	36	36.25
Mean	37.22	37.4
Lower quartile (25%)	24	24.5
Upper quartile (75%)	48	49.4
Inter-quartile range (middle 50%)	25–47	24.5–49.4
Mean deviation	12.57	13.28
Standard deviation	15.54	15.82
Variance	241.5	250.24

briefly here upon another important and related statistic known as the *standard error of the mean*. Often referred to notationally as the 'SE', this can be defined as:

$$\text{SE (Mean)} = \frac{\text{Standard deviation of the sample (s)}}{\sqrt{\text{sample size (n)}}}$$

Utilizing the properties of the normal distribution, it can be shown the true mean of a population lies within different intervals of the sample mean with different levels of probability. For example, the standard error of the mean relating to our salon customers equals: $15.54 / \sqrt{50} = 15.54 / 7.07 = 2.2$ years. Thus it is likely 68 times out of 100 (or approximately 2 in 3 times) that the true mean of the population lies within the range 37.22 ± 2.2. That is between 35 and 39 years (or the Mean $\pm 1 \times$ SE). If we wish to predict the range with greater confidence then the rule of plus or minus two standard errors (or strictly a value of 1.96) can be applied to give a 95 per cent level of confidence to our estimate. In this case, it is estimated the true mean of the population lies between 33 and 42 years.

Coefficient of variation

Just as the standard deviation and variance indicate the spread in values of a data set, the *coefficient of variation* may be used to compare the spread of two separate data sets. It is a particularly useful statistic where the units of measurement differ or where the same unit of measurement is employed but the values for the two data sets vary so much in magnitude as to make any direct comparison misleading (Fleming and Nellis 1993: 48–49).

To calculate the coefficient of variation for a data set the standard deviation is described relative to its mean. Thus, the coefficient of variation can be expressed as:

Coefficient of Variation $= \frac{s}{\bar{x}} \times 100$ (where it is expressed as a percentage value)

For our ungrouped data the coefficient of variation is: $(15.54/37.22) \times 100 = 41.8$ which reflects the fact that, in this case, the standard deviation is reasonably large or almost half the value of the mean.

Let us now assume relevant statistics relating to the ages of a sample of customers visiting one of the other salons in the Style group are as follows: mean $= 51.2$ and standard deviation $= 12.54$. In this case the coefficient of variation is: $(12.54/51.27) \times 100 = 24.5$. In other words, although the average age is higher in the second sample the data is less widely distributed around its mean. Comparison between the two coefficients of variation reflects this difference.

Summary

This chapter has introduced the reader to many different methods for describing data sets. It has discussed ways in which arrays of numbers can be presented and grouped. It has highlighted the desirability of presenting data in tabular and graphical form and, while outlining the advantages of each method, has shown certain pitfalls to be avoided. Various charts have demonstrated how the frequency distributions of different data sets can be constructed. This led to considering the more important statistics a researcher may compute in order to show how a data set is distributed about its points of central tendency incorporating relevant measures of dispersion. Finally, the reader's attention has been drawn to the powerful benefits to be derived from statistics based on random samples especially where the concepts of the normal distribution and probability theory apply. The next two chapters discuss the benefits and methods involved in conducting principal statistical tests.

17

Statistical tests

In the last chapter considerable attention was given to ways in which various data sets can be described incorporating statistical measures. These measures, while permitting the researcher to explain the nature of a data set in terms of its frequency distribution and points of central location do not enable him or her to make deductions of an inferential nature. In Chapter 15 it was shown there are many situations which arise in the context of business and management studies where it is useful to draw inferences from sample data and place probability values on the likelihood of particular outcomes. In this chapter and the next we will explore further the area of inferential statistics. In particular, we will look at some of the techniques available for making deductions from sample data based on the application of statistical tests. Before doing this, it is first necessary to outline the meaning of specialized terms and concepts relating to the area of inferential statistics.

Purpose of statistical tests

The purpose of a statistical test is to enable a researcher to make some deduction about a data set. Statistical tests are devices contrived by mathematicians which permit analysts to determine whether or not some observed phenomenon is likely to be true. Note, the emphasis is on 'likely to be true' because, as with many things in life, we cannot always state a situation exists or an outcome will be achieved with absolute certainty. Thus, with reference to our example (see Chapter 16) we may want to infer facts about the average age of customers visiting the Style Hairdressing Salon in London during the survey period using the sample data. Discussions in Chapter 16 relating to the properties of the normal distribution showed deductions of this nature can be made providing the sample is selected at random from a normally distributed population. Furthermore, it was shown that probability values can be assigned to indicate the likelihood of various estimates falling within a given range of the mean.

Looking now at a different situation, we might progress to asking whether or not the average age of all customers visiting the Style Hairdressing Salon in London is similar to or distinctly different from the average age of customers visiting another salon in the group. Using the data already provided we note the average age of the sample of guests visiting the London salon was 37.2 years, while the average age of those visiting at a second salon in Glasgow was 51.3 years. On visual inspection, it would seem reasonable to hypothesize there is a difference. The value of a statistical test is it permits the researcher, given certain data conditions, to test this hypothesis.

In fact, what mathematicians have done is devise a series of statistical tests to suit different situations and data conditions. From the results of these tests researchers can make deductions regarding a whole set of research issues. Moreover, they can place a confidence factor or probability measure on the likelihood that a certain deduction is true.

Range of statistical tests

There are a large number of statistical tests that can be employed. Each one has been devised to cope with different types of data or research situations. Thus, it will be found there are groups of tests that are particularly applicable to selected disciplines. For example, there are tests applicable to dealing with experimental situations involving small samples. These include the range of tests employed by medical researchers or psychologists. On the other hand, there are tests that are suited to field trials such as the types of tests carried out by agriculturists. Because business and management studies cover a wide range of issues there are a number of different types of statistical tests that can be employed by students of these subjects.

Which test to choose

It was suggested in the initial paragraphs of Chapter 14 that for many students the problem of analysing statistical information seems frightening and often over-whelming. Likewise, the thought of conducting some form of statistical test may fill the student with fear and feelings of grave doubt. One of the reasons for this may be the rather daunting mathematical formulae that are often associated with such tests. Another may be the problem of knowing which test to choose from the sizeable list on offer. In fact, certain tests are only applicable when dealing with certain issues. This will become evident as the purpose of individual tests is described. Furthermore, certain tests can only be applied to certain types of data. Just as it is inappropriate to calculate an arithmetic mean in respect of nominal data, even when numerical values are assigned to each category, so it is inappropriate to use certain statistical tests in respect of certain types of data. This aspect will be explained more fully as the chapter progresses.

In fact, one of the principal considerations in deciding upon which test to use is to decide first of all upon the level of data being manipulated. That is, is it of a nominal, ordinal or interval nature and does it conform approximately to a normal distribution? These considerations are important and the principal distinction drawn between types of statistical tests is the distinction drawn between 'parametric' and 'non-parametric' tests.

'Parametric' and 'non-parametric' tests

Parametric tests can only be performed where the data conforms to a normal distribution and is of an interval or ratio nature. This range of tests includes the important and well-known student's t-test which is used to test differences between means of two data sets. In a different form, a 't-test' may also be used to assess whether or not some influence, or treatment, has resulted in a changed outcome such as whether or not a new diet has affected people's weight. Non-parametric tests, as might be expected, involve less rigorous conditions. These may be used on data of lower level not conforming to a normal frequency distribution.

Null hypotheses

Prior to conducting a statistical test it is necessary to establish what is known as a null hypothesis. This is expressed mathematically as H_0 and the alternative as H_1. In effect, the researcher sets up a hypothesis, or makes a statement which the test then challenges. When stating a null hypothesis, the normal procedure is to start by assuming no difference or change really exists. For instance, in our hairdressing salon example we may state the null hypothesis (H_0) as being that no real difference exists between the average age of customers visiting the London salon and the average age of those visiting the Glasgow unit. That is, the two samples have come from one general population of people spanning a wide age range.

In another quite different situation relating to a study measuring the effect of a diet on people's weights, we might state the null hypothesis by saying the change in diet effects no increase or decrease in people's weights The value of a statistical test is that it helps the researcher to decide whether or not the null hypothesis is true, or more precisely, whether or not it should be accepted. If the result of the test shows the null hypothesis should *not* be accepted, that is it should be rejected, then we can go on to say, with some degree of confidence, a difference does exist or a change has occurred.

Significance levels

It has been said that the results of a statistical test enable the researcher to state whether or not they believe the null hypothesis to be true. Moreover, reference to specialized statistical tables enables the researcher to state whether or not they believe a null hypothesis to be true with a given level of confidence or significance value. This is a probability measure. It will be seen that for each type of statistical test there is an appropriate table and publications containing comprehensive lists of tables can be purchased (Murdoch and Barnes 1986). These tables enable the researcher to decide whether or not the result they have obtained from a particular statistical test is significant and at what level. We will come back to this later with reference to specific examples.

First, however, it may be helpful to make it clear to the reader that just as we calculated such measures as the arithmetic mean, variance or standard deviation for a data set (see Chapter 16), so we can calculate a measure or value applicable to a certain type of statistical test. There are formulae for doing this and the initial step is to decide which test is appropriate to the research aspect being investigated and the type of data being analysed. In other words it is necessary, in the case of the latter, to establish whether the data is nominal, ordinal, or interval in nature (see Chapter 14) and whether or not the data is normally distributed. The researcher can then progress to calculating the required test statistic for the investigation under consideration. The next step is to refer to the appropriate statistical table for that test and obtain what is known as the relevant significance or probability level. To do this you may also need to state the number of degrees of freedom (df) appropriate to the data set. This is simply a number computed to indicate aspects about the size of the data set or the number of values involved. Example calculations are given with reference to the specific examples.

The significance level is presented in the statistical tables as a probability value normally in decimal terms i.e. 0.05 and 0.01. The value 0.05 is particularly important as it indicates the 95 per cent confidence limit. This limit is normally taken as the minimum for deciding upon whether or not a particular result is significant and whether or not the null hypothesis should be accepted or rejected. Thus, if we were to calculate the t-test statistic (shown later) in respect of the mean ages of the customers at our two hairdressing salons and found the value to be equal to or higher than that stated in the appropriate statistical table for the 0.05 level of significance, we would state the mean ages to be significantly different at the 95 per cent confidence level. Put another way, we would be 95 per cent confident in rejecting the null hypothesis, that is in making the statement that the average ages of the guests visiting the London and Glasgow salons are different. In other words, the two samples come from different populations.

It should be noted that anything lower than the 95 per cent confidence level, that is where the level is computed to be 94 per cent or less, means the null hypothesis is normally accepted and the result is regarded as not significant. Conversely, if the significance level is found to be higher, that is, it indicates a confidence level of 95 per cent or more has been achieved, then we say the observed difference or change is significant. The figure of 0.01 in a statistical table indicates, for instance, a 99 per cent level of confidence, or a highly significant result. For further explanation on this point the reader should consult Hinton (1995: 38).

Type I and II errors

It will be seen that in making statements regarding statistical tests and their associated significance levels there is an element of risk involved. For example, we may state on the basis of our test statistic that the average ages of the salon customers are different according to the 95 per cent confidence level. There would, however, be a 5 per cent chance that in making such a statement we would be wrong.

Let us consider this for a moment. It was said that in setting up a statistical test it is necessary to state a null hypothesis and normally this is phrased in a way that indicates no difference exists or change has occurred. In other words, with reference to the salon example, we would state the null hypothesis as saying the average ages of the customers visiting the two salons are not different. If it is then found that the value of the test statistic indicates there is a significant difference at the 95 per cent level, we would reject the null hypothesis and state a difference does exist. Because we are dealing with probabilities, however, there is a chance that in making such a statement we will be wrong five times out of one hundred. This leads to defining two types of error which can arise when conducting significance tests.

The *Type I error* occurs when the researcher rejects the null hypothesis when in fact they should have accepted it. In other words, we state a significant difference does exist in the average ages of the two groups when it does not. Or, put rather differently, we state the two samples come from different populations when they in fact relate to the same population. In visual terms we can see this situation arising when the value of a test statistic falls by chance at one extreme end of a continuum. For example, we noted in Chapter 16 with reference to the normal distribution (represented here as Figure 17.1) that the two ends, shown as shaded areas and known as the 'two tails' of the distribution, encompass together 5 per cent of the distribution (or 2.5 per cent each). Thus, although a value of 'x' may fall at one extreme end or another of the continuum described by the horizontal axis, its value is still consistent with belonging to the population described by the frequency distribution. In other words, in drawing

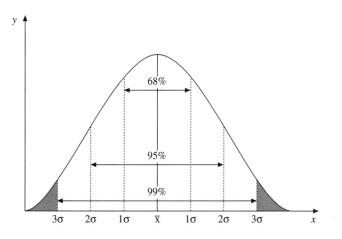

FIGURE 17.1 The standard normal distribution

our samples and conducting our statistical test we may have arrived at an extreme result on this occasion. It is this concept which underlies the meaning of a Type I error.

The alternative situation known as a *Type II error* is where the null hypothesis is accepted when in fact it should have been rejected. To describe how this situation can arise, let us take the example based on the potential weight change in a sample of people due to the introduction of a new diet consisting of a range of products developed by a large food manufacturer. Let us suppose the result of our statistical test indicates that on average no weight change has taken place. We would therefore accept the null hypothesis and state no difference or change has occurred. However, once again there is a chance we would be wrong in making this deduction. It is possible the diet does have an effect but in this instance the weight change did not show up with this particular sample or the measurement or test used to detect the change were not sufficiently sensitive to identify subtle differences.

One- and two-tailed tests

Before conducting a series of selected tests there is one further aspect it is important to note when stating a significance level. It relates to how a hypothesis is precisely worded. Taking our hairdressing salons example and assuming we have made no initial review of the data, so we have no idea whether or not one mean is higher than the other, we may state the null hypothesis in one of three ways. We may say the average ages of customers visiting the London salon is:

(a) no lower;
(b) no higher; or
(c) no different

from that of the customers visiting the Glasgow salon. Similarly, in the case of the study relating to the effects of a new diet, we might pose three different null hypotheses which state that the diet does not:

(a) reduce;
(b) increase people's weight; and/or
(c) effect any weight change at all.

The first two statements in each case indicate a direction to the null hypothesis. These are the conditions required for establishing a one-tailed test. The third statement, which indicates no direction, forms the basis for conducting a two-tailed test. In this latter instance, we are only interested in stating whether or not a difference exists or a change has occurred.

In the statistical tables for evaluating significance levels for different tests, the probability values are stated according to whether or not it is a one- or two-tailed test which is being conducted. Although the actual method for calculating the test statistic is not influenced by the nature of the null hypothesis, i.e. whether or not it is a one- or two-tailed test which is being conducted, the effect of stating a direction is to impose a more rigorous test which in turn affects the significance level that can be quoted. In effect by stating a direction to the null hypothesis we are setting up a more precise test.

Calculations relating to specific types of tests

The rest of this chapter is devoted to describing the calculations involved in conducting different types of statistical tests and the data conditions involved. The tests are described by reference broadly conceived business and management examples or research issues. Within a text such as this it is only possible to describe a limited number of tests relating to a small number of examples. By implication it will be seen the same tests could be applied in a wider range of circumstances.

T-test

This is a particularly useful and well-known test and one that the business and management student will want to note. It is most useful for testing whether or not a significant difference exists between the means of two samples or, put another way, whether or not two samples come from one population. There are two principal versions of a t-test (sometimes known as student's t-test). One relates to samples involving independent data sets and the other to samples which involve paired comparisons. An example of the first is where we wish to test whether or not there is any significant difference between the average age of the sample of customers visiting the Style Hairdressing Salon in London and the average age of the sample of customers visiting the Glasgow unit. For the second situation, we can take the example based on evaluating the effect of a new diet on people's weight. In this instance, we weigh the people first before putting them on the diet which is intended to reduce their weight. After a given period of, say, one month their weights are then re-checked and a t-test conducted to ascertain whether or not there has been any significant reduction.

Basic assumptions

In both cases the t-test is based on certain assumptions about the data sets. The data must be of an interval nature, randomly chosen and normally (or near normally) distributed. The variances of the two data sets should also be similar. However, like certain other aspects that arise in statistics, it is not always entirely clear how strictly the criteria regarding normality and comparative sizes of variances should be adhered to. For example, what is meant by 'nearly normal 'or 'variances that are similar'? No precise definitions exist which tell the researcher to what extent such criteria may be violated without jeopardizing the validity of the test (sophisticated software packages such as SPSS offer guidance on such decisions). Where there is considerable doubt an alternative is to conduct one of the less-refined non-parametric tests. In these cases the criteria are less stringent. With reference to the t-test there are two non-parametric tests which, in a sense, parallel the t-test. These are the Mann-Whitney and Wilcoxon tests. The first relates to independent samples and the second to paired comparisons. These tests will be described following those dealing with the calculations relevant for conducting the two t-tests.

T-test for independent samples

In order to avoid unnecessary computations, we shall use the information already calculated on ages as given in Chapter 16. This information gives full details of the mean, variance and standard deviation for the sample of customers visiting the Style Hairdressing Salon in London based on the raw data (see Table 16.11). For the sample of customers visiting the Glasgow salon, it was assumed the mean age was 51.3 years. We will also assume the variance was 270 and the standard deviation 16.4 years based on a sample of 30 customers. These figures are set out in Table 17.1.

These figures provide enough information to calculate the t-test statistic. The formula can be presented in various ways. The simplest version is perhaps:

$$t = \frac{|\bar{x}_1 - \bar{x}_2|}{S_p\sqrt{1/n_1 + 1/n_2}}$$

Where:

- $\bar{x}_1$ and $\bar{x}_2$ represent the two mean values for the two samples and $|\bar{x}_1 - \bar{x}_2|$ their absolute differences ignoring the sign;
- n_1 and n_2 represent the two samples sizes; and
- $S_p{}^2$ is the pooled variance and S_p is the square root of that variance.

The latter variance is represented by:

$$S_p{}^2 = \left[(n_1 - 1)_{S_1{}^2} + (n_1 - 1)_{S_2{}^2}\right]/(n_1 + n_2 - 2)$$

where $S_1{}^2$ and $S_2{}^2$ are the variances of the two samples. Inserting the values given in Table 17.1 it is found the pooled variance equals 252 and S_p equals 15.9. The value of 't' is therefore:

$$t = \frac{|37.2 - 51.3|}{15.9\sqrt{0.02 + 0.033}} = \frac{14.1}{15.9 \times 0.23} = \frac{14.1}{3.66} = 3.85$$

TABLE 17.1 Statistics relating to samples of customers visiting Style Hairdressing Salons in London and Glasgow

	London	Glasgow
Sample size	50	30
Mean age	37.2	51.3
Variance	241.5	270
Standard deviation	15.5	16.4

The next step is to refer to the table giving the appropriate values of 't' for different degrees of freedom. In this case the number of degrees of freedom is $50 + 30 - 2 = 78$. This value is based on first looking at the number of observations given for the first sample and subtracting one and then doing the same for the second sample and adding the two values together. In each case the number of degrees of freedom is based on the knowledge that if we know every value except one in each data set plus the total of all values for the data set, then we can calculate the missing value. In other words, if for the first sample we know the ages of 49 of the customers and the total of all ages is 1861 (see Chapter 16), we can calculate the age of the 50th member of the sample. The same applies in the case of the second sample.

Since we are only interested in knowing whether or not the average ages of the two samples are different we are only concerned with conducting a two-tailed test and only the absolute difference between the means is noted. For a one-tailed test it can be useful to observe the actual rather than the absolute difference between the means as this will immediately assist in determining whether or not the null hypothesis has been met. For example, if we had decided to test at the outset whether or not the Glasgow salon's customers had a higher average age than the sample of customers from the London salon, then taking the actual difference in means would have given a negative result, i.e. -14.1, and this would be consistent with our belief that the second group had a higher mean age while a positive result would have immediately discounted such a claim without proceeding further with the test. Once proceeding with the test, it is the absolute value of 't' which must be taken when referring to the significance tables, and reference to appropriate statistical tables as described show that for 't' to be significant at the 99 per cent level (i.e. $p = 0.01$), the computed value of 't' must be greater than or equal to 2.66; thus in our case it is significant and we reject the null hypothesis. Thus, we conclude the average ages of the customers are different or, put another way, the samples relate to two different populations.

T-test relating to paired data

This test is illustrated with reference to the data given in Table 17.2. This shows for a small sample of nine women their weights before and after the introduction of the diet referred to earlier. It is worth noting, at this point, that the t-test can be conducted in situations where the size of the samples are not large. This is one of the benefits of this test. We compute from Table 17.2 the average weight before the experiment was 69.33 kilograms and afterwards 67.33 kilograms. So on average the women lost two kilograms over the study period.

To calculate the t-value we need to review not just the difference in the overall means but the difference in weights before and after for each individual in the sample. The formula for 't' in this instance is:

$$t = \frac{|\bar{x}_1 - \bar{x}_2|}{S_D / \sqrt{n}}$$

where $\bar{x}_1$, and $\bar{x}_2$ are the two overall means for samples one and two, and S_D represents the standard deviation of the observed differences in weight. In effect, we are creating

TABLE 17.2 Weight of sample of women (in kilograms)

	1	2	3	4	5	6	7	8	9
Before	62	66	70	76	64	62	76	83	65
After	57	71	70	75	60	65	76	73	59

a new variable d_i (where i runs from 1, 2, ... 9) and where d_i is the difference between the first and second observation for each of the nine cases in our sample. To calculate S_D we apply the formula:

$$S_D{}^2 = \sum_{i=1}^{n}(d_i - \bar{d})^2/n - 1$$

where 'n' equals the number of paired observations and $\bar{d}$ is the mean difference in weight calculated over all values of d_i divided by 'n'. Table 17.3 shows the different steps.

In this case:

$$\bar{d}(or \sum_{i=1}^{n} d_i/n) \text{ equals } 18/9 = 2.0;$$

$$\sum_{i=1}^{n}(d_i - \bar{d})^2 \text{ equals } 176; \text{ and}$$

$$S_D{}^2 \text{ equals } 176/8 = 22.0$$

Thus, S_D equals 4.69 and $S_D\sqrt{n} = \dfrac{4.69}{3} = 1.56$ and the value of 't' can be computed as:

$$t = 2/1.56 = 1.28$$

TABLE 17.3 Calculations relating to paired data

	x_{1i}	x_{2i}	d_i	$(d_i - d)$	$(d_i - d_2)^2$
1	62	57	5	3	9
2	66	71	−5	−7	49
3	70	70	0	−2	4
4	76	75	1	−1	1
5	64	60	4	2	4
6	62	65	−3	−5	25
7	76	76	0	−2	4
8	83	73	10	8	64
9	65	59	6	4	16

Note: $\Sigma^d/_n = \bar{d} = 2$ kilogrammes

The number of degrees of freedom is eight since in this case we are dealing with nine paired differences, i.e. df $= 9 - 1$. It is also a one-tailed test since we are concerned in knowing whether or not the diet has resulted in a reduction in weight. Looking at the table of t-values, it is found that 't' must be equal to or greater than 1.86 to give a significant result. Thus it is evident that the value of 't' is no where near significant and the null hypothesis is accepted, that is the diet resulted in no significant weight loss. This does not mean, as we can see, that some women did not lose weight; some in fact did rather well while others actually gained weight but the overall result was not significant. This in itself may be a cause for further investigation and re-evaluation of the diet among different groups of women observed perhaps over a longer period.

Related non-parametric tests

We now turn to describing selected 'non-parametric' tests which are allied to the two t-tests in that they also deal with comparisons between two independent or paired samples of data. Their advantage is that they can be conducted on data of a lower level than interval data. In each instance the data need only be of an ordinal status and the requirements relating to normality do not apply. The tests are therefore useful in situations which involve rating scales or where scored values are applicable. You will be pleased to learn the calculations involved are also simpler than those for the t-test. The disadvantage with such tests is that because they are less rigorous mathematically, they may not result in detecting small differences between two data sets.

Mann-Whitney U-test

This test can be used on independent samples of data. In addition, the number of observations in each set need not be equal. It can therefore be useful when examining differences between two groups of customers who have been asked to give their opinion on some particular product. It may be used, for example, to distinguish between the views of men and women, or customers of different ages, or between the views of visitors categorized by nationality or social class. To demonstrate how the test operates we will take an example based on two sets of customers visiting the Style Hairdressing Salon in London. Let us suppose the management of the salon are concerned to know customers' views regarding the salon's quality of service. They also state they would like to know whether men or women have different views of the quality of this service.

In looking at such a situation there are many factors we might take into consideration. In a detailed analysis it might be appropriate to evaluate customers' opinions regarding individual services such as (a) booking of appointments; (b) consultation with stylists; (c) hairwash or (d) the styling process (e.g. cut, colour, perm and so on).

In a 'real' situation the researcher will want to take into account as many different aspects as possible that could affect the evaluation. Let us suppose, however, that as a starting point the management have identified five areas of service standards they wish to evaluate. These are identified as obtaining customers' opinions on the:

- efficiency of appointment booking procedures;
- efficiency of consultation with a stylist;
- standard and efficiency of hair wash;
- standard of cleanliness and presentation of the salon; and
- efficiency and standard of the styling process (e.g. cut, colour, perm and so on).

These are aspects every customer is likely to have an opinion on.

The next step is to ask each customer in the sample to give a rating, or score, expressing their opinion on a scale of 1 to 10 where 1 = very poor and 10 = excellent. These scores are then aggregated in order to ascertain an overall score for each customer. Thus, the minimum score will be 5 and the maximum 50. It is assumed for the purpose of describing the calculations only a small number of customers were approached. Table 17.4 lists the aggregated responses for 10 men and 15 women visiting the salon during the survey period. Thus the study is based on two independent samples of unequal size. The data is of an ordinal nature and the null hypothesis states that there is no difference between the two groups in respect of their opinion of the salon's services. Thus the test is a two-tailed test as no particular direction is indicated. That is, it is assumed the sample of men express no better or worse an opinion of the salon's services than the sample of women. In fact, a visual inspection of the data gives the impression that the women were more satisfied with the service than the men.

TABLE 17.4 Result of customers' opinions on standards in the Style Hairdressing Salon, London

Men (1)	Women (2)
10	26
15	20
12	25
14	30
20	36
13	40
9	45
8	32
16	36
22	28
	44
	28
	36
	29
	41

Where the samples are of unequal size, it is usual to list the data values for the smaller sample first although this is not essential. The next step is to rank the scores taking the two samples together. This ranking procedure, which is also applicable to the calculation procedures for other non-parametric tests, is conducted as follows.

Each data value is placed in ascending order. In this case, the 25 values (covering both samples) are listed ranging from the lowest score of 8 to the highest score of 45. Table 17.5 presents the figures in an ordered list. Under each value is a count representing the order of the observation in the overall data set.

It will be found in this example that certain numbers are tied, i.e. the 9th and 10th values with a value of 20, the 14th and 15th values with a value of 28, and the 19th, 20th and 21st values with a value of 36. The ranked value which is the number we wish to calculate is related to the ordering, i.e. 1–25, and where data values are tied their order numbers are added and divided by the number of tied values involved. For example, the 9th and 10th values are tied so their rank is calculated as $(9 + 10)/2 = 9.5$. Where there are three tied values as in the case of the 19th, 20th and 21st data values in the ordered set, the orderings are added, i.e. $19 + 20 + 21$, and divided by 3 giving a rank of 20 in each case.

We can now assign to each score in Table 17.5 a ranked value. These are shown in Table 17.6 with the scores listed in ascending order.

The generalized formula for the Mann Whitney U-test is:

$$(A) \quad N_1 N_2 + \frac{N_1(N_1 + 1)}{2} - \sum R_1$$

Where N_1 and N_2 equal the number of observations in the two samples as shown in columns (1) and (2) of Table 17.6, i.e. 10 and 15 in this case, and $\sum R_1$, is the sum of the ranks for the first column, i.e. 56.5.

Thus we obtain, in the case of our example, a value of:

$$(10 \times 15) + \frac{10(11)}{2} - 56.5 = 150 + \frac{110}{2} - 56.5$$
$$= 150 + 55 - 56.5$$
$$= 148.5$$

We also need to make one further calculation which is:

$$(B) \quad N_1 N_2 - [N_1 N_2 + N_1(N_1 + 1)/2 - \sum R_1]$$

TABLE 17.5 Scores rounded in ascending order

8	9	10	12	13	14	15	16	20	20	22	25	26
1	2	3	4	5	6	7	8	9	10	11	12	13

28	28	29	30	32	36	36	36	40	41	44	45
14	15	16	17	18	19	20	21	22	23	24	25

TABLE 17.6 Mann-Whitney U-test: scores shown together with rankings

Men (1)		Women (2)	
Score	Rank	Score	Rank
8	1	20	9.5
9	2	25	12
10	3	26	13
12	4	28	14.5
13	5	28	14.5
14	6	29	16
15	7	30	17
16	8	32	18
20	9.5	36	20
22	11	36	20
		36	20
		40	22
		41	23
		44	24
		45	25

In other words $N_1 \times N_2$ minus the value just calculated above under (A). The result is $10 \times 15 - 148.5 = 1.5$. These two figures give the test statistics for the Mann Whitney U-test, namely, the value of U and U'. The latter is pronounced U prime. The smallest value is the value of U and the larger U'. Thus U = 1.5 and U' = 148.5.

The significance level for the test is ascertained by establishing the positioning of U in the appropriate statistical table for given sample sizes N_1 and N_2. These tables show U must not exceed 39, based on a two-tailed test. Thus, there is a highly significant difference between the two sets of scores as might be expected, and in fact a confidence level of over 99 per cent is indicated. In practice, we would have been advised in this case, based on a visual inspection of the data, to have stated at the outset a null hypothesis for a one-tailed test. This would have stated an expectation that the sample of men were no less satisfied with the salon's services than the sample of women.

In calculating the Mann-Whitney U-test, it is possible to do the same type of calculations in respect of the larger sample of data shown in column (2) of Table 17.6. The generalized formula is then:

$$N_1 N_2 + N_2(N_2 + 1)/2 - \sum R_2$$

where $\sum R_2$ is the sum of the ranks for column (2) relating to the larger data set. It will be found the results for U and U' result, in fact, in the same values as before. The reason for choosing the smaller sample is to reduce the length of the calculations.

Wilcoxon test

Like the t-test for related samples, the Wilcoxon test is based on paired data sets. For the Wilcoxon test to be applied the data need, however, only be of an ordinal status. So once again, like the Mann-Whitney U-test, the Wilcoxon test is useful for analysing data based on ranked scores. Another advantage is that the paired data may relate either to (a) the same groups of individuals as in a 'before and after' situation or to (b) samples matched on the basis of selected characteristics. In the case of, for example, market research, such characteristics might include age, gender, social class or nationality or other characteristics identified by the researcher as important to potentially influencing the results of a study. For example, it could be said, rather obviously, that a person's opinion of an airline's in-flight service will be affected by their experience of flying. If they are frequent fliers and/or have experience of many differnet airlines, then they are likely to be more discerning than the person who flies infrequently and/or has experienced flying with few airlines. In conducting a study of this nature using the Wilcoxon test, the first step would be to match people on their flying experiences before questioning them for their opinions on the standard of in-flight service on the particular airline under review.

These considerations form part of the design aspects of the study and need to be thought through prior to conducting fieldwork. There are a number of texts which discuss design concepts relating to the research process to which the reader can refer. Often these are described with reference to studies involving experimental situations where samples of people are subjected to various 'treatments'. In a business research context such a study might include a situation where a sample of people are first asked for their views regarding a particular product. They are then shown a promotional video before being asked again for their views. The aim would be to see whether or not the video affected their opinion or disposition towards that product. Clearly in setting-up such an evaluation, which in this case is known as a 'before and after' study, there are important considerations to take into account when both designing the study and interpreting the results. In this case, the two sets of results, i.e. the opinions obtained before and after showing the video, are effectively matched because the 'treatment' is applied to the same group of people. A problem may arise, however, when people are aware they are taking part in an experiment and their second opinion is influenced by that fact. They may, for example, think it incumbent on them to express a changed view. This is just one example of a design problem that can arise in experimental research. It is beyond the scope of this text to go into all the steps a researcher can take to eliminate or reduce the risk of bias in survey results due to design problems. Many aspects of survey design have been touched upon and there are a variety of texts giving further guidance on this matter.

To return to the Wilcoxon test, we show how this is conducted with reference to a 'before and after' situation. We assume the management of the Style Hairdressing Salon in London are concerned about complaints they have received regarding the salon's appointments booking system. There appears to be a feeling of discontent among customers about the way in which appointments are being booked. These complaints have come particularly from regular female customers who have joined the 'Cleopatra' Club. Because of the importance of these loyal customers to the salon, the management of the salon decide they must tackle the situation with urgency. They resolve to send their receptionist on a two-day intensive training programme.

Coupled with this action, the management decide they would like to conduct a short survey among members of the 'Cleopatra' Club to establish more systematically their views to date regarding the salon's appointment booking system. In setting up the study the management decide not to advise Club members of the changes they are instituting. The reason is they wish to avoid biasing the results of the survey. Thus, this action constitutes part of the design considerations in setting up the survey.

A short questionnaire is devised to assess views on:

- courtesy of staff when making appointments;
- speed of the appointments booking system; and
- efficiency of the booking system.

A sample of the 'Cleopatra' Club members is then selected at random. Each selected person is asked to grade their views on the above services on a scale of 1 to 10 based on their experience of booking appointments and prior to the changes taking place. As before, a score of $1 =$ very poor and $10 =$ excellent, and scores are aggregated over the three categories of service. A sample of 12 customers is selected. These same people are then approached one month later, after the changes have taken place, when they are asked for their views again regarding their more recent experiences of utilizing the booking system. In reality, it would be difficult for the management not to announce they had changed procedures, but if they do they must assume the announcement does not in itself affect the results of the study. In other words, it is assumed that on both occasions the sample of individuals give their honest unbiased opinion. Table 17.7 details the scores achieved.

A quick visual inspection shows that every customer in the sample except two thought the service had improved. Given this, and the management's desire to effect an improved service, it is pertinent to pose the null hypothesis for a one-tailed test. We state therefore, the null hypothesis as being that the customers' opinions reflect no improvement has occurred in the salon's services due to the changed procedures. This may seem a rather tortuous way of presenting the problem but it will be recalled that the null hypothesis is always stated as indicating no change (or in this case, no improvement) has taken place. We then compute the test statistic as a guide to whether or not we should accept or reject the null hypothesis. For the management of the salon's sake we hope the outcome will be to reject it!

To operate the Wilcoxon test, we first calculate the differences in the score for each sample member. These are:

+10   0   +8   +5   +5   +6   +5   −4   +9   +10   +3   +7

These values are placed in ascending order ignoring the signs. Thus it is the absolute difference that is important in establishing the rankings for the data set. In addition, it should be noted that all zero values are excluded. Thus, the ordering is as follows:

TABLE 17.7 Wilcoxon test: opinions of customers on appointment booking system

Member	Score before	Score after
1	15	25
2	19	19
3	20	28
4	10	15
5	12	17
6	18	24
7	20	25
8	19	15
9	6	15
10	10	20
11	11	14
12	14	21

+3	−4	+5	+5	+5	+6	+7	+8	+9	+10	+10
1	2	3	4	5	6	7	8	9	10	11

The ranking for tied numbers is dealt with as before. Thus, values of 5 are each assigned the rank of 4, i.e. $(3+4+5)/3$, and values of 10 each assume the rank 10.5, i.e. $(10 + 11) / 2$. The ranks for the paired comparisons are shown in Table 17.8.

These ranks are then added according to two groups. That is (a) all ranks relating to positive differences, and (b) all ranks relating to negative differences. In this case, the totals are: (a) 64 and (b) 2. The smallest value represents the T statistic. Thus $T = 2$. The significance value of T is obtained by reference to the appropriate statistical table for the Wilcoxon test. This shows the values of 'T' according to different values of N, where N is equal to the number of paired comparisons involved in the study which did not result in a difference of zero. Thus, in this case $N = 11$ (i.e. $12 - 1$). For significance to be established, T must be equal to or less than 13 and in fact, it can be shown that the result from the test is highly significant at the 99 per cent confidence level given it is a one-tailed test.

Sign S-test

As well as the Wilcoxon T-test, there is an even simpler test which can be used to . evaluate differences based on paired comparisons. It is described briefly here. The test is based on the premise that only the number of positive and negative differences are compared. Thus, in the case of the sample of 'Cleopatra' Club members, the test would examine how many members recorded a higher opinion on the second occasion and how many recorded a lower one. The respective numbers were, in fact, 10 and 1. The 'S statistic' is taken as the lower of these two numbers.

TABLE 17.8 Wilcoxon test: ranks of sample of Club members

Member	Difference in score	Rank
1	+10	10.5
2	0	—
3	+8	8
4	+5	4
5	+5	4
6	+6	6
7	+5	4
8	−4	2
9	+9	9
10	+10	10.5
11	+3	1
12	+7	7

Thus it is equal to 1. Once again, N is defined as the count of the number of paired comparisons excluding the number resulting in zero change. So N is still equal to 11. The significance levels for 'S' can be observed by looking in the appropriate table.

The advantage of the S statistic is it is easy to compute. Compared with the Wilcoxon test it suffers from the fact that it does not take into account the size of the differences in the paired scores as reflected through the ranked values. Thus it is less discerning as a test. However, the S test has particular value when the size of the differences are not known. In our study we might have set up a different method of evaluation or scoring system where we simply asked our sample of customers to indicate whether or not the overall standard of appointment booking had improved in their opinion between the first and second occasions. Each person's views could then have been presented according to one of three options:

- service is about the same as before;
- service appears to have improved; and
- service appears to have got worse.

With reference to the sign test the first would indicate a zero value, the second a positive (+ve) value and the third a negative (−ve) value. Thus, we could compute an S statistic based on this simplified set of data.

Conclusion

This chapter has introduced the reader to the concept of statistical tests and has dealt with some of the basic tests that can be applied when comparing two sets of data. As with any statistical test the nature of the data being examined and the purposes of the test have to be carefully considered at the outset. Different tests apply to different situations and types of data. We have examined the basic tests for comparing first independent and then related data sets under both parametric and non-parametric conditions.

■ □ ■ ■ 18

Measures of association

This chapter is concerned with two rather different groups of statistical tests. Often referred to as 'measures of association' they include the Chi-square test (pronounced 'ky') and the group of tests based on correlation coefficients. The tests differ from those described in the last chapter in a number of ways. The tests described in the last chapter sought to determine whether or not data sets pertaining to two samples could have come from one population or, put another way, whether or not there were significant differences between two sample groups in respect of particular data values.

The tests described in this chapter, on the other hand, examine whether or not there is an association between one characteristic and another. This might be viewed as asking whether or not there is some association between one variable and another. In conducting such tests and describing how they operate, it is important to emphasize that the tests are not proof of 'causality'. They are purely measures describing the strength of the associations between variables. We will return to this aspect with reference to specific examples to make the point clearer.

Chi-square tests (χ^2)

Chi-square tests can assume different levels of complexity and may be known by names other than a 'measure of association'. Sometimes Chi-square tests are regarded as tests relating to 'goodness of fit'. This is because the test can usefully be applied to determine whether or not an observed set of frequencies matches some expected or desired distribution.

Chi-square calculations, unlike the tests described in the previous chapter, are based on frequency distributions. They seek to determine whether or not the frequency distribution for a particular data set is similar to or significantly different from that expected by chance or some predetermined pattern. The following paragraphs describe some of the principal ways in which Chi-square tests can be applied in business and management research. They are particularly valuable tests because they are relatively simple to understand and apply, and the data can be of any level, i.e. nominal, ordinal, interval or ratio. Also the conditions regarding normality do not apply.

Simple contingency tables

The simplest form of the Chi-square test is that based on a 2×2 contingency table. Table 18.1 describes such a table. It shows, for a sample of air passengers, the number who were classed as business travellers as opposed to holidaymakers. It also shows how many business travellers slept well during the flight and how many did not compared with the experiences of the holidaymakers.

The sample sizes of the two groups are the same in this case but this is not essential for the Chi-square test to be conducted. It is possible to have unequal size groups.

Table 18.1 is known as a 2×2 contingency table because each variable involves only two categories and therefore there are four principal cells making up the body of the table. The totals shown in the final column and row are known as marginal totals. The table describes a simple frequency distribution and visual inspection suggests that, in general, the holidaymakers slept rather better during the flight than the business travellers. We have taken a simplistic example in order to show how the test statistic is computed and to illustrate how the findings should be interpreted.

In setting up our test we state once again a null hypothesis. In general, the null hypothesis with any Chi-square test involving contingency tables is the same. It states there is no association between the two variables. That is, in this case, there is no association between the type of traveller and whether or not they slept well during the flight. To test this hypothesis we proceed to calculate another contingency table which shows the expected frequencies for each cell assuming no association exists. This is calculated by multiplying the appropriate marginal totals together and dividing by the aggregated sample size. The first cell – relating to the expected frequency for the number of business passengers who slept well – is calculated as follows:

$$
\begin{aligned}
\text{Expected frequency Cell A} &= (100 \times 105)/200 \\
&= 52.5
\end{aligned}
$$

Table 18.2 shows the calculations in generalized notational form and Table 18.3 gives the computed values in respect of our example.

TABLE 18.1 Sleeping patterns of passengers on a long-haul flight

Slept well	Business travellers	Holidaymakers	Total
Yes	45	60	105
No	55	40	95
Total	100	100	200

TABLE 18.2 Calculations for expected frequencies

Slept well	Business travellers	Holidaymakers	Total
Yes	Cell A = $(N_1 \times T_1)/T$	Cell C = $(N_2 \times T_1)/T$	T_1
No	Cell B = $(N_1 \times T_2)/T_0$	Cell D = $(N_2 \times T_2)/T_0$	T_2
Total	N_1	N_2	T_0

TABLE 18.3 Expected frequencies in relation to Table 18.1

Slept well	Business travellers	Holidaymakers	Total
Yes	52.5	52.5	105
No	47.5	47.5	95
Total	100	100	200

In effect, we are saying that of the total sample of all passengers (200), 105 (52.5 per cent) slept well and 95 (47.5 per cent) did not. Thus, if there is no difference between the two groups of passengers in respect of how they slept during the flight, then we would expect these same proportional patterns to be reflected in the expected frequency values for each of the cells. The Chi-square test is based on evaluating the difference between the observed and expected frequencies or the values given in Tables 18.1 and 18.3. It thus tests the null hypothesis, which states that no association exists. The generalized formula for the Chi-square test is:

$$\chi^2 = \sum_{i=1}^{n}(0_i - E_i)^2/E_i$$

where 0_i is the observed frequency in respect of cell i and E_i is the expected frequency in respect of cell i. Table 18.4 shows the calculations in respect of our example.

As well as calculating the value of the Chi-square test statistic, it is necessary to determine the relevant number of degrees of freedom for the contingency table. This is calculated as: degrees of freedom (df) equals the number of categories for the row variable minus one, multiplied by the number of categories for the column variable minus one.

TABLE 18.4 Calculations for Chi-square statistic (See Tables 18.1 and 18.3)

Cell	$(O - E)$	$(O - E)^2$	$(O - E)^2/E$
A	45 − 52.5 (−7.5)	56.25	1.07
B	55 − 47.5 (+7.5)	56.25	1.18
C	60 − 52.5 (+7.5)	56.25	1.07
D	40 − 47.5 (−7.5)	56.25	1.18

χ^2 equals the total for the last column ,that is, $\chi^2 = 4.5$

In this case, there are only two categories for each variable, i.e. type of passenger (business and holidaymaker) and whether or not they slept well (yes or no). Thus the number of degrees of freedom is one, i.e. $(2 - 1) \times (2 - 1) = 1$. Reference to the applicable table for the χ^2 test shows that for χ^2 to be significant at the 95 per cent confidence level (i.e. $p = 0.05$) its value must be equal to or greater than 3.841. Thus, there is an association between the type of passenger and their sleeping pattern. Before progressing to other examples where a Chi-square test may be used but in a more complex situation, it is important to enlarge on several aspects of the test. This can be done with reference to other simple examples.

Degrees of freedom (df)

In the simple 2×2 contingency table, the degrees of freedom were calculated as one. The principle involved in deciding degrees of freedom is not dissimilar to that applicable to other tests. In our example there were four marginal totals denoted in Table 18.2 as N_1, N_2, T_1 and T_2. Assuming these values are known and the frequency relative to one cell, say A, is known then the frequency values for all the other cells can easily be calculated. Thus, the degrees of freedom represent the number of cells whose frequency value needs to be known in order to compute the frequency values of the remaining cells given the marginal totals are also known.

In subsequent paragraphs we will compute values of χ^2 for a contingency table where the variables are divided into more than two categories. The number of degrees of freedom will then assume a higher value taking account of the larger number of categories involved. For example, we may have divided passengers into three types: business travellers, holidaymakers and those taking the flight in order to visit family and friends (VFR). Table 18.1 would now have had six principal cells, i.e. 3×2. In this case, the degrees of freedom using the generalized formula is $(3 - 1) \times (2 - 1) = 2$. Thus, if in our new table we knew the observed frequencies in respect of two of the cells (say those with brackets in Table 18.5) plus the marginal totals, the frequencies for the other cells could be computed.

Another extension would be to provide for more options on passenger sleeping patterns. Let us say they could indicate one of three categories: (i) Yes, slept well; (ii) slept fairly well; or (iii) slept badly. In this case we would expand our table into a 3×3 contingency table with $(3 - 1) \times (3 - 1) = 4$ degrees of freedom.

Yates correction factor

There is one situation where it is appropriate to introduce the Yates correction factor into the computation of the χ^2 statistic. This is where you are dealing with a 2×2 contingency table, especially where the total aggregated sample size is small, say, less than 50 observations (see Fleming and Nellis 1993: 299). The procedure involves deducting the value 0.5 from the observed frequencies in the calculation relating to the χ statistic (see below). Thus the generalized formula, in these circumstances, is amended to:

TABLE 18.5 Chi-square test: showing number of values (bracketed) necessary to compute other cell values taking account of marginal totals

Slept well	BT	Holidaymakers	VFR	Totals
Yes	45	(60)	50	155
No	(55)	40	50	145
Total	100	100	100	300

TABLE 18.6 Revised calculations for Chi-square statistic incorporating Yates correction factor

Cell	$(|0 - E| - 0.5)$	$(|0 - E|\ 0.5)^2/E$
A	7.5 – 0.5 (7)	49/52.5 (0.93)
B	7.5 – 0.5 (7)	49/47.5 (1.03)
C	7.5 – 0.5 (7)	49/52.5 (0.93)
D	7.5 – 0.5 (7)	49/47.5 (1.03)

$$\chi^2 = \sum_{i=1}^{n}(|0_i - E_i| - 0.5)^2/E_i$$

where $|0_i - E_i|$ is the absolute difference between the observed and expected frequency for the 'ith' cell. In our example, based on the frequencies shown in Table 18.1, the revised value of χ^2 incorporating Yates correction factor is given in Table 18.6.

Thus:

$\chi^2 = 0.93 + 1.03 + 0.93 + 1.03$
$\chi^2 = 3.92$ with (1df)

The effect of the Yates correction is to introduce greater accuracy into the calculation and evaluation of the χ^2 statistic. In our example, using the Yates correction factor we find the χ^2 statistic is just significant at the 95 per cent confidence level. Thus, the null hypothesis would still be rejected. That is, we would say there is an association between the type of passenger and their sleeping pattern.

Conditions necessary for conducting a χ^2 test

It has been shown that the cells in a Chi-square contingency table relate to an observed frequency distribution. The values, therefore, represent counts and each observed frequency assumes a discrete value. It has also been shown, however, that the expected frequency values, as computed by the procedures described, need not assume whole integer numbers. They are continuous data and may be calculated to several decimal places. In calculating the Chi-square statistic it is best not to round up expected frequencies into whole numbers as this can result in important losses of accuracy. The statistical table showing significance values for χ^2 gives values up to two decimal places. It is therefore meaningful to work on expected frequency values involving up to three places of decimal.

Another important point to note is the particular conditions under which a Chi-square statistic should not be computed. It is only appropriate to compute the statistic based on observed frequencies. It is not correct to use figures relating to proportional distributions or relative frequency distributions. The cells should not represent percentage (%) values. Each cell value should also be independent of another. People cannot, for instance, appear in more than one group.

Expected frequencies below five

Where an expected frequency falls below five, it is generally considered advisable to regroup the data to overcome this situation before conducting the Chi-square test. This can best be demonstrated with reference to a 5×2 contingency table which shows for two samples of customers their opinions in respect of a computer shop's after-sales service on a scale of $1-5$ (see Table 18.7).

Calculation of the expected frequencies show that the values for the first row of cells falls below five (i.e. 2.43 and 2.57, see Table 18.8(a)). We can overcome this by regrouping. We can define a new class which includes customers who rated the shop's after-sales service as either 'poor or very poor'. Thus, we add the frequencies shown in the first two rows together for each sample of customers. The result is a revised 4×2 contingency table as shown in Table 18.8(b). The figures in brackets are the expected frequencies.

Regrouping the data inevitably results in some loss of information. The Chi-square statistic can, however, now be safely computed and the calculations are shown in Table 18.9.

Thus the value of χ^2 using the same formula $\sum_{i=1}^{n}(O_i - E_i)^2/E_i$ yields:

$\chi^2 = $ 1.297 (or the sum of values in the final column of Table 18.9)

The number of degrees of freedom is 3, i.e. $(4-1) \times (2-1)$. The table of significance shows that for χ^2 to be significant its value must be equal to or greater than 7.815.

TABLE 18.7 Customers' opinions of a computer shop's after-sales service

Rating of services	Corporate customers	Non-corporate customers	Total
1 Very poor	2	3	5
2 Poor	10	15	25
3 Adequate/acceptable	23	25	48
4 Good/efficient	30	27	57
5 Very good	20	20	40
Total	85	90	175

TABLE 18.8(a) Expected frequencies relating to Table 18.7

Rating of services	Corporate customers	Non-corporate customers	Total
1 Very poor	2.43	2.57	5
2 Poor	12.14	12.86	25
3 Adequate	23.31	24.69	48
4 Good	27.69	29.31	57
5 Very good	19.43	20.57	40
Total	85	90	175

TABLE 18.8(b) Regrouped contingency table relating to Tables 18.7 and 18.8(a)

Rating of services	Corporate customers	Non-corporate customers	Total
Poor or very poor	12 (14.57)	18 (15.43)	30
Adequate	23 (23.31)	25 (24.69)	48
Good	30 (27.69)	27 (29.31)	57
Very good	20 (19.43)	20 (20.57)	40
Total	85	90	175

TABLE 18.9 Calculations for Chi-square based on regrouped data as given in Table 18.8(b)

$|0_i - E_i|$		$(0_i - E_i)^2$	$(0_i - E_i)^2/E_i$
12 − 14.57	(= 2.57)	6.60	0.453
23 − 23.31	(= 0.31)	0.096	0.004
30 − 27.69	(= 2.31)	5.336	0.193
20 − 19.43	(= 0.57)	0.325	0.017
18 − 15.43	(= 2.57)	6.60	0.428
25 − 24.69	(= 0.31)	0.096	0.004
27 − 29.31	(= 2.31)	5.336	0.182
20 − 20.57	(= 0.57)	0.325	0.016

Thus, as might be expected, the difference between the observed and expected frequencies is not significant. We can therefore say there is no association between the type of customer and their opinion of the shop's after-sales service.

Clearly, regrouping may result in subtle differences between two data sets being obscured. Therefore, regrouping should be avoided if at all possible and thus larger sample sizes are recommended. Moreover, it can be seen that the way in which the categories are constructed may determine whether or not significant associations are detected. It can also be seen that as the size of the contingency table increases so the number of calculations that need to be conducted in order to compute the χ^2 statistic become more demanding.

With the development of sophisticated computer software many of the tedious procedures are eliminated. Indeed, the flexibility offered by computers enables several tests to be conducted at once. Suppose, for example, you wish to conduct a Chi-square test for several different groupings of your data. Perhaps you have observed that young people's intentions to buy a particular magazine appears to be associated with their age. You therefore take a sample of young people aged between 10 and 25 and question them on their purchasing intentions. You then group the data to show how the young people expressed their intention to buy or not to buy according to an age distribution. Given that you have the raw data you are in a position to group the data according to a variety of age bands. You may choose:

- 10 and under 15;
- 15 and under 20; and
- 20 and up to and including 25.

The problem here is whether such a division obscures important differences in young people's purchasing intentions. Perhaps narrower bands would show up more distinctions. We might therefore choose alternative bands such as:

- 10 and under 12;
- 12 and under 14;
- 14 and under 16;
- 16 and under 20; and
- 20 and up to 25.

Note also the classes are not necessarily of the same interval width. This does not matter for the Chi-square test. It is an extremely accommodating test for different types of data. Moreover, with the facility of computer power a variety of options as described by the magazine example can be examined. Although, it is beyond this text to go into precise methods, the researcher will find specialist software programmes dealing with these aspects. For instance, a programme referred to as CHAID within the Software Package for the Social Sciences (SPSS) enables the researcher to conduct a whole series of χ^2 tests on data using different groupings. The procedure is highly effective in studies involving market segmentation.

Causality

In interpreting the results of a Chi-square test it is important to remember that the test is one that measures associations and not causality. In other words, it tests whether or not there are any statistical grounds for saying variable A is associated with variable B. If the χ^2 statistic proves significant, we can then go on to describe in various ways how the association reveals itself based on the sample results. In respect of Table 18.5 we decided, using the Yates correction factor, that χ^2 had a significant value at the 95 per cent level. We might have described this result by saying the sample of holidaymakers were shown by the test to have slept better during a flight compared with the sample of business travellers. Using descriptive statistics, we could have then said that 60 per cent of the holidaymakers slept well compared with only 45 per cent of the business travellers.

Clearly we cannot say, however, that being a holidaymaker causes the person to sleep better! Causality is a very difficult issue to deal with. There are many factors that can impinge upon or influence a situation. Business travellers may not sleep so well because they are more tense. Perhaps they are concerned about the business problems they expect to face the next day, or perhaps they are overworked and cannot relax properly. Another possibility is they had too much wine at last night's corporate dinner party! All Chi-square tests do is look at associations between two variables. Causality is a much more complex issue to tackle. The most a researcher can expect to do is make reasoned deductions about relationships between variables and only after exhaustive examination of the data when viewed from a wide range of perspectives.

Interpreting test statistics

There are certain other important points to bear in mind when reviewing the results of a Chi-square test, or indeed, any statistical test. It must be remembered that the test statistic and significance level or result achieved are based on the data used. Thus, if the number of observations are small, this must be borne in mind when attempting to make inferences regarding the population of people or things as a whole. Studies based on small samples can usefully provide in-depth understanding of particular situations, but if we then wish to infer from the results characteristics regarding the whole population, we must resort to the appropriate considerations regarding random sampling procedures and the rationale of qualitative versus quantitative studies.

Another consideration is to decide whether or not the samples are in any way biased. In selecting samples of customers of style Hairdressing Salons in London and Glasgow, the consultants were careful to select people based on systematic random sampling procedures. Let us suppose, however, the consultants had not been so thorough and simply selected the first 50 customers visiting each salon on day one of the survey. Suppose, at the same time, the Style Hairdressing Salon in Glasgow was offering a special promotion deal to university students. Imagine the effect on the sample data. The sample of customers drawn from the Glasgow salon is likely to include a disproportionately large number of young customers. Unless these events are normal occurrences, there is a real danger the samples will be biased and not representative of the population of customers visiting the salons. Moreover, although we may conduct a series of statistical tests on this data , the results and conclusions drawn will only extend to the quality of the data provided and the situations observed during the survey period.

Goodness of fit

Before leaving the topic of Chi-square tests, it is useful to touch briefly on one other area in which a form of Chi-square is used. This is often referred to as the 'goodness of fit' test. It determines whether or not an observed frequency distribution fits an expected pattern. Observe the results shown in Table 18.10.

TABLE 18.10 Corporate customers' rating of a bank's services

Very poor	Poor	Adequate	Good	Very good
10	15	20	25	15

TABLE 18.11 Revised figures on ratings of bank services

Very poor	Poor	Adequate	Good	Very good
10	17	23	19	16
(17)	(17)	(17)	(17)	(17)

The sample relates to 85 corporate customers who expressed their views regarding a bank's services. It shows the majority (71 per cent) viewed the service as adequate to very good and almost half thought the service good. Supposing, however, the frequencies had been rather less convincing and expressed greater feelings of dissatisfaction as shown in the first row of Table 18.11.

The management of the bank are not clear how to view this data. Does it indicate a tendency towards a particular opinion or not?

A Chi-square test will assist. First we set up a null hypothesis. This states that the corporate customers expressed no clear opinion in respect of the bank's services. This suggests that the expected frequencies will therefore be evenly distributed between the five categories. These are shown in brackets in the second row of Table 18.11. The value of χ^2 is then computed in a similar manner as before. The value, using this data, is:

$$\chi^2 = (7^2 + 0^2 + 6^2 + 2^2 + 1^2)/17$$

$$\chi^2 = 5.29$$

The number of degrees of freedom is calculated as the number of categories in the observed data minus one, i.e. $(5-1) = 4$. Reference to the appropriate statistical table shows the value is non-significant and the management can therefore make no deductions on how corporate customers in the sample viewed their banking services. They have drawn a blank!

The test is referred to, as stated above, as a 'goodness of fit' test since it evaluates how one (observed) distribution matches another based on some pre-determined or expected pattern. This pattern may be determined by the researcher. Thus, the test may be used to evaluate whether or not an observed frequency distribution is normally distributed.

Correlation coefficients

The following discussion deals with the measures of association known as correlation coefficients. They differ from Chi-square tests in that correlation coefficients are concerned with actual values and not frequency distributions. Most people are aware of the meaning of the general term 'correlation'. It is a word we use in everyday parlance to describe whether or not one characteristic or phenomenon is associated with another. We are also mostly aware of the problems of spurious correlations such as the tales involving the number of storks and the number of babies! But, what do we mean by correlation in statistical terms and by measures involving the calculation of correlation coefficients?

We can start by taking a simple everyday example. We might say, for instance, that the amount of money people spend on holidays and leisure is associated with their net income. To test this hypothesis we could then take a random sample of people and plot on a chart their expenditure on last year's holiday against their net income for last year.

Each person's data would be plotted on two continuous scales as shown in Figure 18.1. If there were an association we would expect the plotted points to fall, or almost fall, along one straight line and, we would expect the amount spent on holidays to increase with net income. Thus, we would be looking for a positive (+ve) correlation. In cases where one value decreases while the other increases a negative (−ve) correlation occurs. For instance, the general manager of the Style Hairdressing Salon in London might hypothesize that the more the management spends on upgrading the salons within the group, the fewer will be the number of complaints received from customers!

Range of correlation values

Where one occurrence or data value is always associated with another occurrence or data value, we can say there is a perfect correlation. This is expressed mathematically as the value '+1' or '−1' depending on the direction of the association. Between these two extremes a range of other values can occur. When the correlation coefficient assumes the value zero, we state no correlation or association exists between the two

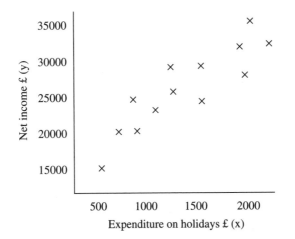

FIGURE 18.1 Scatter plot showing net income (£) against expenditure on holidays

variables. Thus, we can describe a correlation coefficient as a measure ranging between −1 and +1 on a continuum.

−1   **Negative correlation**
(i.e. as the value of one variable increases the other decreases)

0   **Positive correlation**
(i.e. increases in value for one variable is associated with increases in value for the other)

+1

In conducting evaluations involving correlation coefficients we are always dealing with paired comparisons or scores. To determine whether or not a correlation exists, the value of one variable (x) must always be plotted against the value of another variable (y). When analysing data sets it may also be appropriate to calculate a whole series of correlation coefficients. For instance, we may examine data on holiday spending against net income and then against other measures reflecting social class or a tourist's age. Each will involve a separate set of calculations. Thus we can piece together a fuller insight into a whole range of associations that may exist within one data set. The correlation coefficient is designed to indicate how strong the association is and once again we can ascertain significance levels through reference to appropriate statistical tables.

Scatter plots

The following paragraphs describe how correlation coefficients may be calculated. In addition to making such calcluations the researcher may find it also helpful, where the number of observations is not too large, to draw first a scatter plot. This will help decide visually whether or not an association exists. Consider the three simple diagrams given in Figure 18.2.

Plot A indicates a strong positive correlation between two variables x and y. Plot B indicates a similar strong association but in a negative direction, while Plot C indicates no association or correlation. It is not always clear, however, from single visual inspection what the strength of an association is between two variables and it may not be clear where the line, known as the 'line of best fit', should be drawn. In such cases, it is best not to attempt to draw any lines. Instead proceed to the calculation of the correlation coefficient. This will help you to be more precise.

Spearman's rho and Pearson's product moment correlation coefficient (r)

There are two types of correlation coefficient. The first, Spearman's rho, is particularly useful for calculating correlations in respect of ordinal data. It can therefore be used to assess associations between data involving rating scales. The second type of correlation coefficient can only be applied to data of interval or ratio status. The underlying aspect being investigated in the case of both tests is that the relationship between the two variables is linear, although in the case of Spearman's rho a simple curvilinear relationship can be tolerated. Where relationships between two sets of

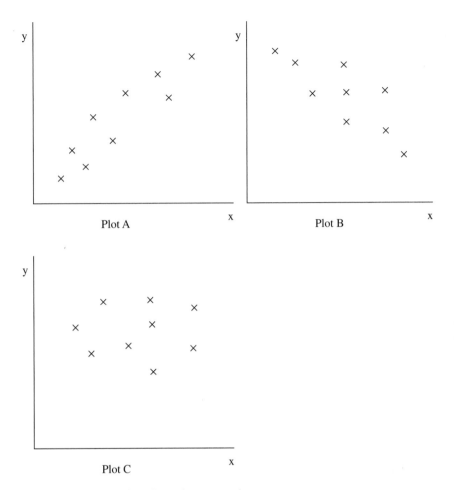

FIGURE 18.2 Examples of simple scatter plots

data are clearly not linear, that is, they are U shaped or follow an even more complex pattern, other more sophisticated techniques need to be considered.

Spearman's rho

We will look at two examples of how this test can be applied. The first is a simple example relating to a catering competition. The organizers of the competition employ two judges who are asked to decide at a preliminary trial on the rankings of eight sponge cakes. The judges are asked to evaluate the quality of the cakes in relation to:

- lightness/texture;
- colour; and
- flavour.

They are asked to then place the cakes in order from 1 to 8. The cake placed first is the best. The reason why the organizers decide to conduct this exercise, is they want to see

TABLE 18.12 Placing of cakes at a competition

Cake	Judge A	Judge B
A	4	3
B	2	1
C	1	2
D	3	4
E	5	5
F	7	8
G	6	6
H	8	7

to what extent the judges agree on the placings. They are aware placings or scores can differ between judges.

The data is of an ordinal status in that the first cake cannot be viewed as being eight times better than the cake placed eighth. In this example the scores already constitute ranked values and the calculation for Spearman's rho is simplified. The next step is to calculate the differences between the ranks as shown in Table 18.12 by applying the formula:

$$\text{rho} = 1 - [6 \sum_{i=1}^{N} D_i^2 / (N^3 - N)]$$

where $\sum_{i=1}^{N} D_i^2$ equals the sum of the differences between the ranked scores for each paired comparison; and

N   is the number of paired comparisons.

The values in this case are easily determined as follows:

$$\sum_{i=1}^{N} D_i^2 = (+1)^2 + (+1)^2 + (-1)^2 + (-1)^2 + (0)^2 + (-1)^2 + (0)^2 + (+1)^2$$

$$= 6$$

and $N = 8$ and $N^3 = 8 \times 8 \times 8 = 512$

Thus, the value of rho is:

$$\text{rho} = 1 - (6 \times 6)/504 \quad = 1 - 0.071$$
$$= 0.93$$

This is a two-tailed test as the organizers simply wished to establish whether or not the rankings were positively correlated. Reference to the appropriate statistical table shows that a value of rho equal to or greater than 0.881 gives a highly significant result at the 99 per cent confidence level. Thus, the judges although not identical in their evaluations are not widely different. We now take a different situation which shows how ranked values can be determined from different types of data.

Table 18.13 describes the outcome of a short monitoring exercise the manager of the Style Hairdressing Salon in London has been carrying out in respect of his receptionists. He is inclined to think his older staff are more reliable. One way in which this is reflected is in their promptness for work. The table shows against the age of each employee the number of times they have been late over the last six months.

A simple scatter plot indicates to the manager that there may be some basis for his thinking (see Figure 18.3) and the association if it exists indicates a negative correlation.

To calculate the value of rho, it is first necessary to calculate the ranks of the scores shown in Table 18.13. This is because Spearman's rho works on these values and not on the original data. The method for calculating ranks has been described in Chapter 17. Each row of scores is ranked separately. The calculations are:

TABLE 18.13 Number of times receptionists were late for work over the last six months

Staff member	Nos times late in last 6 months	Age
1	15	35
2	25	30
3	18	25
4	30	20
5	40	22
6	9	45
7	2	50
8	10	55
9	25	18
10	8	42
11	30	25
12	17	35

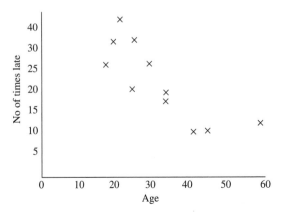

FIGURE 18.3 Scatter plot of number of times receptionists are late against their age, based on the figures given in Table 18.13

No of times late (in ascending order)

2	8	9	10	15	17	18	25	25	30	30	40
1	2	3	4	5	6	7	8	9	10	11	12
1	2	3	4	5	6	7	8.5	8.5	10.5	10.5	12

Note : Middle and bottom rows equal order and rank respectively.

Ages (in ascending order)

18	20	22	25	25	30	35	35	42	45	50	55
1	2	3	4	5	6	7	8	9	10	11	12
1	2	3	4.5	4.5	6	7.5	7.5	9	10	11	12

Note: Middle and bottom rows equal order and rank respectively.

We now replace the actual values or scores in Table 18.13 by the ranked values and calculate the differences as shown on Table 18.14.

The generalized formula for Spearman's rho can now be applied, i.e:

$$\text{rho} = 1 - 6 \sum_{i=1}^{N} D_i^2 / (N^3 - N)$$

where $\sum_{i=1}^{N} D_i^2$ is the sum of the squared differences shown in the final column of the table and N equals the number of paired scores.

In the case of this example:

TABLE 18.14 Ranked values relating to receptionist example

Staff no	Ranks Lateness	Age	Difference (D)
1	5	7.5	−2.5
2	8.5	6	+2.5
3	7	4.5	+2.5
4	10.5	2	+8.5
5	12	3	+9.0
6	3	10	−7.0
7	1	11	−10.0
8	4	12	−8.0
9	8.5	1	+7.5
10	2	9	−7.0
11	10.5	4.5	+6.0
12	6	7.5	−1.5

$$\sum_{i=1}^{12} D_i^2 = (-2.5)^2 + (2.5)^2 + (2.5)^2 + (8.5)^2 + (9)^2 + (-7)^2 + (-10)^2$$
$$+ (-8)^2 + (7.5)^2 + (-7)^2 + (6)^2 + (-1.5)^2$$
$$= 6.25 + 6.25 + 6.25 + 72.25 + 81 + 49 + 100 + 64 + 56.25 + 49 + 36 + 2.25$$
$$= 528.5$$

Thus, the value of rho is:

$$\text{rho} = 1 - \frac{6 \times 528.5}{(12^3 - 12)}$$

$$= 1 - \frac{3171}{1716}$$

$$= 1 - 1.848$$

$$= -0.848$$

The null hypothesis was based on a one-tailed test since the manager believed older staff were more punctual than younger staff. The result is significant and the manager can be confident at the 99 per cent level. Therefore, he is correct in his thinking.

Pearson's product moment correlation (r)

We next proceed to examine the other type of correlation coefficient, the Pearson's correlation coefficient, where the scores or values must be of at least interval status. The data used in the last example as shown in Table 18.14 in fact satisfies this condition and so we will calculate the value of Pearson's correlation coefficient on this same data by way of interesting comparison.

Pearson's correlation coefficient involves a more complex set of calculations, but has the advantage of using the actual data values and not just the ranked scores. It is therefore a more rigorous or discerning test. In looking at the generalized formula for 'r' the researcher may feel it somewhat daunting. It is:

$$r = \frac{\sum_{i=1}^{n}(x_i - \bar{x})(y_i - \bar{y})}{\sqrt{\left[\sum_{i=1}^{n}(x_i - \bar{x})^2\right]\left[\sum_{i=1}^{n}(y_i - \bar{y})^2\right]}}$$

In fact, it is no worse than calculating a standard deviation and we can simplify the notation to:

$$r = \frac{\sum d_x d_y}{\sqrt{\sum d_x^2 \sum d_y^2}}$$

where d_x and d_y represent the difference between each score and its appropriate arithmetic mean. In the case of our example the arithmetic mean for the first variable

TABLE 18.15 Calculation of Pearson's correlation coefficient (r) in respect of data shown in Table 18.13

Staff no	dx (1)	dy (2)	dxdy (3)	dx^2 (4)	dy^2 (5)
1	−4.08	+1.5	−6.12	16.65	2.25
2	5.92	−3.5	−20.72	35.05	12.25
3	−1.08	−8.5	+9.18	1.17	72.25
4	10.92	−13.5	−147.42	119.25	182.25
5	20.92	−11.5	−240.58	437.65	132.25
6	−10.08	11.5	−115.92	101.61	132.25
7	−17.08	16.5	−281.82	291.73	272.25
8	−9.08	21.5	−195.22	82.45	462.25
9	5.92	−15.5	−91.76	35.05	240.25
10	−11.08	8.5	−94.18	122.77	72.25
11	10.92	−8.5	−92.82	119.25	72.25
12	−2.08	1.5	−3.12	4.33	2.25

(numbers of times late) is 19.08 times and for the second variable (age) is 33.5 years. Each value in the two columns of Table 18.13 is then deducted from its appropriate mean to obtain the values of d_x or d_y. The subsequent step-by-step procedures for calculating 'r' are described by reference to Table 18.15.

Thus:

$\sum d_x d_y$ equals the sum of column (3) = −1280.5;
$\sum d_x^2$ equals sum of column (4) = 1366.96; and
$\sum d_y^2$ equals sum of column (5) = 1655.

$r = -1280.5/\sqrt{(1366.96 \times 1655)} = -1280.5/1504.1$
$r = -0.851$

The number of paired comparisons N is still 12 and it is a one-tailed test that is being conducted. Reference to the appropriate statistical table shows 'r' must be equal to or greater than 0.497 for a significance level of p = 0.05. hence the result is highly significant and it is a negative correlation as denoted by the −ve sign given to 'r'. When referring to the statistical tables reference should be made to the appropriate entry for N−2 which in this case is 10.

Interpreting correlation coefficients

Before finalizing this section on correlation coefficients it is relevant to point out certain aspects to consider when interpreting these statistical measures as well as some of the pitfalls to avoid. To do this we will also look briefly at certain situations where correlation coefficients can be used in conducting business research studies.

Causality

As with Chi-square tests, it is important to appreciate that a significant correlation between two variables does not imply causality. A correlation coefficient is purely a mathematical measure of association between two sets of numbers. We found, for example, that the general manager of the Style Hairdressing Salon in London was correct in his thinking that the age of his receptionists and their promptness for work were associated. This does not mean, however, that age in itself makes people more prompt. The greater reliability among the older staff may be associated with other factors such as a requirement for less sleep among older people, or more regular habits in going to bed at night rather than socializing and dancing the night away as may be favoured by those of a younger generation. Another factor may be that the older employees are more concerned about losing their jobs and therefore do not wish to give the manager cause for dismissing them.

All of these are possibilities and the fun of research is to explore the different options through different investigative approaches. Having established a correlation, it would be possible, for instance, to conduct an interview survey and discuss with the receptionists reasons for their behavioural patterns. It is also possible, as suggested earlier, to conduct a whole series of correlation measures to see how a range of variables are associated. Thus, we can begin to isolate the more significant relationships.

Chance correlations

One aspect to be wary of when reviewing correlation values is to note that significant correlations can occur by chance. This can arise particularly where sample sizes are small or where a large number of comparisons are being made. This is because correlation coefficients are measures which show how two sets of numbers in a paired comparison behave. However, it is possible the result obtained from a particular sample reflects an exceptional result. With small samples, for instance, there is always a possibility that two sets of numbers will arise which indicate a relationship which is, in fact, atypical. For example, we may throw a die and achieve a six. We then throw another die with the expectation of achieving any number from 1–6 with equal probability. Supposing, we in fact throw another six and then repeat the exercise on five more occasions. It is just possible that the result could look like that in Table 18.16.

In other words, every time we attained one value on the first throw it matched the value attained for the second throw. If we then proceed to calculate a correlation coefficient it can be seen the result would be to produce a value for 'r' equal to +1, or in other words the result would indicate a perfect match. However, it is unlikely such an occasion could easily be replicated. Thus, the result would be referred to in statistical parlance as atypical or an unreliable result. In rejecting the null hypothesis, that is, that the score achieved on the first throw is independent of the score achieved on the second, we would be making a Type II error. In effect we would be saying there is significant association between the two dice since the result from throwing the first

TABLE 18.16 Results from tossing a die

Throw	Die 1	Die 2
1	6	6
2	5	5
3	4	4
4	2	2
5	1	1
6	3	3

implies an equal score will be obtained when throwing the second, when in fact, common knowledge tells us this situation reflects an extreme outcome that has arisen by chance. Obviously, as the sample size increases the danger of making such a mistake becomes less, but obtaining an exceptional result is a situation which can also arise when making comparisons among many different variables within one data set.

Meaning of a particular correlation

Just as we can obtain a significant correlation by chance, so we can achieve correlations where the result is significant but there is no direct meaning in the association when viewed in the context of the 'real world'. As with all statistical interpretations never abandon that useful in-built factor called 'common sense'. Also, be thoughtful about whether or not an association although identified as significant has any real meaning in the context of your study.

We view these two aspects with reference to various examples. The first, which has been quoted in statistical circles in some form or another for years may seem rather puerile, but it makes the point clear. Let us suppose Professor Newton who is a geneticist has observed that the number of babies born in his home state each day correlates with the number of storks observed and counted in the vicinity on those days. Now some mothers may tell their young children they were originally delivered by a stork, but common sense and a knowledge of the 'facts of life' tell us in later years otherwise! The point is that two totally unconnected incidents can give rise to meaningless but significant correlations simply because two sets of numbers behave in a similar way.

Another less ludicrous example helps us to understand a development of the above argument as well as another point which is that variables may be associated but the knowledge of the association may not offer any real benefit when we come to interpret the results or present the findings for a particular study. Suppose United Newspapers decide to set up a newspaper stand in the West End of London. The new stand is positioned close to the Piccadilly Theatre which has a series of plays running throughout the season. The owner of the stand decides to conduct a short exercise and finds that the sales of newspapers each day are correlated with the number of people attending the Piccadilly Theatre each evening. In other words, he finds high sales are associated with 'full-houses' and low sales with 'poor-houses'. He thus concludes the position of his stand in close proximity to the theatre must be important to his business. In making such a deduction, would he be right or wrong? The question that he must next ask is whether or not his clientele are the same as the people who go to the theatre. If they are, he may be justified in making his deductions as there appears to be a direct connection. On the other hand, suppose the theatregoers are not, in fact, the purchasers of his newspapers. Perhaps, purchasers are tourists and other passers-by who frequent the streets more readily when the weather is fine and when, it so happens, the theatre is staging good plays. In short, another factor is at play.

We can try and resolve these matters through further investigation and that is why it is good to look at as many factors as possible when conducting your research. It is also important to consider which statistical associations are most meaningful in the context of your study. In the theatre example, let us suppose your real aim is to investigate the characteristics of the theatregoers and the reasons as to why they choose to see a particular type of play. As a basis for the study you may decide to collect a range of information on people's characteristics and reasons for choice. In analysing this data using computers to calculate correlation measures, it is not uncommon to produce a correlation matrix which shows how every variable correlates with every other variable. Clearly, based on what has been said so far, it is necessary to apply care and considerable thought to interpreting the results. You may find not unreasonably that theatregoers' ages and incomes are correlated. The question, however, is whether or not this piece of information is useful to you in your study. You may think that it is and want to emphasize the finding in presenting your results. On the other hand, you may decide other associations are more important such as an association between age and preference for certain types of plays, or income and frequency of theatregoing.

Correlation as a predictor

Setting aside the problems which can arise in interpreting correlation coefficients, it can be seen that correlation coefficients can be extremely useful when identifying associations across a range of variables. They can also assist with predicting data values. Returning to the scatter plots, we can see that where a perfect linear relationship exists then the value of one variable can be determined precisely from knowing the value of the other.

In practice, such perfect matches rarely exist, but we can nevertheless often use correlation analysis to predict data values with reasonable accuracy. It is beyond the scope of this text to go into the various types of prediction techniques. For those interested in such technical developments a useful next step would be to look at the procedures involved in conducting regression analysis. The simplest form of regression analysis is that based on the relationship between two variables 'y' and 'x' as shown in the scatter plots. It is usually assumed 'y' denotes the dependent variable – the one we are trying to predict – and 'x' is the independent variable (see Chapter 14). The prediction is then based on determining the regression line or 'line of best fit' and ascertaining values of 'y'.

Where it is useful to look at the values of a variety of independent variables in order to determine the value of one, this is referred to as multiple regression. In this case, the aim is to predict 'y' based on the values of a number of independent variables x_1, x_2, x_3 ... and so on. As stated earlier, it is not appropriate to go into these techniques here, but as with simple linear regression the concept of multiple regression is founded on the construction and theory relating to correlation coefficients. It takes account of measures which reflect the strength of associations between different variables.

Beyond correlation

This section of the book has introduced the student to some of the more important basic principles involved in conducting statistical evaluations in respect of business and management studies. It is impossible, within the context of this book, to provide an exhaustive description of all types of tests and statistical appraisals that can be conducted. The aim has been to provide basic guidelines with descriptions relating to the most common techniques. We have also attempted to introduce the reader to some of the problems that can arise when conducting statistical analyses.

Thus, the chapters on descriptive statistics, significance tests and tests of association should enable the student researcher to conduct a number of evaluations for themselves. Beyond this, there are a range of more complex techniques including analysis of variance, multiple regression, factor analysis, cluster analysis, trend analysis and principal components to name but some. All of these techniques have potentially wide-ranging applications. In addition, there are techniques that might be regarded as being of a more specialist nature. To gain an understanding of these more sophisticated techniques, the student will need to consult specialized texts relevant to the methodologies concerned.

References and further reading for Part Three

Clark, L. J. (1993) *The Essentials of Business Statistics Part I*, New Jersey: Research and Education Association.

Clegg, F. (1990) *Simple Statistics: A Course Book for the Social Sciences*, Cambridge: Cambridge University Press.

Cunningham, S. (1991), *Data Analysis in Hotel Catering Management*, Oxford: Butterworth-Heinemann.

Emden, J. V. and Easteal, J. (1987) *Report Writing*, Maidenhead: McGraw-Hill Book Company.

Fleming, M. C. and Nellis, J. G. (1993) *Principles of Applied Statistics*, London: Routledge.

Hannagan, T. J. (1988) *Mastering Statistics*, Basingstoke and London: Macmillan.

Harper, W. M. (1991) *Statistics*, London: Longman.

Hinton, P. R. (1995) *Statistics Explained: A Guide for Social Science Students*, London: Routledge.

Kanji, G. K. (1993) *Statistical Tests*, London: Sage.

Milewski, E. G. (1994) *The Essentials of Statistics Part I*, New Jersey: Research and Education Association.

Moser, C. A. and Kalton, G. (1993) *Survey Methods in Social Investigation*, Aldershot: Dartmouth.

Murdoch, J. and Barnes, J. A. (1986) *Statistical Tables*, Basingstoke and London: Macmillan.

Oakshott, L. (1994) *Essential Elements of Business Statistics*, London: D. P. Publications Ltd.

Rowntree, D. (1981) *Statistics Without Tears*, Harmondsworth: Penguin.

Part Four

Writing the Dissertation

19

Key techniques in writing up your dissertation

Now you have arrived at the great moment when you are going to put down all your thoughts and findings on paper in a form that will allow your examiners, internal and external, to assess your abilities to do certain things. For some of you this may be where the real test comes. You know the objective of your research, you know the outcome. You have masses of data in a variety of shapes and forms. You have done all the analysing, and evaluation that you feel is necessary. Would it not be nice just to transfer all of that straight from your mind to that of your examiners without the tedious process of putting it on paper? Perhaps that day will come, but meanwhile you have to tackle the transmission of your findings in the traditional way. This means putting everything together on paper in the most easily assimilated form, with clarity and precision of language, and in a manner which shows your examiner that you, have, more or less on your own initiative and independent judgement:

- identified and isolated an issue or problem;
- established some hypothetical construct in order to investigate it;
- developed an appropriate research methodology in carrying out the investigation;
- carried out critical searches of appropriate source material to support your analysis;
- implemented your methodology through the collection, collation and analysis of data; and
- deduced valid and reliable conclusions.

Perhaps you will receive the following ideas and advice more sympathetically if you realize that all the conventions and patterns which have been developed for the presentation of dissertations are in place precisely because they make it as painless as possible for the reader of your dissertation to extract from it the evidence that you have all the abilities outlined above. In other words it is not for the good of your soul we ask that numbering and referencing is of a certain style, that data is presented in a certain way, that your process of thought follows a certain order. This does not mean that there is one rigid format to be followed, but there are general guidelines that are consistently adhered to. This chapter outlines these and hopefully will therefore absolve you of the responsibility of having to think any more than you need about 'formalities' when you should be directing your intellectual energies towards the academic content of your dissertation. It may be that your own university or department has specific presentational requirements over and above, or which reflect a slight reorganization, of what follows. For example, there can be minor variations in the format of references, and a summary or abstract as such may be forgone because the content it would have is contained within the conclusions. However, we assume that you have already established what might be called 'local' conventions, and thus the following guidelines can be ignored or adapted as required. And in the long term, the skills and techniques outlined here will also be of value to you in your careers, when you have to prepare reports of varying length and complexity and on a variety of subjects in your role as business professionals.

You will no doubt be thinking at this stage that the least of your problems is whether a certain cluster of thoughts you have produced is called a summary or a conclusion, or whether you present a book title in your bibliography in italics or underlined. Your primary thoughts relate to more pressing problems, which in contemporary jargon can be encapsulated in the phrase 'How do I get my act together?' Meaning 'How do I get to grips with the enormity of the task set me, never before having written more than a 2000 word essay?' 'How do I organize my time – it looks like lots, but is it really?' 'How do I begin to get all this material into nice flowing English – this blank sheet of paper or empty screen is looking at me balefully?' It is useful at the outset therefore to remember that (a) thousands of undergraduates have been there before you and (b) these undergraduates are now graduates. The following advice is based on the experiences of a number of undergraduates, and should provide you with a 'short cut' to success.

Language and style

The language and style of writing requires to be just as carefully considered as it would be if you wanted to compete with Shakespeare. You may be writing a dissertation, instead of a play which you plan to become a classic for at least five hundred years, but that does not alter the fact that the ability to write clear and interesting prose contributes greatly to the success of your dissertation. After all, to paraphrase the philosopher Wittgenstein, if you cannot articulate what you are thinking, then the thoughts are not even in your head and, as we noted above, the very reason you have to produce this formal document we call a dissertation (or perhaps a project in some courses) is to prove to others you do have certain thoughts and ideas in your head! 'You know what I mean' may be quite an acceptable response in everyday conversation – it is not so for your examiners

The goal is to engage your readers' thinking in a way which will stimulate and interest them, maybe not quite in the manner of an 'airport blockbuster', but because you have recognized that whatever the market for the writing, the style and register of the content must reflect that market. Thoughts and ideas must be presented as directly, clearly and elegantly as you can manage. The word 'elegantly' is deliberately used to emphasize the stance that a good 'business style' or a good 'academic style' of writing can be just as elegant, or graceful, as a good 'literary' style. The difference is that literature, poetry and drama are usually written for the entertainment or amusement of others. Indeed, some texts may even be written for the deliberate mystification of others, but that is not the objective of your dissertation. However, because a dissertation is about 'scientific' understanding, students often fall into the trap of feeling they have to produce obfuscatory, convoluted, turbid, jargon-laden prose or they will not be taken seriously. Using two-syllable words instead of four, using sentences with 25 words instead of 50, using appropriate formal but everyday language instead of jargon, not only gets your message over faster, but also implies that you have sufficient confidence in that message to deliver it straight without any 'camouflage' of the sort the Plain English Campaign delight in drawing attention to. As it happens the word-processing package being used to type this has a 'test' to establish just the level one is writing at, which is to some extent based on how 'big' or difficult the words are and thus what age/educational background is required for understanding. Which is not quite the same thing as style, but certainly is a part of it. Of course, within any scientific study there must be some words and phrases, concepts and theories which are probably not easily (if at all!) comprehended by the layperson, but they are there for good reasons which you are very well aware of and can be explained by a brief addition to the text or in a glossary (see below). However, this is not the place to embark on a course in how to write good English, merely to draw attention to the above points if only because experience shows that students can have a big mental block about the actual writing style of a dissertation by virtue of the importance attached to its readership. The 'authority' over your subject matter which you hope to demonstrate to your examiners should come from the power of the ideas and the clarity and precision with which you express them.

The presentation of your dissertation

The point has been already made that the apparently arbitrary conventions which exist with regard to the actual written presentation of your dissertation are there for a purpose – to allow the reader to find his or her way round a mass of information in a logical order, or in a chosen order only extracting what the reader requires. Thus there are only very slight variations between universities' 'house styles', and these variations will no doubt have already been presented to you. For example, the length of the dissertation demanded of you can vary slightly, although generally at undergraduate level it is about 10,000 words. The important factor is that you have a consistent and coherent approach, based on certain academic conventions, to how you organize, produce and present your dissertation, because that will be considered part of the test of whether you have achieved your place in the academic 'sun'! And as the most important reader(s) of your dissertation will be your supervisor and the external examiner, they will be even more sympathetic to an intellectual effort if its presentation also shows care and attention. Thus ease of reading is an aspect truly appreciated. What follows is designed to be a blueprint or checklist for a conventional dissertation, and should ensure that your technical communication skills satisfy the above two objectives.

The obvious starting point is the order of content. Comprehensively, this would be as follows (different universities emphasize different orders for what follows: not all items are required by each university for every type of thesis – less widely included items are marked below with an asterisk).

(1) Title page
(2) Copyright statement and author declarations*
(3) Acknowledgements*
(4) Table of contents (including appendices)
(5) List of tables*
(6) List of figures*
(7) Abstract/summary/executive summary
(8) Preface*
(9) Main body of dissertation
(10) Glossary*
(11) Appendices
(12) Bibliography

Note that the table of contents (4) must present headings and sub-headings exactly as they appear in the next, but (1) and (7) are not included in this. Before proceeding to examine each of the above in turn, having commented on the relationship between *language* and style, it is worthwhile making a few general comments about *presentation* and style in constructing your dissertation.

This is another area which generally follows an almost international convention as to details about the page size, page margins, page numbers, abbreviations, style of numbers and numbering used, and how tables, diagrams, and figures, are presented. If you have not been given this information by your department, you can either check the style of dissertations by former undergraduates which may kept in your institution's library, or you can consult any number of specialist books, some of which are in the references at the end of this section. There may be very slight variations as to how your dissertation has to be bound, and titled on the binding, but again you will have been given such instructions at the outset. It is also likely a bookbinder will be recommended, if the work is not done 'in house.' Although you may be very proficient with a typewriter or word-processor, employing a typist who is a specialist in producing dissertations for your department is well worth the cost when it comes to the final production. When you are working to a deadline, it is a relief to know that you do not have to worry about the niceties of layout and correct spacing. However, it is extremely important to remember that the typist, just like your examiners, is not telepathic, so the following points must be kept in mind.

• Make sure that your draft manuscript is either typed, even if badly, by you or is handwritten as clearly as possible. If your typist has to guess at the translation of your bad writing, you might get a result like that of a game of Chinese Whispers!
• Remember that the necessary formal 'jargon' of your discipline or study may have its own conventions, abbreviations and spellings, and your typist might need some help with these, however good his or her formal English and spelling may be, and

despite the spell and grammar checks on word-processing packages. (For example, 'sociology' as a word on the spell check for this word-processing programme comes up as 'not found', and it is suggested it could be replaced with 'social outcast', 'socks', or ' soda fountains'!)

- Review your time and task-management schedule, and work out the timing of your delivery of material to the typist. It does not need to go to the typist in the final order, or all in one package, so you could plan to submit work for typing in several chunks. Find out from the typist what the optimum time is for production of the document, and discuss together how you intend to progress with handing over the manuscript.
- Maintain a regular oversight of the typing, so that you know it is of the style and quality you are required to hand over. It is also good for your morale – what you have written will always read better when it is professionally typed!

We now turn to examine each of the elements of the structure of the dissertation contained in the list above.

1 The title page

An example of a title page is shown in Figure 19.1. Your university will no doubt have laid down quite specifically what information should be given on a title page, although it is unlikely to be radically different from this.

AN INVESTIGATION INTO THE EFFECTIVENESS OF OUTWARD BOUND
SURVIVAL COURSES IN MANAGEMENT TEAM BUILDING

Mary Charlotte Crippen

A dissertation/thesis submitted in part fulfilment of the requirements of the degree of
Bachelor of Arts with Honours in Business and Management Studies

UNIVERSITY OF SOUTH-WEST CORNWALL

June 2000

FIGURE 19.1 Example of a dissertation title page

2 Copyright statement and author declaration

Your dissertation serves only one direct purpose. It has been produced exclusively by you in order to achieve your specific degree. Thus you normally have to state 'up front' that is the case, that you have not been listed for any other academic award during your period of study, nor has any of the material you have written up been submitted for another academic award. Whereas a formal unseen written examination, in front of an invigilator, is obviously your own unaided work, you may have to register publicly that this is the case with regard to your dissertation. And you will be considered to be held to that, otherwise it would be like committing perjury in a court of law. Figure 19.2 shows an example of a Declaration and Figure 19.3 a copyright statement. Many universities now insist on the latter as a means of ensuring that material is appropriately protected in the interests of student and institution – this is especially true at postgraduate level.

It is probably unnecessary but still well worth reminding you that implicit in any declaration is acknowledgement of the 'sin' of plagiarism. This is presenting the work of another as if it were your own, using the same language, and without referencing the source. The word 'perjury' was used above. The legal analogy here is that plagiarism is considered to be stealing someone else's intellectual property, and is thus a serious academic offence. Plagiarism is a bit like stealing the blueprint for someone else's invention, which is why we have patent laws. Using the ideas of others to support your discussion is perfectly acceptable as long as you acknowledge the fact, which is why appropriate referencing, to be examined later, is so important. Because of its length and the amount of reading involved, producing, a dissertation can result in your having reams of notes and quotes, and it is quite easy when writing up the dissertation to copy down something from your notes which you do not even realize you were plagiarizing, but will be recognized as such by your examiners. So this is another reason for keeping all your raw data and notes as well referenced as possible.

> I, MARY CHARLOTTE CRIPPEN, declare that I am the sole author of this dissertation, that during this period of registered study I have not been registered for any other academic award or qualification, nor has any of the material been submitted wholly or partly for any other award. I have personally carried out all the work of which this is a record. The programme of study of which this is a part has been delivered by the School of Business and Management, University of South-West Cornwall.
>
>
> Signed:
>
> Date: June 30th, 2000

FIGURE 19.2 Example of an author's declaration for a dissertation

School of Business and Management, University of South-West Cornwall

---

Reproduction of Undergraduate Dissertation/Project

The University Library receives requests from other libraries to supply photocopies of theses, dissertations, reports, etc. Such requests are normally complied with provided that the consent of the author can be obtained. Occasionally, however, it is difficult or impossible to contact an author especially in the case of graduates from overseas.

It would greatly assist the Library if authors of such papers would complete the lower section of this form indicating whether or not they are prepared to sanction the reproduction of their work, subject to the appropriate safeguards. Further reference to an author in this connection would then be unnecessary.

It is emphasized that, if this permission is given, it in no way affects an author's interests in his/her work under copyright.

AUTHOR'S DECLARATION

Name .... (capitals please)
Title of work ....
....
Qualification ....
Department/School ....
Delete whichever does not apply.

1. I am willing that my thesis/dissertation/report should be available for reproduction at the discretion of the Librarian of the School of Business and Management and on the understanding that users are made aware of their obligations under copyright.

2. I am not willing that my thesis/dissertation/report be made available for reproduction.

Signed ....
Date ....

FIGURE 19.3 Example of a dissertation copyright declaration

Another document which will generally be attached is one which gives your university library 'permission to copy' extracts from your dissertation for other researchers if you cannot be got hold of personally. However, signing such a statement in no way affects your interests or rights as the author of the dissertation.

3 Acknowledgements

As a matter of courtesy you will wish to include a 'thank you' to those who helped you with your dissertation or thesis. Acknowledgements come in a variety of styles and forms, and can often be just as interesting or as witty as the work to which they are referring. But in the case of a piece of academic work, being witty is not the prime objective. Restrain your journalistic tendencies until after you graduate, and give

Acknowledgements

I would like to thank the following for their contribution to the production of this dissertation. Dr Caitlin Fraser, my supervisor, gave her academic and moral support over the whole period of production of this work, and especially during the final tense weeks. My tutor, Andrew Penarth, exercised great patience whilst helping me with my statistical analyses. The management of the Information West International showed great forbearance in putting up with me and responded amicably and helpfully to all my questions. Finally, to my parents, for all the tea and sympathy with which they overwhelmed me through these long months of creation, thank you.

FIGURE 19.4 Example of a dissertation acknowledgements page

recognition without over-embellishment. Generally, however, you will want to thank those who gave you specific and in-depth help or support, such as your supervisor, and any other members of the academic staff, and additionally, if you were involved in, say, a survey, those who co-operated in that. It may also be good social skills to thank mum/dad/partner/children/friends and so on, who put up with your strange or preoccupied behaviour over the period of production (see Figure 19.4).

4–6 Table of contents (including appendices; list of tables; list of figures)

As was pointed out earlier, although you would certainly have a table of contents, you may not necessarily have tables and/or figures to list. Again, you may have to conform to a local 'house style', but the following is a relatively conventional sample contents page.

Contents

Title page	
Copyright statement and author declaration	ii
Acknowledgements	iii
Table of contents (including appendices)	iv
List of tables	v
List of figures	vi
Abstract/summary/executive summary	vii

(it is conventional to use Roman numbering until you get to the start of Chapter 1)

Chapter One: Management Development

Chapter Two: Literature Review

etc.

(Use actual headings and sub-headings as they appear in your dissertation).

Illustrative material is normally placed as near as possible to the appropriate text, and tables should be typed into the text and given a number, a title and a source, if not derived from original research work.

7 The Abstract, summary or executive summary

Writing your abstract (or summary/executive summary depending on your institution's preference) is an intellectual exercise in itself, as it must explain precisely yet clearly to the reader the nature and scope of your research, your findings and the particular contribution you have made to the sum of human knowledge in your chosen field of study in around 300 words. This conventional length, approximately one-thirtieth the length of your complete dissertation, sounds a horrendous task, but you will already have gone most of the way towards doing that when you first established what you were going to do and had to present a synopsis to your supervisor. Since that first synopsis you may have refined your objectives to some extent, even to a great extent, and your research findings may now be quite unrelated to what you proposed initially to demonstrate. But at least the core of your thinking is likely to be still there. It is useful to remember that the purpose of the abstract, apart from it being an assessment of your ability for examination purposes, is to let a potential reader, such as another researcher, determine whether what you have written is worth reading for his or her purposes. You can think of it as a sort of 'marketing' exercise through which you show the relevance and importance of your study by pinpointing its key elements.

8 Preface

A preface is not normally found in undergraduate dissertations but may be seen in research theses for higher degrees. An author's preface is normally a short 'scene-setting' section prior to the first chapter which draws attention to any special or unique points contingent upon the reasons for selection of topic, the importance of the topic, and/or the topic's relevance.

9 The content or main body of the dissertation

Again there is a conventional order of presentation, which is unlikely to vary unless there is something particularly unusual about the style or method of research. In a sense the order of presentation is 'no big deal' as they say, as it follows a pattern you are already well familiar with when it comes to writing essays. That is, you have an introduction, an outline of your method of approach, the presentation and evaluation of your data, and then a conclusion based on your findings. Of course, this will be sub-divided into chapters and the actual number of chapters you have will again depend how you have developed your investigation. A good way to think about this is to imagine that you are just writing an essay, but each paragraph becomes a 'chapter'. Just as a paragraph consists of linked and related sentences that focus on the same idea or topic, amplify it, explain it, evaluate it, so a chapter looks at one aspect of your research and develops it in detail. You will find too that your chapter 'headings' usually follow naturally from the necessary elements of your dissertation. The actual number of chapters you produce will (for a 10,000 word dissertation) generally be from four to seven, with each chapter being around the same length. If you go by this yardstick, then you have at the outset a rough guide as to how many words you should produce for each chapter. For example, if the required length of your dissertation is around 10,000 words, the likelihood is that you will have six chapters, each around 1700 words.

The manner in which these chapters are evolved will depend entirely on how you have personally planned your discussion, but your supervisor will have given you guidance on this. However, it is extremely unlikely that you will get by without the following components.

- *Introduction*: in which you outline and explain the purpose and extent of your research and why you embarked upon it – why you were interested in the topic in the first place.
- *Aims*: in which you spell out specifically the aims you hope to achieve, and the hypothesis, or hypotheses you have set up, wish to test, whether of your own construction, or that of another academic whose assumptions you might be challenging, or building upon.
- *The context or background*: this is sometimes referred to as the 'literature search', or 'literature review' although in fact it should cover more than a search of all relevant literature. Additionally it should also be a critical appraisal of what you have found, and how your ideas are related to or stem from any previous research related to the topic.
- *The methodology*: this is arguably the most important component of your dissertation, as you no doubt have been told *ad nauseam*! It is the element which shows how you have gone about your research, which particular research methods and techniques you have used and why, and how you have implemented them. If you can present this with clarity and cogency, then you will have predisposed your examiners to receiving the rest of your intellectual effort positively. This is because an examiner can (almost) determine the mark likely to be gained by the

dissertation by the methodology alone – this is the 1 per cent inspiration which precedes the 99 per cent perspiration!

- *Execution*: now the 99 per cent perspiration. What you actually did in practice, described comprehensively and systematically. How you gathered your data, how you resolved your research questions, how you analysed and evaluated your findings in relation to the research questions or hypotheses you set yourself. Either within this component or within your conclusion it is necessary to assess critically the effectiveness of your chosen research methodology.
- *Conclusion*: the summing up of your stance, what you have added to the aggregate of human knowledge and why. This will also reflect the impact of the theoretical material on your findings, and can also suggest wider implications, new question which have been raised. What must *never* come into your conclusion is any new material or new arguments.

10 Glossary

A glossary is a list of specialist terms and definitions thereof employed in a dissertation or thesis. Only essential, specialist, terms should be included. Local regulations vary as to where in a dissertation the glossary should appear so it is wise to check your institution's practice in this regard.

11 Appendices

This section of your dissertation holds all the information which you considered to be key supportive material for your investigation, but is not required to be an essential part of it. Again you will have to judge for yourself exactly what you feel is important enough in terms of helping the reader to understand further where your thoughts have come from. It might be raw data, which is summarized, analysed or extrapolated from in the main body of the dissertation, or the full results of questionnaires, tests, verbatim interviews, or a glossary of technical terms. It could be lists of institutions visited or important individuals and groups consulted. What is included will in fact depend upon how and where you collected your data from, what type of data it is, and how you have gone about analysing it. Appendices are usually numbered in Roman numerals – I, II, III, or letters – A, B, C.

12 Referencing and constructing a bibliography

During your research you will have read, and made use of, a very wide range of literature, probably from a huge variety of sources. Not all of it would necessarily have been helpful to you, but that which was directly relevant and applicable to your project must be formally referenced. The extent of your reading shows that you have a good knowledge of the field in which your research is located and it also serves as framework or context for your own findings. However, present your references with discretion, meaning do not include *everything* you have looked at, down to the *Yellow*

Pages. You might just get queried about the contribution a particular article made to your dissertation and if you have only included it to boast, and to boast about the extent and breadth of your reading, you could be in deep trouble. The references you include should mainly be those which offer some evidence to support, amplify, or in some other way relate to what you yourself are writing about.

Within the main body of your dissertation, specific references to the work of others can be made in a number of ways, depending upon the sentence structure you have chosen. The main rule is that you do not give any more than is necessary to identify the full information in your bibliography, thus all that is required is a name and a date of publication. The following are examples of the different types of presentation.

As Macdonald (1992) pointed out ...

... such a position was taken some years ago (Macdonald, 1992) when it was argued that ...

Research undertaken at the Cornish Institute of Business Research (Duncan, 1985; Gordon, 1989; Penarth, 1992) suggests that ...

... however generally the findings did not seem to support this hypothesis (Campbell, 1991: 72).

Note that when reference is made to work by several authors, on the first reference, all names are given, and further references thus:

Cameron, Robert and Stewart (1983) .... then ... Cameron *et al.* (1983)

Note also (as in the Campbell example above) that some references need to be precise and thus a page reference or references is inserted after the date. Such page references are always required prior to a quotation.

The bibliography

A widely used system of referencing in the academic world is the so-called 'Harvard' system, which we have employed in the examples above. These translate to the bibliography as in Figure 19.5. The list is alphabetical by author surnames, or names if it is an organization.

Proctor, T. (1995) *The Essence of Management Creativity*, Hemel Hempstead: Prentice Hall International (UIC) Limited.

Scottish Tourist Board (1992) *Tourism and the Scottish Environment: A Sustainable Partnership*, Edinburgh: Scottish Tourist Board.

Welsch, H. (1998) 'American North', in Morrison, A. (Ed) *Entrepreneurship: an International Perspective*, Oxford: Butterworth-Heinemann, pp. 58–75.

Wilkins, B. and Anderson, P. (1991) 'Gender differences and similarities in management communication: *Managerial Communication Quarterly*, Vol. 5, No. 1, pp. xxx–xxx.

Note: in the above Figure, pp. indicates pages numbers (from-to) which would replace the 'xxx–xxx' format, e.g. pp. 201–249. It is increasingly the case that the 'pp.' Latinism is omitted.

FIGURE 19.5 Example of an extract from a list of references or bibliography

You will of course have realized that there are variations in style – even within the Harvard system. In dissertations and theses, the titles of books and journals may be underlined instead of italicized in the publishing world to underline a word is, in effect, an instruction to italicize. It is becoming increasingly common to simply italicize these items directly (a trend resulting mostly from the advent of advanced word-processing technology). As always, the most important consideration is to be *accurate and consistent*.

This brief discussion of dissertation writing conventions brings the present chapter to a conclusion. In Chapter 20, the final chapter of the book, we examine the various issues attendant on the oral presentation of project and dissertation findings, a skill that is becoming increasingly important in the modern world.

20

The oral presentation of dissertation findings

It is sometimes the case that you have to give a formal oral presentation of your dissertation, though this is still unusual at undergraduate level and is a practice more commonly associated with higher degrees (masters and doctorates). If you do have to talk about your dissertation, it is likely that it will be within a viva voce the (Latin) academic term for such procedures. This in itself is an ordeal, mainly because you do not know what questions are to be asked of you, and thus the only preparation you can undertake is first, to ensure you know your material almost off by heart, and second, to try to get into your examiner's mind and foresee what he or she might be likely to ask. This could be questions about material you did not write up, data you did not collect, methodologies you did not consider, so even being familiar with every word of your dissertation may not be enough. Basically, then, a viva voce is about thinking on your feet, defending your thesis or dissertation in a constructive way, expanding on its content for the benefit of your examiner(s).

A viva voce is a special form of oral presentation for examination purposes. Other kinds of oral presentation include the mini-lecture and the seminar presentation. This chapter is to remind you of how to go about planning and delivering an effective oral presentation. We focus primarily on the viva voce. You will no doubt have done this many times before in your undergraduate progress, but this is the most important session and you want to get it absolutely right. Thus a checklist is essential in order that you not only make the best use of your time but also of your knowledge, and your ability to propound it. This requires particular technical skills and considerable interpersonal skills, including the ability to empathize with your audience, however constituted, and to monitor how it is responding to your presentation so you can adjust your stance accordingly. The psychology of verbal and non-verbal communication is immensely important here because it is likely you will be assessed not only on your academic knowledge and intellectual understanding, but also on how you present yourself as a human being. How you handle a question which you cannot answer can reveal more about both these aspects of you than the rehearsed answer to the predictable question.

Let us look first at some of the technical aspects of the delivery. At the outset you will almost certainly know who your 'audience' is. There may be one or several examiners, and it is possible there may also be your fellow students present. Thus you can be fairly sure of the general level of knowledge and understanding of your subject matter, although not everyone may actually have read your dissertation (although your examiner(s) certainly will have!). The objective of the communications process is a formal or informal assessment of your academic effort. You know how long you have for your session, and perhaps even the actual format. Perhaps you have to speak for 10 minutes and then be prepared to answer questions for 20 minutes. You know where you have to give the presentation, although you may not be told what audio or visual equipment is available. And you know what time you are on, and what 'running order', if any, you occupy. What questions do you have to ask yourself about the above? The following are indicative.

- How can I ensure that in the time I have been given I can draw out the most important points in my dissertation?
- How can I ensure that the points I draw out are those which will engage the audience, who might have had to sit through a considerable number of similar presentations that day, and probably over a period of days'?
- How can I compensate, if I have to, for a physical and spatial environment which may be a distraction, either to my audience or to me? For example, background noise, a seating arrangement which could be 'threatening' to me because I am too close to the audience, or because I have to stand or sit in a very formal position.
- What is the best way to get over the key points I would wish to, and how do I ensure that any discussion and/or questions fit into a specified time.
- What technical equipment is available if I require it, and is it positioned conveniently, and working properly? For example, a flip chart, a white board (with the right kind of marker pens) an overhead projector (OHP). The positioning of an OHP could be crucial if you intend using acetates because you must ensure that the font you use is the appropriate size for the distance between the OHP and the screen.
- If I do not or cannot have answers to the above questions, how much does it affect my plans for my presentation?
- Finally, what is it about me, as opposed to the practical and intellectual aspects of the presentation, which might be used positively towards a good performance, or which might adversely affect one, and how do I deal with that?

What do I do next? Some technical issues in structure and strategy

Keep right at the front of your mind when you are preparing for your presentation that you are trying to fulfil three objectives. You have to keep your audience listening, by sparking and then retaining its interest You have to make an impact with your academic and intellectual talents. Further, you have to support that impact with your personal attitude and demeanour, in order to reinforce belief that you are on top of your subject. This requires that you employ all the technical and interpersonal skills at your command, directed towards these objectives. 'Technical' may be also interpreted as 'practical' or 'operational' skills or issues, as opposed to the 'human' or psychological aspects, and we will start with these.

As your audience is knowledgeable, you will be able to speak to them in their own 'language'. This will save time, although you may need to have by you at least a glossary of concepts, or of perhaps lesser known academics whom you have referred to in your dissertation. This could be put on an acetate or on a sheet for a flip chart for ease of access. As the key people in the audience will have read your dissertation, you do not need to reiterate word for word what you were about and how you went about it. So what you do say is more of a 'storyline' which draws out the most important points or issues you feel you have investigated, and why. Thus a very effective way in which to engage the audience, and one that serves you as a structure for your presentation, is to present that storyline, with these key issues, in note form to your audience, so that they keep to your train of thought, and thus allow you to control the presentation as closely as possible. Again this could be done either on an acetate, or quickly copied from your brief notes on to a white board or flip chart.

You will, of course, have your actual dissertation by you, so have, along with the notes you have constructed, the appropriate reference to the full detail in the dissertation should you be asked about it. These can be jotted down on a sheet of paper, as well as indicated on the dissertation with markers. Frantically checking for references not only wastes time, it is also bad psychology.

The amount of information you present your audience with at the outset obviously depends upon how you have been briefed as to time allowance and content. This is then a matter of your judgement. But if we again think about the psychology of the presentation, your audience may respond less positively to what you say if your notes look as if you are going to talk endlessly. Photocopying a typed set of notes onto an acetate always looks more professional than handwritten notes, unless your writing is of copybook quality. This also applies if you are using supporting graphs or diagrams which can now be constructed so effectively with computer graphics programmes. Whether handwritten or typed, a truly professional visual presentation generally will be all the better for colour, even if this is not essential. Remember, too, the point about the size of font. It can be extremely frustrating to see a screenful of type that one cannot read because it is so small, having been designed for a much larger lecture theatre with much greater magnification. Have a practice if you can to check what is the optimum size. And if you do not know, err on the safe side – better to use too large a font than too small. If you intend to use some other form of presentational aid perhaps an audio tape or a videotape, if your research has encompassed interviewing, then ensure that you are properly familiar with the equipment, so that you do not waste time or lose the impact of some aspect of your work through technical problems. All audio or visual equipment may work the same way, but the buttons and switches are not necessarily in the same place!

The simplest way to construct your 'storyline' is to re-write your abstract in note form, and then think of each chapter heading as a secondary section of notes, with sub-sections of further notes. However, it might be worth standing back from the formal written organization of your dissertation and think about presenting it in a way which is more in tune with it being an oral presentation designed to hold your audience's interest. For example, after outlining the dissertation's aims, you could discuss why you chose particular methodologies, or new questions thrown up by your findings, or problems with regard to the collection or collation of certain data. Not only does this approach allow you to concentrate on those areas with which you are most familiar, and thus most comfortable about being questioned upon, but it will also lengthen your audience's attention span. If you do not have access to an OHP, then use the pre-technology trick of writing down the main points of your presentation on separate index cards. Each card should have a main heading, with three or four sub-headings. Constructing this will encourage you to break down what could be a complex argument into a simple sequence of ideas or strands of thought. Think of these cards as prompt cards, which will allow you to speak more naturally when you develop each idea, rather than reading direct from a script, which not only sounds more stilted, but also suggests that you are not so on top of your material as you ought to be. If you have not already used this technique, then practise before the formal occasion. Prepare any aids you intend to use as professionally as time allows, but equally do not embellish them with unnecessary detail. Simplicity and directness will have more impact. Remember too that whilst you are using any aids keep good eye contact with your audience, and do not stand silent for too long at any one time.

Basically then, the structure of your presentation should be as follows:

- an introduction which gets your audience's attention, gives them a flavour of what is to come, and informs them of the content and structure of your presentation;
- the main detail; and
- a review and summary of what you have said, with your evaluation of the work you have undertaken and the conclusions you have drawn

Your examiners will decide for themselves what they find interesting, or important to question you on, and have probably made that decision before they even saw you, so your presentation should be rather more of a general overview to remind them again what they have read.

Dealing with the human element of the process

In some respects, to separate out the technical and the human element in this communications process is an artificial exercise, as very often how you choose to deal with the technical requirements of an oral presentation will be because you have taken account of the human requirements. For example, if you are speaking in a room in which the seating arrangement is not conducive to good interaction (problem of eye contact, perhaps) then you might want to position yourself in a particular way or at a particular angle. Although the main objective of the process is to convince the audience that you are of an appropriate intellectual calibre, you know that if you can additionally entertain it with your presentation, then psychologically it will be more predisposed to be supportive of what you say – or at least less critical. A borderline 'fail' can quite easily become a clear pass if the student's self-presentation and handling of the situation shows confidence, involvement with his or her subject matter, and the ability to cope with challenges to his or her intellectual rigour with maturity. The place and manner in which you position yourself can also be a function of how nervous you are likely to be. If you can choose to sit at a desk or table, or stand at a lectern, it can be quite comforting because there is a physical barrier between you and the audience. If you can sit down, you can unobtrusively sit on your hands, or tuck them between your knees to stop them shaking. Standing by an overhead projector not only gives you something to 'hold on to' instead of wondering what to do with your hands, but also allows the angle of the eye contact to give you some psychological control over your audience as you look down on them. Do not be frightened to say that you would prefer to sit or stand in a certain place.

When you are constructing your notes, do not feel you need continually to use the complex academic or technical language of your written work. Of course you must be absolutely clear about definitions, concepts, how you have employed theories, references to the work of other academics and so on in case you are questioned on them. But far better that you do not get tongue-tied during your presentation. The style of the spoken word is generally more colloquial than that of the written word, whatever the context.

Similarly, keep a regular check on how your time is going. Answering a question may take more time than you thought, but it is better not to run over or even look like running over. The minute your audience start thinking about the length of time you have been performing, the minute they start getting distracted from your presentation. Better to finish off on a 'high', in which you explicitly spell out that you are choosing to finish on a certain point, whilst leaving others untouched. This in itself shows that you are command of the situation.

Your delivery technique – the 'you' in your presentation

As mentioned above, the presentation of your dissertation will certainly not be the first time you have undertaken such an exercise, so you will have a fair idea of your competence and confidence in such situations. This is not the place to go into sophisticated analyses of perfect presentation skills – there are many textbooks which do exactly that if you do not already know – however, a brief checklist should help you re-assess your strengths and weaknesses. Consider the following.

- Can you build into your voice clarity, confidence and be at ease with the situation?
- Can you project enthusiasm, sincerity, conviction?
- Is your pronunciation and articulation good – very important if you are handling a great deal of jargon or specialist language? A regional accent is no barrier, despite what some people may think, as long as words are articulated properly.
- Is your general appearance appropriate to the situation as you see it?

- Can you identify whether you have any distracting mannerisms which might interfere with audience attention?
- Are you good at identifying and dealing with 'cues' given by an audience which will ensure that your flow of ideas is not interrupted through negative perceptions of either the content or presentation?

Finally here, what if you suffer generally from 'stage fright' in such situations, however often you have undertaken the task? 'Stage fright' comes from having a higher than usual level of adrenaline in your blood, which prepares the body for expending extra energy. Think of that extra energy working for you, to help you produce the performance of your life! Do not envy those of your colleagues who can go in and be totally relaxed on such occasions – they just may come over to their audience as so 'laid back' that they appear lacking in enthusiasm and vitality. Think of what Jean Paul Sartre was saying when he commented that a speech was as a 'slight fever.' First, remember that careful preparation will give you confidence for your presentation and confidence in your ability to deliver it effectively. Second, remember that you have put enormous effort into your dissertation, and you have 'lived' with it for some considerable time. Have the courage of your convictions, faith in what you have written, and remember that it has been produced in order to contribute to what you most want to achieve, a good degree. If you believe in what you are saying, then that is the best antidote for fear of failure or of sounding foolish.

Lastly, force yourself to look calm. Think about the body language that gives away nervousness on your part (you know that you fiddle with your hair, or rattle keys in your pocket) and consciously practise controlling that. Practise keeping your voice level and your breathing even. Remember too that nervousness can be contagious, so try not to let your audience see that you are suffering. Concentrate on the situation and what its purpose is for you, rather than worry about them.

In conclusion, conclude with impact! Leave a good impression by looking directly at your audience (meaning that you should know exactly what you are going to say without reference to your notes) and sounding as if you have offered up – albeit with humility – equivalent findings to that of Einstein's Theory of Relativity. After all, you just might have done … but even if you have not, we hope this book has at least been worthwhile for you in a variety of other ways.

Further reading for Part Four

Berry, R. (1994) *The Research Project: How to Write It*, London: Routledge.

Hampson, L. (1994) *How's Your Dissertation Going? Students Share the Rough Reality of Dissertation and Project Work*, Lancaster: Unit for Innovation in Higher Education, School of Independent Studies, University of Lancaster.

Sharpe, H. K. (1983) *The Management of a Student Research Project*, Aldershot: Gower.

Wolcott, H. (1990) *Writing up Qualitative Research*, London: Sage Publications.

■ □ ▨ ■ Appendix A

Statistical tables

TABLE A.1 Standard normal distribution. The entries in this table are the probabilities that a random variable having the standard normal distribution assumes a value between 0 and z_1; the probability is represented by the area under the curve (the shaded area). Areas for negative values of z are obtained by symmetry.

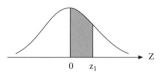

					Second decimal place in z					
z	0.00	0.01	0.02	0.03	0.04	0.05	0.06	0.07	0.08	0.09
0.0	0.0000	0.0040	0.0080	0.0120	0.0160	0.0199	0.0239	0.0279	0.0319	0.0359
0.1	0.0398	0.0438	0.0478	0.0517	0.0557	0.0596	0.0636	0.0675	0.0714	0.0753
0.2	0.0793	0.0832	0.0871	0.0910	0.0948	0.0987	0.1026	0.1064	0.1103	0.1141
0.3	0.1179	0.1217	0.1255	0.1293	0.1331	0.1368	0.1406	0.1443	0.1480	0.1517
0.4	0.1554	0.1591	0.1628	0.1664	0.1700	0.1736	0.1772	0.1808	0.1844	0.1879
0.5	0.1915	0.1950	0.1985	0.2019	0.2054	0.2088	0.2123	0.2157	0.2190	0.2224
0.6	0.2257	0.2291	0.2324	0.2357	0.2389	0.2422	0.2454	0.2486	0.2517	0.2549
0.7	0.2580	0.2611	0.2642	0.2673	0.2704	0.2734	0.2764	0.2794	0.2823	0.2852
0.8	0.2881	0.2910	0.2939	0.2967	0.2995	0.3023	0.3051	0.3078	0.3106	0.3133
0.9	0.3159	0.3186	0.3212	0.3238	0.3264	0.3289	0.3315	0.3340	0.3365	0.3389
1.0	0.3413	0.3438	0.3461	0.3485	0.3508	0.3531	0.3554	0.3577	0.3599	0.3621
1.1	0.3643	0.3665	0.3686	0.3708	0.3729	0.3749	0.3770	0.3790	0.3810	0.3830
1.2	0.3849	0.3869	0.3888	0.3907	0.3925	0.3944	0.3962	0.3980	0.3997	0.4015
1.3	0.4032	0.4049	0.4066	0.4082	0.4099	0.4115	0.4131	0.4147	0.4162	0.4177
1.4	0.4192	0.4207	0.4222	0.4236	0.4251	0.4265	0.4279	0.4292	0.4306	0.4319
1.5	0.4332	0.4345	0.4357	0.4370	0.4382	0.4394	0.4406	0.4418	0.4429	0.4441
1.6	0.4452	0.4463	0.4474	0.4484	04495	0.4505	0.4515	0.4525	0.4535	0.4545
1.7	0.4554	0.4564	0.4573	0.4582	0.4591	0.4599	0.4608	0.4616	0.4625	0.4633
1.8	0.4641	0.4649	0.4656	0.4664	0.4671	0.4678	0.4686	0.4693	0.4699	0.4706
1.9	0.4713	0.4719	0.4726	0.4732	0.4738	0.4744	0.4750	0.4756	0.4761	0.4767
2.0	0.4772	0.4778	0.4783	0.4788	0.4793	0.4796	0.4803	0.4808	0.4812	0.4817
2.1	0.4821	0.4826	0.4830	0.4834	0.4838	0.4842	0.4846	0.4850	0.4854	0.4857
2.2	0.4861	0.4864	0.4868	0.4871	0.4875	0.4878	0.4881	0.4884	0.4887	0.4890
2.3	0.4893	0.4896	0.4898	0.4901	0.4904	0.4906	0.4909	0.4911	0.4913	0.4916
2.4	0.4918	0.4920	0.4922	0.4925	0.4927	0.4829	0.4931	0.4932	0.4934	0.4936
2.5	0.4938	0.4940	0.4941	0.4943	0.4945	0.4946	0.4948	0.4949	0.4951	0.4952
2.6	0.4953	0.4955	0.4956	0.4957	0.4959	0.4960	0.4961	0.4962	0.4963	0.4964
2.7	0.4965	0.4966	0.4967	0.4968	0.4969	0.4970	0.4971	0.4972	0.4973	0.4974
2.8	0.4974	0.4975	0.4976	0.4977	0.4977	0.4978	0.4979	0.4979	0.4980	0.4981
2.9	0.4981	0.4982	0.4982	0.4983	0.4984	0.4984	0.4985	0.4985	0.4986	0.4986
3.0	0.4987	0.4987	0.4987	0.4988	0.4988	0.4989	0.4989	0.4989	0.4990	0.4990
3.1	0.4990	0.4991	0.4991	0.4991	0.4992	0.4992	0.4992	0.4992	0.4993	0.4993
3.2	0.4993	0.4993	0.4994	0.4994	0.4994	0.4994	0.4994	0.4995	0.4995	0.4995
3.3	0.4995	0.4995	0.4995	0.4996	0.4996	0.4996	0.4996	0.4996	0.4996	0.4997
3.4	0.4997	0.4997	0.4997	0.4997	0.4997	0.4997	0.4997	0.4997	0.4997	0.4998
3.5	0.4998									
4.0	0.49997									
45	0.499997									
5.0	0.4999997									

Reprinted with permission from *Standard Mathematical Tables*, 15th edn, © 1964 CRC Press Inc., Boca Raton, FL.

TABLE A.2 *t*-distribution. Critical points (t_α) for different probability levels (α) and different number of degrees of freedom (v). Example: For $v = 19$, $P(t > 2.0930)$ 0.025 and $P(|t| > 2.0930) = 0.05$.

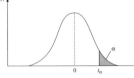

α v	0.4	0.25	0.15	0.1	0.05	0.025	0.01	0.005	0.001	0.0005
1	0.3249	1.0000	1.9626	3.0777	6.3138	12.7062	31.8205	63.6567	318.3087	636.6189
2	0.2887	0.8165	1.3862	1.8856	2.9200	4.3027	6.9646	9.9248	22.3271	31.5991
3	0.2767	0.7649	1.2498	1.6377	2.3534	3.1824	4.5407	5.8409	10.2145	12.9240
4	0.2707	0.7407	1.1896	1.5332	2.1318	2.7764	3.7469	4.6041	7.1732	8.6103
5	0.2672	0.7267	1.1558	1.4759	2.0150	2.5706	3.3649	4.0321	5.8934	6.8688
6	0.2648	0.7176	1.1342	1.4398	1.9432	2.4469	3.1427	3.7074	5.2076	5.9588
7	0.2632	0.7111	1.1192	1.4149	1.8946	2.3646	2.9980	3.4995	4.7853	5.4079
8	0.2619	0.7064	1.1081	1.3968	1.8595	2.3060	2.8965	3.3554	4.5008	5.0413
9	0.2610	0.7027	1.0997	1.3830	1.8331	2.2622	2.8214	3.2498	4.2968	4.7809
10	0.2602	0.6998	1.0931	1.3722	1.8125	2.2281	2.7638	3.1693	4.1437	4.5869
11	0.2596	0.6974	1.0877	1.3634	1.7959	2.2010	2.7181	3.1058	4.0247	4.4370
12	0.2590	0.6955	1.0832	1.3562	1.7823	2.1788	2.6810	3.0545	3.9296	4.3178
13	0.2586	0.6938	1.0795	1.3502	1.7709	2.1604	2.6503	3.0123	3.8520	4.2208
14	0.2582	0.6924	1.0763	1.3450	1.7613	2.1448	2.6245	2.9768	3.7874	4.1405
15	0.2579	0.6912	1.0735	1.3406	1.7531	2.1314	2.6025	2.9467	3.7328	4.0728
16	0.2576	0.6901	1.0711	1.3368	1.7459	2.1199	2.5835	2.9208	3.6862	4.0150
17	0.2573	0.6892	1.0690	1.3334	1.7396	2.1098	2.5669	2.8982	3.6458	3.9651
18	0.2571	0.6884	1.0672	1.3304	1.7341	2.1009	2.5524	2.8784	3.6105	3.9216
19	0.2569	0.6876	1.0655	1.3277	1.7291	2.0930	2.5395	2.8609	3.5794	3.8834
20	0.2567	0.6870	1.0640	1.3253	1.7247	2.0860	2.5280	2.8453	3.5518	3.8495
21	0.2566	0.6864	1.0627	1.3232	1.7207	2.0796	2.5176	2.8314	3.5272	3.8193
22	0.2564	0.6858	1.0614	1.3212	1.7171	2.0739	2.5083	2.8188	3.5050	3.7921
23	0.2563	0.6853	1.0603	1.3195	1.7139	2.0687	2.4999	2.8073	3.4850	3.7676
24	0.2562	0.6848	1.0593	1.3178	1.7109	2.0639	2.4922	2.7969	3.4668	3.7454
25	0.2561	0.6844	1.0584	1.3163	1.7081	2.0595	2.4851	2.7874	3.4502	3.7251
26	0.2560	0.6840	1.0575	1.3150	1.7056	2.0555	2.4786	2.7787	3.4350	3.7066
27	0.2559	0.6837	1.0567	1.3137	1.7033	2.0518	2.4727	2.7707	3.4210	3.6896
28	0.2558	0.6834	1.0560	1.3125	1.7011	2.0484	2.4671	2.7633	3.4082	3.6739
29	0.2557	0.6830	1.0553	1.3114	1.6991	2.0452	2.4620	2.7564	3.3962	3.6594
30	0.2556	0.6828	1.0547	1.3104	1.6973	2.0423	2.4573	2.7500	3.3852	3.6460
35	0.2553	0.6816	1.0520	1.3062	1.6896	2.0301	2.4377	2.7238	3.3400	3.5911
40	0.2550	0.6807	1.0500	1.3031	1.6839	2.0211	2.4233	2.7045	3.3069	3.5510
45	0.2549	0.6800	1.0485	1.3006	1.6794	2.0141	2.4121	2.6896	3.2815	3.5203
50	0.2547	0.6794	1.0473	1.2987	1.6759	2.0086	2.4033	2.6778	3.2614	3.4960
60	0.2545	0.6786	1.0455	1.2958	1.6706	2.0003	2.3901	2.6603	3.2317	3.4602
70	0.2543	0.6780	1.0442	1.2938	1.6669	1.9944	2.3808	2.6479	3.2108	3.4350
80	0.2542	0.6776	1.0432	1.2922	1.6641	1.9901	2.3739	2.6387	3.1953	3.4163
90	0.2541	0.6772	1.0424	1.2910	1.6620	1.9867	2.3685	2.6316	3.1833	3.4019
100	0.2540	0.6770	1.0418	1.2901	1.6602	1.9840	2.3642	2.6259	3.1737	3.3905
120	0.2539	0.6765	1.0409	1.2886	1.6577	1.9799	2.3578	2.6174	3.1595	3.3735
150	0.2538	0.6761	1.0400	1.2872	1.6551	1.9759	2.3515	2.6090	3.1455	3.3566
200	0.2537	0.6757	1.0391	1.2858	1.6525	1.9719	2.3451	2.6006	3.1315	3.3398
300	0.2536	0.6753	1.0382	1.2844	1.6499	1.9679	2.3388	2.5923	3.1176	3.3233
∞	0.2533	0.6745	1.0364	1.2816	1.6449	1.9600	2.3263	2.5758	3.0902	3.2905

Reproduced from Z. W. Kmietowicz and Y. Yannoulis (1988) *Statistical Tables for Economics, Businesss and Social Studies,* Harlow: Longman.

TABLE A.3 Critical values of the Mann–Whitney U statistic. The calculated value of U must be smaller than or equal to the table value for significance. Dashes in the table indicate that no value is possible for significance.

0.05 Level of significance: One-tailed Test

n_2	1	2	3	4	5	6	7	8	9	10	11	12	13	14	15	16	17	18	19	20
1	–	–	–	–	–	–	–	–	–	–	–	–	–	–	–	–	–	–	0	0
2	–	–	–	–	0	0	0	1	1	1	1	2	2	2	3	3	3	4	4	4
3	–	–	0	0	1	2	2	3	3	4	5	5	6	7	7	8	9	9	10	11
4	–	–	0	1	2	3	4	5	6	7	8	9	10	11	12	14	15	16	17	18
5	–	0	1	2	4	5	6	8	9	11	12	13	15	16	18	19	20	22	23	25
6	–	0	2	3	5	7	8	10	12	14	16	17	19	21	23	25	26	28	30	32
7	–	0	2	4	6	8	11	13	15	17	19	21	24	26	28	30	33	35	37	39
8	–	1	3	5	8	10	13	15	18	20	23	26	28	31	33	36	39	41	44	47
9	–	1	3	6	9	12	15	18	21	24	27	30	33	36	39	42	45	48	51	54
10	–	1	4	7	11	14	17	20	24	27	31	34	37	41	44	48	51	55	58	62
11	–	1	5	8	12	16	19	23	27	31	34	38	42	46	50	54	57	61	65	69
12	–	2	5	9	13	17	21	26	30	34	38	42	47	51	55	60	64	68	72	77
13	–	2	6	10	15	19	24	28	33	37	42	47	51	56	61	65	70	75	80	84
14	–	2	7	11	16	21	26	31	36	41	46	51	56	61	66	71	77	82	87	92
15		3	7	12	18	23	28	33	39	44	50	55	61	66	72	77	83	88	94	100
16	–	3	8	14	19	25	30	36	42	48	54	60	65	71	77	83	89	95	101	107
17	–	3	9	15	20	26	33	39	45	51	57	64	70	77	83	89	96	102	109	115
18	–	4	9	16	22	28	35	41	48	55	61	68	75	82	88	95	102	109	116	123
19	0	4	10	17	23	30	37	44	51	58	65	72	80	87	94	101	109	116	123	130
20	0	4	11	18	25	32	39	47	54	62	69	77	84	92	100	107	115	123	130	138

0.05 Level of significance: Two-tailed Test

n_2	1	2	3	4	5	6	7	8	9	10	11	12	13	14	15	16	17	18	19	20
1	–	–	–	–	–	–	–	–	–	–	–	–	–	–	–	–	–	–	–	–
2	–	–	–	–	–	–	–	0	0	0	0	1	1	1	1	1	2	2	2	2
3	–	–	–	–	0	1	1	2	2	3	3	4	4	5	5	6	6	7	7	8
4	–	–	–	0	1	2	3	4	4	5	6	7	8	9	10	11	11	12	13	13
5	–	–	0	1	2	3	5	6	7	8	9	11	12	13	14	15	17	18	19	20
6	–	–	1	2	3	5	6	8	10	11	13	14	16	17	19	21	22	24	25	27
7	–	–	1	3	5	6	8	10	12	14	16	18	20	22	24	26	28	30	32	34
8	–	0	2	4	6	8	10	13	15	17	19	22	24	26	29	31	34	36	38	41
9	–	0	2	4	7	10	12	15	17	20	23	26	28	31	34	37	39	42	45	48
10	–	0	3	5	8	11	14	17	20	23	26	29	33	36	39	42	45	48	52	55
11	–	0	3	6	9	13	16	19	23	26	30	33	37	40	44	47	51	55	58	62
12	–	1	4	7	11	14	18	22	26	29	33	37	41	45	49	53	57	61	65	69
13	–	1	4	8	12	16	20	24	28	33	37	41	45	50	54	59	63	67	72	76
14	–	1	5	9	13	17	22	26	31	36	40	45	50	55	59	64	67	74	78	83
15	–	1	5	10	14	19	24	29	34	39	44	49	54	59	64	70	75	80	85	90
16	–	1	6	11	15	21	26	31	37	42	47	53	59	64	70	75	81	86	92	98
17	–	2	6	11	17	22	28	34	39	45	51	57	63	67	75	81	87	93	99	105
18	–	2	7	12	18	24	30	36	42	48	55	61	67	74	80	86	93	99	106	112
19	–	2	7	13	19	25	32	38	45	52	58	65	72	78	85	92	99	106	113	119
20	–	2	8	13	20	27	34	41	48	55	62	69	76	83	90	98	105	112	119	127

From: Table K of Siegel, S. (1956) *Nonparametric Statistics for the Behavioural Sciences,* New York: McGraw-Hill.

TABLE A.3 Critical values of the Mann–Whitney U statistic (continued). The calculated value of U must be smaller than or equal to the table value for significance. Dashes in the table indicate that no value is possible for significance.

0.01 Level of significance: One-tailed Test

n_2	\ n_1 1	2	3	4	5	6	7	8	9	10	11	12	13	14	15	16	17	18	19	20
1	–	–	–	–	–	–	–	–	–	–	–	–	–	–	–	–	–	–	–	–
2	–	–	–	–	–	–	–	–	–	–	–	–	0	0	0	0	0	0	1	1
3	–	–	–	–	–	–	0	0	1	1	1	2	2	2	3	3	4	4	4	5
4	–	–	–	–	0	1	1	2	3	3	4	5	5	6	7	7	8	9	9	10
5	–	–	–	0	1	2	3	4	5	6	7	8	9	10	11	12	13	14	15	16
6	–	–	–	1	2	3	4	6	7	8	9	11	12	13	15	16	18	19	20	22
7	–	–	0	1	3	4	6	7	9	11	12	14	16	17	19	21	23	24	26	28
8	–	–	0	2	4	6	7	9	11	13	15	17	20	22	24	26	28	30	32	34
9	–	–	1	3	5	7	9	11	14	16	18	21	23	26	28	31	33	36	38	40
10	–	–	1	3	6	8	11	13	16	19	22	24	27	30	33	36	38	41	44	47
11	–	–	1	4	7	9	12	15	18	22	25	28	31	34	37	41	44	47	50	53
12	–	–	2	5	8	11	14	17	21	24	28	31	35	38	42	46	49	53	56	60
13	–	0	2	5	9	12	16	20	23	27	31	35	39	43	47	51	55	59	63	67
14	–	0	2	6	10	13	17	22	26	30	34	38	43	47	51	56	60	65	69	73
15	–	0	3	7	11	15	19	24	28	33	37	42	47	51	56	61	66	70	75	80
16	–	0	3	7	12	16	21	26	31	36	41	46	51	56	61	66	71	76	82	87
17	–	0	4	8	13	18	23	28	33	38	44	49	55	60	66	71	77	82	88	93
18	–	0	4	9	14	19	24	30	36	41	47	53	59	65	70	76	82	88	94	100
19	–	1	4	9	15	20	26	32	38	44	50	56	63	69	75	82	88	94	101	107
20	–	1	5	10	16	22	28	34	40	47	53	60	67	73	80	87	93	100	107	114

0.01 Level of significance: Two-tailed Test

n_2	\ n_1 1	2	3	4	5	6	7	8	9	10	11	12	13	14	15	16	17	18	19	20
1	–	–	–	–	–	–	–	–	–	–	–	–	–	–	–	–	–	–	–	–
2	–	–	–	–	–	–	–	–	–	–	–	–	–	–	–	–	–	–	0	0
3	–	–	–	–	–	–	–	–	0	0	0	1	1	1	2	2	2	2	3	3
4	–	–	–	–	–	0	0	1	1	2	2	3	3	4	5	5	6	6	7	8
5	–	–	–	–	0	1	1	2	3	4	5	6	7	7	8	9	10	11	12	13
6	–	–	–	0	1	2	3	4	5	6	7	9	10	11	12	13	15	16	17	18
7	–	–	–	0	1	3	4	6	7	9	10	12	13	15	16	18	19	21	22	24
8	–	–	–	1	2	4	6	7	9	11	13	15	17	18	20	22	24	26	28	30
9	–	–	0	1	3	5	7	9	11	13	16	18	20	22	24	27	29	31	33	36
10	–	–	0	2	4	6	9	11	13	16	18	21	24	26	29	31	34	37	39	42
11	–	–	0	2	5	7	10	13	16	18	21	24	27	30	33	36	39	42	45	48
12	–	–	1	3	6	9	12	15	18	21	24	27	31	34	37	41	44	47	51	54
13	–	–	I	3	7	10	13	17	20	24	27	31	34	38	42	45	49	53	56	60
14	–	–	1	4	7	11	15	18	22	26	30	34	38	42	46	50	54	58	63	67
15	–	–	2	5	8	12	16	20	24	29	33	37	42	46	51	55	60	64	69	73
16	–	–	2	5	9	13	18	22	27	31	36	41	45	50	55	60	65	70	74	79
17	–	–	2	6	10	15	19	24	29	34	39	44	49	54	60	65	70	75	81	86
18	–	–	2	6	11	16	21	26	31	37	42	47	53	58	64	70	75	81	87	92
19	–	0	3	7	12	17	22	28	33	39	45	51	56	63	69	74	81	87	93	99
20	–	0	3	8	13	18	24	30	36	42	48	54	60	67	73	79	86	92	99	105

TABLE A.4 Critical values of the Wilcoxon T statistic. The calculated value of T must be lower than or equal to the table value for significance. Dashes in the table indicate that no value is possible for significance.

	0.05 Level of significance		0.01 Level of significance	
n	One-tailed Test	Two-tailed Test	One-tailed Test	Two-tailed Test
5	0	–	–	–
6	2	0	–	–
7	3	2	0	–
8	5	3	1	0
9	8	5	3	1
10	10	8	5	3
11	13	10	7	5
12	17	13	9	7
13	21	17	12	9
14	25	21	15	12
15	30	25	19	15
16	35	29	23	19
17	41	34	27	23
18	47	40	32	27
19	53	46	37	32
20	60	52	43	37
21	67	58	49	42
22	75	65	55	48
23	83	73	62	54
24	91	81	69	61
25	100	89	76	68
26	110	98	84	75
27	119	107	92	83
28	130	116	101	91
29	140	126	110	100
30	151	137	120	109
31	163	147	130	118
32	175	159	140	128
33	187	170	151	138
34	200	182	162	148
35	213	195	173	159
36	227	208	185	171
37	241	221	198	182
38	256	235	211	194
39	271	249	224	207
40	286	264	238	220
41	302	279	252	233
42	319	294	266	247
43	336	310	281	261
44	353	327	296	276
45	371	343	312	291
46	389	361	328	307
47	407	378	345	322
48	426	396	362	339
49	446	415	379	355
50	466	434	397	373

From: Table J of Runyan, R. P. and Haber, A. (1991) *Fundamentals of Behavioral Statistics,* 7th edition, New York: McGraw-Hill.

TABLE A.5 Critical values of S for the sign test. S must be equal to or less than the stated value to be significant.

N	Level of significance for one-tailed test				
	0.05	0.025	0.01	0.005	0.0005
	Level of significance for two-tailed test				
	0.10	0.05	0.02	0.01	0.001
5	0	–	–	–	–
6	0	0	–	–	–
7	0	0	0	–	–
8	1	0	0	0	–
9	1	1	0	0	–
10	1	1	0	0	–
11	2	1	1	0	0
12	2	2	1	1	0
13	3	2	1	1	0
14	3	2	2	1	0
15	3	3	2	2	1
16	4	3	2	2	1
17	4	4	3	2	1
18	5	4	3	3	1
19	5	4	4	3	2
20	5	5	4	3	2
25	7	7	6	5	4
30	10	9	8	7	5
35	12	11	10	9	7

Reproduced from F. Clegg (1990), *Simple Statistics*, Cambridge: Cambridge University Press.

TABLE A.6 χ^2 (Chi-squared)-distribution. Values of χ^2_α giving area (α) in the right-hand tail for different number of degrees of freedom (v).
Example: For $v = 15$ area beyond $\chi^2_{0.95} = 7.261$ is 0.950 and beyond $\chi^2_{0.10} = 22.307$ is 0.100.

v \ α	0.995	0.990	0.975	0.950	0.900	0.750	0.500	0.250	0.100	0.050	0.025	0.010	0.005
1	$0.0^4 3927^*$	$0.0^3 1571^*$	$0.0^3 9821^*$	$0.0^2 3932^*$	0.01579	0.1015	0.4549	1.323	2.706	3.841	5.024	6.635	7.879
2	0.01003	0.02010	0.05065	0.1026	0.2107	0.5754	1.386	2.773	4.605	5.991	7.378	9.210	10.597
3	0.07172	0.1148	0.2158	0.3518	0.5844	1.213	2.366	4.108	6.251	7.815	9.348	11.345	12.838
4	0.2070	0.2971	0.4844	0.7107	1.064	1.923	3.357	5.385	7.779	9.488	11.143	13.277	14.860
5	0.4117	0.5543	0.8312	1.145	1.610	2.675	4.351	6.626	9.236	11.070	12.833	15.086	16.750
6	0.6757	0.8721	1.237	1.635	2.204	3.455	5.348	7.841	10.645	12.592	14.449	16.812	18.548
7	0.9893	1.239	1.690	2.167	2.833	4.255	6.346	9.037	12.017	14.067	16.013	18.475	20.278
8	1.344	1.646	2.180	2.733	3.490	5.071	7.344	10.219	13.362	15.507	17.535	20.090	21.955
9	1.753	2.088	2.700	3.325	4.168	5.899	8.343	11.389	14.684	16.919	19.023	21.666	23.589
10	2.156	2.558	3.247	3.940	4.865	6.737	9.342	12.549	15.987	18.307	20.483	23.209	25.188
11	2.603	3.053	3.816	4.575	5.578	7.584	10.341	13.701	17.275	19.675	21.920	24.725	26.757
12	3.074	3.571	4.404	5.226	6.304	8.438	11.340	14.845	18.549	21.026	23.337	26.217	28.300
13	3.565	4.107	5.009	5.892	7.041	9.299	12.340	15.984	19.812	22.362	24.736	27.688	29.819
14	4.075	4.660	5.629	6.571	7.790	10.165	13.339	17.117	21.064	23.685	26.119	29.141	31.319
15	4.601	5.229	6.262	7.261	8.547	11.036	14.339	18.245	22.307	24.996	27.488	30.587	32.801
16	5.142	5.812	6.908	7.962	9.312	11.912	15.338	19.369	23.542	26.296	28.845	32.000	34.267
17	5.697	6.408	7.564	8.672	10.085	12.792	16.338	20.489	24.769	27.587	30.191	33.409	35.718
18	6.265	7.015	8.231	9.390	10.865	13.675	17.338	21.605	25.989	28.869	31.526	34.805	37.156
19	6.844	7.633	8.907	10.117	11.651	14.562	18.338	22.718	27.204	30.143	32.852	36.191	38.582

continued

α / v	0.995	0.990	0.975	0.950	0.900	0.750	0.500	0.250	0.100	0.050	0.025	0.010	0.005
20	7.434	8.260	9.591	10.851	12.443	15.452	19.337	23.828	28.412	31.410	34.170	37.566	39.997
21	8.034	8.897	10.283	11.591	13.240	16.344	20.337	24.935	29.615	32.670	35.479	38.932	41.401
22	8.643	9.542	10.982	12.338	14.041	17.240	21.337	26.039	30.813	33.924	36.781	40.289	42.796
23	9.260	10.196	11.688	13.090	14.848	18.137	22.337	27.141	32.007	35.172	38.076	41.638	44.181
24	9.886	10.856	12.401	13.848	15.659	19.037	23.337	28.241	33.196	36.415	39.364	42.080	45.558
25	10.520	11.524	13.120	14.611	16.473	19.939	24.337	29.339	34.382	37.652	40.646	44.314	46.928
26	11.160	12.198	13.844	15.379	17.292	20.843	25.336	30.434	35.563	38.885	41.923	45.642	48.290
27	11.808	12.879	14.573	16.151	18.114	21.749	26.336	31.528	36.741	40.113	43.194	46.963	49.645
28	12.461	13.565	15.308	16.928	18.939	22.657	27.336	32.620	37.916	41.337	44.461	48.278	50.993
29	13.121	14.256	16.047	17.708	19.768	23.567	28.336	33.711	39.087	42.557	45.722	49.588	52.336
30	13.787	14.954	16.791	18.493	20.599	24.478	29.336	34.800	40.256	43.773	46.979	50.892	53.672
35	17.192	18.509	20.569	22.465	24.797	29.054	34.336	40.223	46.059	49.802	53.203	57.342	60.275
40	20.707	22.164	24.433	26.509	29.050	33.660	39.335	45.616	51.805	55.758	59.342	63.691	66.766
45	24.311	25.901	28.366	30.612	33.350	38.291	44.335	50.985	57.505	61.656	65.410	69.957	73.166
50	27.991	29.707	32.357	34.764	37.689	42.942	49.335	56.334	63.167	67.505	71.420	76.154	79.490
55	31.735	33.571	36.398	38.958	42.060	47.611	54.335	61.665	68.796	73.311	77.381	82.292	85.749
60	35.535	37.485	40.482	43.188	46.459	52.294	59.335	66.981	74.397	79.082	83.298	88.379	91.952
70	43.275	45.442	48.758	51.739	55.329	61.698	69.334	77.577	85.527	90.531	95.023	100.425	104.215
80	51.172	53.540	57.153	60.391	64.278	71.144	79.334	88.130	96.578	101.879	106.629	112.329	116.321
90	59.196	61.754	65.647	69.126	73.291	80.625	89.334	98.650	107.565	113.145	118.136	124.116	128.299
100	67.328	70.065	74.222	77.929	82.358	90.133	99.334	109.141	118.498	124.342	129.561	135.807	140.169
120	83.829	86.909	91.568	95.705	100.627	109.224	119.335	130.051	140.228	146.565	152.214	158.963	163.670
150	109.122	112.655	117.980	122.692	126.278	137.987	149.334	161.288	172.577	179.579	185.803	193.219	198.380
200	152.224	156.421	162.724	168.279	174.828	186.175	199.334	213.099	226.018	233.993	241.060	249.455	255.281
250	196.145	200.929	208.095	214.392	221.809	234.580	249.334	264.694	279.947	287.889	295.691	304.948	311.361
Z_α	-2.5758	-2.3263	-1.9600	-1.6449	-1.2816	-0.6745	0.0000	0.6745	1.2816	1.6449	1.9600	2.3263	2.5758

*E.g. $0.0^43927 = 0.00003927$.

Interpolation : For $v > 100$, $\chi^2_\alpha = \frac{1}{2}(Z_\alpha + \sqrt{2v-1})^2$ where Z_α is the standardized normal variable shown in the bottom line of the table.

Reproduced from Z. W. Kmietowicz and Y. Yannoulis (1988) *Statistical Tables for Economic, Business and Social Studies*, Harlow: Longman.

TABLE A.7 Critical values of the Spearman r_s ranked correlation coefficient.

N	0.05 Level of significance		0.01 Level of significance	
	One-tailed Test (directional)	Two-tailed Test (non-directional)	One-tailed Test (directional)	Two-tailed Test (non-directional)
5	0.900	1.000	1.000	–
6	0.829	0.886	0.943	1.000
7	0.714	0.786	0.893	0.929
8	0.643	0.738	0.833	0.881
9	0.600	0.683	0.783	0.833
10	0.564	0.648	0.746	0.794
12	0.506	0.591	0.712	0.777
14	0.456	0.544	0.645	0.7 15
16	0.425	0.506	0.601	0.665
18	0.399	0.475	0.564	0.625
20	0.377	0.450	0.534	0.591
22	0.359	0.428	0.508	0.562
24	0.343	0.409	0.485	0.537
26	0.329	0.392	0.465	0.515
28	0.317	0.377	0.448	0.496
30	0.306	0.364	0.432	0.478

The calculated value of r_s must be larger than or equal to the table value for significance.

Reproduced from Hinton, P. R. (1995) *Statistics Explained: A Guide for Social Science Students,* London: Routledge. *Adapted from:* Olds, E. G. (1949) 'The 5% significance levels for sums of squares of rank differences and a correlation', *Annals of Mathematical Statistics,* vol. 20, pages 117–18. Olds, E. G. (1938) 'Distribution of sums of squares of rank differences for small numbers of individuals', *Annals of Mathematical Statistics,* vol. 9, pages 133–48. With the permission of the Institute of Mathematical Statistics.

TABLE A.8 Critical values of the Pearson *r* correlation coefficient.

df	0.05 Level of significance		0.01 Level of significance	
	One-tailed Test (directional)	Two-tailed Test (non-directional)	One-tailed Test (directional)	Two-tailed Test (non-directional)
1	0.9877	0.9969	0.9995	0.9999
2	0.9000	0.9500	0.9800	0.9900
3	0.8054	0.8783	0.9343	0.9587
4	0.7293	0.8114	0.8822	0.9172
5	0.6694	0.7545	0.8329	0.8745
6	0.6215	0.7067	0.7887	0.8343
7	0.5822	0.6664	0.7498	0.7977
8	0.5494	0.6319	0.7155	0.7646
9	0.5214	0.6021	0.6851	0.7348
10	0.4973	0.5760	0.6581	0.7079
11	0.4762	0.5529	0.6339	0.6835
12	0.4575	0.5324	0.6120	0.6614
13	0.4409	0.5139	0.5923	0.6411
14	0.4259	0.4973	0.5742	0.6226
15	0.4124	0.4821	0.5577	0.6055
16	0.4000	0.4683	0.5425	0.5897
17	0.3887	0.4555	0.5285	0.5751
18	0.3783	0.4438	0.5155	0.5614
19	0.3687	0.4329	0.5034	0.3487
20	0.3598	0.4227	0.4921	0.5368
25	0.3233	0.3809	0.4451	0.4869
30	0.2960	0.3494	0.4093	0.4487
35	0.2746	0.3246	0.3810	0.4182
40	0.2573	0.3044	0.3578	0.3932
45	0.2428	0.2875	0.3384	0.3721
50	0.2306	0.2732	0.3218	0.3541
60	0.2108	0.2500	0.2948	0.3248
70	0.1954	0.2319	0.2737	0.3017
80	0.1829	0.2172	0.2565	0.2830
90	0.1726	0.2050	0.2422	0.2673
100	0.1638	0.1946	0.2301	0.2540

The calculated value of *r* must be larger than or equal to the table value for significance.

Reproduced from Hinton, P. R. (1995) *Statistics Explained: A Guide for Social Science Students*, London: Routledge.
Adapted from: Table VII of Fisher, R. A. and Yates, F. (1974) *Statistical Tables for Biological, Agricultural, and Medical Research,* 6th edition. London: Longman Group UK Ltd (previously published by Oliver and Boyd Ltd, Edinburgh)

# Index